THE RO   D0196469

BUDAPEST

Forthcoming titles include

Baltic States • Chicago
First-Time Round the World • Grand Canyon
Philippines • Skiing & Snowboarding in North America
South America • The Gambia • Walks Around London

Forthcoming reference titles include

Chronicle series: China, England,
France, India • Night Sky

read Rough Guides online

www.roughguides.com

Rough Guide Credits

Text editor: Ruth Blackmore
Series editor: Mark Ellingham
Production: Rachel Holmes and Zoe Nobes
Cartography: Melissa Baker

Publishing Information

This second edition published August 2002
by Rough Guides Ltd,
62–70 Shorts Gardens, London, WC2H 9AH

Distributed by the Penguin Group:

Penguin Books Ltd, 80 Strand, London WC2R ORL
Penguin Putnam, Inc. 375 Hudson Street, New York 10014, USA
Penguin Books Australia Ltd, 487 Maroondah Highway,
PO Box 257, Ringwood, Victoria 3134, Australia
Penguin Books Canada Ltd, 10 Alcorn Avenue,
Toronto, Ontario, Canada M4V 1E4
Penguin Books (NZ) Ltd,
182–190 Wairau Road, Auckland 10, New Zealand

Typeset in Bembo and Helvetica to an original design by Henry Iles.
Printed in Spain by Graphy Cems.

© Charles Hebbert and Dan Richardson
320pp, includes index
A catalogue record for this book is available from the British Library.

ISBN 1-85828-889-4

THE ROUGH GUIDE TO

BUDAPEST

by Charles Hebbert
and Dan Richardson

ROUGH
GUIDES

We set out to do something different when the first Rough Guide was published in 1982. Mark Ellingham, just out of university, was travelling in Greece. He brought along the popular guides of the day, but found they were all lacking in some way. They were either strong on ruins and museums but went on for pages without mentioning a beach or taverna. Or they were so conscious of the need to save money that they lost sight of Greece's cultural and historical significance. Also, none of the books told him anything about Greece's contemporary life – its politics, its culture, its people, and how they lived.

So with no job in prospect, Mark decided to write his own guidebook, one which aimed to provide practical information that was second to none, detailing the best beaches and the hottest clubs and restaurants, while also giving hard-hitting accounts of every sight, both famous and obscure, and providing up-to-the-minute information on contemporary culture. It was a guide that encouraged independent travellers to find the best of Greece, and was a great success, getting shortlisted for the Thomas Cook travel guide award, and encouraging Mark, along with three friends, to expand the series.

The Rough Guide list grew rapidly and the letters flooded in, indicating a much broader readership than had been anticipated, but one which uniformly appreciated the Rough Guide mix of practical detail and humour, irreverence and enthusiasm. Things haven't changed. The same four friends who began the series are still the caretakers of the Rough Guide mission today: to provide the most reliable, up-to-date and entertaining information to independent-minded travellers of all ages, on all budgets.

We now publish more than 200 titles and have offices in London and New York. The travel guides are written and researched by a dedicated team of more than 100 authors, based in Britain, Europe, the USA and Australia. We have also created a unique series of phrasebooks to accompany the travel series, along with an acclaimed series of music guides, and a best-selling pocket guide to the Internet and World Wide Web. We also publish comprehensive travel information on our website: **www.roughguides.com**

Help us update

We've gone to a lot of trouble to ensure that this Rough Guide is as up to date and accurate as possible. However, things do change. All suggestions, comments and corrections are much appreciated, and we'll send a copy of the next edition (or any other Rough Guide if you prefer) for the best letters.

Please mark letters "Rough Guide Budapest Update" and send to:

Rough Guides, 62–70 Shorts Gardens, London, WC2H 9AH, or Rough Guides, 4th Floor, 345 Hudson St, New York NY 10014.

Or send an email to mail@roughguides.com
Have your questions answered and tell others about your trip at www.roughguides.atinfopop.com

Acknowledgements

Dan Richardson would like to thank Lila, Bea, Kriszta and Csilla for their kindnesses, and the staff at Tourinform for their patient assistance.
Charles Hebbert would like to thank Rachel Appleby, Balassa Peter, Biber Krisztina, Biczok Anna, Bodrogi Bea, Eileen G. P. Brown, Bob Cohen, Peterjon Cresswell, Mark Epstein, Jack Falk, Fazakas Pèter, Fenyő Krisztina, Pearl R. Gluck, Hangyl Judit, Heather Hermant, Liszka Tamas, Lőrincz Anna, Lucy Mallows, Peter Pallai, Tom Popper, Richard Robinson, Szűcs Dúra, Tamás Amaryllis, the staff at Tourinform, everyone else who has been so generous with their help, and above all Caroline Hoare.
In addition, the editor would like to thank Rachel Holmes for typesetting, Jan Wiltshire for proofreading and Melissa Baker for maps.

Readers' letters

Many thanks to readers who wrote in with comments on the last edition: Chris and Margaret Begg, Jane Brace, Dara Breathnach, Jeroen Bruggeman, David Cahill, Elizabeth Dick, John Duffy, Elizabeth l'Estrange, Jean Grier, Peter Henshaw, Debbie Lewis, Sarah Nicholls, Deborah O'Byrne, Beck Pitt, Francesca Raphaely, Brian Roper, Tatyana Stewart, Derek Wilde, Milva Zupan, Johan Bolhuis, Jaime Browne, Mike Dean, Sally Dunkley, Jean Grier, Coral Hoyos, Rosemary Johnston, Ildiko Joo, Edwin Kuipers, Paul Kurucz, Ann Layzell, Juliet Lehair, Sandra Mason, Katalin Matrai, Colin Pidgean, Cathy Platt, Yizhar Regev, Daniel Sardi, Ron Sonnet, Zzuzsi Snarey, Zsuzsanna Varga, John Chapman, Mrs. F. Rabinowitz, Peter Beglin.

READERS' LETTERS • PHOTO CREDITS

CONTENTS

CONTENTS

Contents

MAP LIST

Introduction

With its wonderful natural setting, straddling the River Danube, its beautiful architecture and excellent Magyar cuisine, Budapest is one of the most satisfying cities in Europe to visit. Its magnificent waterfront and boulevards invite comparisons with Paris, Prague and Vienna – as do many features of its cultural life such as its coffee houses, its love of opera and its wine-producing tradition. However, the city is also distinctively Hungarian, its inhabitants displaying fierce pride in their Magyar ancestry. Their language too, whose nearest European relatives are Finnish and Turkish, underlines the difference.

Ironically, provincial Hungarians have long regarded Budapest as a hotbed of alien values and loose morals – a charge that misses the point. Foreigners have played a major role in the city since its inception, and the Chinese and Arab communities established since the end of Communism simply bring it up to date as an international city. Even the sex trade that has earned it the reputation of the "Bangkok of Europe" is nothing new, having been a feature of life during Habsburg times. In politics, art and much else, Budapest is not only the capital but a catalyst for the country, without which Hungary would be a far duller place.

Fundamental to the city's layout and history is the **River Danube** – which is seldom blue. It separates **Buda** on the hilly west bank from **Pest** on the eastern plain. **Várhegy** (Castle Hill) on the Buda side was for many centuries the seat of monarchs, and its palace, museums, churches and Baroque streets make it the obvious place to start sightseeing. Thereafter, you can wander through the **Víziváros** (Watertown) below the hill, before pushing on to **Gellérthegy** (Gellért Hill), with its crags and towering Liberation Monument. The historic **Turkish baths** in the **Tabán** quarter between the two hills are also well worth experiencing.

Over in **Pest**, you're likely to spend most of your time enjoying the streetlife, bars and restaurants within the **Belváros** (Inner City) and the surrounding districts. In contrast to the medieval street plan of Várhegy and the Belváros, these surrounding districts are defined by two semicircular boulevards – the **Kiskörút** (Small Boulevard) and the **Nagykörút** (Great Boulevard) – and radial avenues such as Andrássy út and Rákóczi út. Exploring the area between them can easily occupy you for several days.

In the **Lipótváros**, the financial and government centre, the interest lies in **St Stephen's Basilica**, the monumental **Parliament** building rivalling the Várhegy across the Danube, and some wonderful buildings around **Szabadság tér** (Liberty Square), including one by Ödön Lechner, whose work is often likened to Gaudí's in Barcelona. In the **Terézváros** one can hardly avoid making comparisons with Paris, as **Andrássy út** and the **Opera House** were clearly inspired by Haussmann's work for Napoleon III. Andrássy út terminates at **Hősök tere** (Heroes' Square), a magnificent imperial set piece that is Budapest's Les Invalides and Nelson's Column rolled into one.

Of the remaining inner-city districts, the **Erzsébetváros** and **Józsefváros** hold the most appeal. The former is traditionally Budapest's **Jewish quarter**, with a rich and tragic history that's still palpable in the backstreets, making them a wonderful place to explore. The great synagogue on Dohány utca provides more historical information. The adjacent Józsefváros is also fascinating but quite seedy in parts, though there's nothing to fear in the vicinity of the **National Museum**, or even at **Kerepesi Cemetery**, out beyond the Nagykörút. In **Ferencváros**, the attractions are the **Great Market Hall** on the Kiskörút, and the **Applied Arts Museum** further out, in an amazing building by Lechner.

Other parts of the city are also rewarding, but you need to be selective. **Óbuda** (Old Buda) really only lives up to its name in one locality, though its postwar sprawl harbours several Roman remains, with the ruins of Aquincum further out in **Római-Fürdő**. More alluringly, there are the **Buda Hills** that encircle the city to the west, with enjoyable **rides** on the Cogwheel and Children's railways, and intriguing **caves** to be visited. In fine weather people also flock to **Margit sziget** (Margit Island) to swim and sunbathe at two enormous lidos.

Further out, but still within the city limits, the **Statue Park** of redundant Communist monuments and the **Rail Heritage Park** of steam trains rate as major attractions, while the **Budakeszi Game Park** and two romantic **cemeteries** might not be everyone's idea of fun, but can claim many admirers.

One of the great things about Budapest is that most of its pleasures are affordable for visitors on a tight budget. Delicious meals can be had all over the city, and discovering things for yourself can be half the fun. Though **Hungarian cuisine** is noted for its richly sauced meat and fish dishes, there are enough alternatives (Indian, Chinese, Italian, Middle Eastern) for vegetarians to enjoy themselves too.

Budapest's **nightlife** is also very affordable and, though small, it caters for a wide range of tastes. There isn't always much of a distinction between clubs and bars, as many bars play live music or have a disco; beer halls, however, usually serve full meals. Generally, the scene is trouble-free and welcoming, with a whole network of events that are surprisingly accessible. This is especially true of the Táncház (Dance House) scene, where Hungarians of all ages perform wild stamping dances to the rhythms of darkest Transylvania, and internationally renowned artists like Márta Sebestyén appear in an informal setting.

In the case of **classical music and opera**, world-class ensembles and soloists can be enjoyed in the palatial settings of the Vigadó and State Opera House, especially during the major festivals in spring, summer and autumn. You can also go to outdoor concerts on Margit sziget (Margit Island) over summer. For fans of **pop, rock and world music**, the two big events are the Budapesti Bucsú, first held to celebrate the departure of Soviet troops in 1991, and the Sziget Festival, which claims to be the largest in Europe.

When to visit

The best times to visit Budapest are **spring** (late March to the end of May) and **autumn** (Sept–Oct), when the weather is mild and there are fewer tourists, except during the Spring Festival (late March/early April). The majority of tourists come in the summer, when residents decamp to Lake Balaton and those who remain flock to the city's pools and parks to escape the heat and dust. Though many concert halls are closed over summer, there are all kinds of outdoor events to compensate – especially in August, when the Sziget Festival, the Formula One Grand Prix and the Opera and Ballet festival all take place around the middle of the month. Winter is cold and may be snowy, but you can still enjoy all the city's sights and cultural attractions (as well as trying roasted chestnuts from street vendors), while the thermal baths take on an extra allure. It's wise to book accommodation in advance for Christmas, New Year, the Spring Festival and Grand Prix.

Budapest's climate

	°F	°C	RAINFALL
	AVERAGE DAILY	AVERAGE DAILY	AVERAGE MONTHLY
			Millimetres
Jan	29	-2	37
Feb	32	0	44
March	42	6	38
April	53	12	45
May	61	16	72
June	68	20	69
July	72	22	66
Aug	70	21	47
Sept	63	17	33
Oct	52	11	57
Nov	42	6	70
Dec	34	1	46

BASICS

BASICS

1

Arrival

Budapest's city centre is well connected to the airport, train and bus stations. The terminal for the airport-shuttle bus and international buses is in downtown Pest, close to metro station Deák tér, the intersection of all three of the city's metro lines, and just a few stops away from here are the major train stations.

For information on booking accommodation and details of the accommodation booking agencies listed below, see p.158.

BY AIR

Ferihegy Airport, 20km from the centre, has two passenger terminals next door to each other: Ferihegy 2A, serving Malév and Malév's joint flights with other airlines; and Ferihegy 2B, which is used by the rest. A **shuttle bus** (*Centrum Minibusz*; every 30min, 5.30am–9pm; 800Ft) runs from outside the terminal buildings to the *Kempinski Hotel* on Erzsébet tér in downtown Pest; tickets can be purchased on board. Alternatively, the more expensive **Airport Minibus** will take you directly to your destination. Tickets (1800Ft) can be bought in the luggage-claim hall while you are waiting for your bags, or in the main concourse; you give your address and then have to wait five to twenty minutes until the driver calls your destination. To book a return trip to the airport call ☎296-8555 some hours beforehand (or a day in advance if you're on an early flight), and allow a couple of hours to get there.

Public transport might be more inconvenient but it's not much slower, and it's certainly cheaper: take the *Reptérbusz* from the stop between the two terminals and stay on board until the final stop, the faded, red-and-yellow metro station at Kőbánya-Kispest; here you switch to the blue metro line, alighting ten stops later at Deák tér. It takes about 45 minutes and costs 106Ft for each of the two tickets. Tickets are available at the airport information desk or from the machine by the bus stop – buying one from the driver on board will cost you 120Ft. **Airport taxis** are mafia-controlled and known to physically threaten other cabs that enter their patch. They charge way above the odds, with fixed rates of 5000–6000Ft, depending on your destination – almost twice the rate of other cabs – though they will charge unsuspecting foreigners many times that. You can order normal city cabs at Ferihegy's **tourist offices**; they can also reserve accommodation in Budapest for you.

The telephone code for Budapest is ☎1. To call Budapest from abroad, dial ☎36, followed by the subscriber's seven-digit number. Mobile phones have the prefix 06-30 or 06-20 followed by a seven-digit number.

BY TRAIN

The Hungarian word *pályaudvar* (abbreviated to *pu.* in writing only) is used to designate the seven Budapest **train stations**, three of which are on the metro and useful for tourists. Translated into English, their names refer to the direction of services handled rather than location, so that Western Station (*Nyugati pu.*) is north of downtown Pest, and Southern Station (*Déli pu.*) is in the west of the city; Eastern Station (*Keleti pu.*), however, is to the east of the city centre.

Nyugati Station is located on the northern edge of Pest's Great Boulevard. Luggage lockers (200Ft) and a 24-hour left-luggage office (160Ft or 320Ft depending on size) can be found next to the ticket office beside platform 13. You can change money and book rooms at Cooptourist (Mon–Fri 9am–4.30pm) and Budapest Tourist (Mon–Fri 9am–5.30pm, Sat 9am–noon), down in the underpass in front of the station near the entrance to the metro, or at the Budapest Tourist Information Office (daily 9am–8pm; ⓣ 302-8580), by the police office (*Rendőrség*) to the left of the main entrance of the station; this is also good for information on the city. To get to downtown Pest, take the blue metro line two stops to Deák tér in the direction of Kőbánya-Kispest.

Trains from Vienna's Westbahnhof terminate at Pest's **Keleti Station** on Baross tér in the VIII district. This station is something of a hangout for thieves and hustlers, but there's also a strong police presence. In summer you can expect long queues at the 24-hour left-luggage office (160Ft or 320Ft) and also at the privately run tourist office, Ibusz (Mon–Fri 8am–4pm) and the Tourist Information Centre (daily: June–Aug 7am–11pm; Sept–May 7am–9pm), both in the Lotz Hall at the side exit of the station down platform 6. Keleti is three stops from Deák tér by the Déli pu.-bound red metro line.

A warning about **taxis** at Keleti Station: the unmarked taxis lining the road outside the doors of the station are best avoided, despite their drivers wearing badges saying "official taxi". Instead, look out for taxis from the companies listed

BY TRAIN

on p.15, such as Főtaxi; you'll find them outside the main doors, on the right.

Déli Station is 500m behind the Várhegy in Buda and four stops from Deák tér on the red metro line. Accommodation and exchange are handled by Budapest Tourist (Mon–Thurs 9am–5pm, Fri 9am–4pm), in the row of shops down the steps past the metro entrance; left-luggage is around the corner.

BY BUS

The majority of **international bus services** wind up at the **Erzsébet tér bus station**, just by Deák tér on the edge of downtown Pest. However, the construction of a new conference centre on Erzsébet tér means the bus station will eventually move elsewhere, probably to the Népliget site (see below), although exactly when this will happen was uncertain at the time of writing. Erzsébet tér bus station's left-luggage office is small but rarely busy, and there are several tourist offices in the vicinity –Tourinform (see p.8) is just around the corner, Cooptourist at Bajcsy-Zsilinszky út 17, 150m north of the bus station (Mon–Fri 9am–5pm), and Ibusz at Dob utca 1, slightly further in the other direction (Mon–Fri 8am–4pm). Ten minutes' walk away by the *Marriott Hotel* on the Pest embankment is a 24-hour exchange office.

Services from Slovakia, Romania and Yugoslavia arrive at the **Népstadion bus station** in the XIV district. Domestic lines also use this station, as well as the **Árpád híd bus station** in the XIII district, the **Etele tér bus station** in the XI district and the **Népliget bus station** in the IX district. None of the four currently has any tourist facilities, but they're all just four or five metro stops from the centre of Pest.

BY HYDROFOIL

Hydrofoils from Vienna (April–Oct) dock at the **international landing stage**, on the Belgrád rakpart (embankment), near downtown Pest. Ibusz (Mon–Fri 8.15am–5pm)
is five minutes' walk north, on Ferenciek tere, inland of the
Erzsébet Bridge, and there's a 24-hour exchange office just
up the river on Petőfi tér.

BY CAR

All things considered, **driving** in Budapest can't be recommended. Road manners are non-existent, parking space is
scarce and traffic jams are frequent. Careering trams, bumpy
cobbles and unexpected one-way systems make things
worse. If you do have a car, you might be better off parking
it somewhere outside the centre and using public transport
to get in and out. It's best not to leave it unattended for too
long, though. Guarded **parking lots** exist at many suburban hotels and campsites, and in each district of the city.

If you want **to rent a car**, you're best off avoiding the old
Russian Ladas and choosing one of the Western models
(offered by most companies); rates for these are in the
region of $70 a day, cheaper if you rent for a whole week.
With some agencies, mileage and insurance are included in
the price, and it's worth checking if there's going to be a
surcharge or not. Most places accept a credit card as a
deposit; if you don't have one, you can expect to pay
upwards of $1000. See p.263 for agency addresses.

BY BICYCLE

Cyclists must contend with the same hazards as drivers, as
well as sunken tramlines, and they are also banned from most
major thoroughfares. However, cycle routes are now appear-

ing – for example, up Andrássy út and along the Buda bank of the Danube to Szentendre and beyond – and the number of cyclists has shot up. Tourinform has free **cycling maps** of Budapest, or you can buy them in map shops. See p.263 for details of bike-repair shops and rental outlets. Bicycles can be carried on HÉV trains and the Cogwheel Railway for the price of a single ticket, but not on buses or trams.

Information and maps

The best source of information is the National Tourist Office's **Tourinform** at V, Sütő utca 2, just around the corner from Deák tér metro (daily 8am–8pm; ☏ 438–8080, ⓦ www.hungarytourism.hu). Their friendly polyglot staff can answer just about any question on Budapest and Hungary in general. If you need information outside these hours you can go to the 24-hour office near-

by at Vigadó utca 6 (☎438-8080); this is also the office of
the tourist police, Policeinform, where you can report any
problems you might have and ask advice. The Budapest
Tourist Office (🌐www.budapestinfo.hu) also has a couple
of information offices in the city: at Liszt Ferenc tér 11
(daily: May–Sept 10am–10pm; Oct–April 10am–6pm;
☎322-4098); and in the Várhegy district on Szentháromság
tér (daily 8am–8pm; ☎488-0453). You can also get maps
and information on the city from the Ibusz, Budapest
Tourist and Cooptourist offices listed on p.158, but these
tend to be less helpful than the Tourinform offices.

It's a good idea to get hold of a proper **map** of the city at
the earliest opportunity. The small freebies supplied by
tourist offices give an idea of Budapest's layout and princi-
pal monuments, but lack detail. Larger, folding maps are
sold all over the place, though their size makes them cum-
bersome. For total coverage you can't beat the wirebound
Budapest Atlasz, available in bookshops for 1300Ft, which
shows every street, bus and tram route, and the location of
restaurants, museums and suchlike. It also contains enlarged
maps of the Vár, central Pest, Margit sziget (Margit Island)
and the Városliget (City Park), plus a comprehensive index.

Details of **what's on** can be found in the magazines *Where
Budapest* (monthly, free in hotels), *Budapest Sun* (weekly,
around 250Ft), *Budapest in your pocket* (bimonthly, 300Ft, or
distributed free on Malév planes), and the Hungarian-lan-
guage listings weeklies, *Pesti Est* (free in cinema foyers, published on Wednesdays) and *Pesti Műsor* (available at
newsagents for 99Ft).

Budapest is divided into 23 districts (*kerület*), designated
on maps and street signs by Roman numerals. Addresses
begin with the number of the district – for example, V,
Petőfi tér 3 – a system used throughout this guide.

SIGHTSEEING TOURS AND BUDAPEST CARD

If you're hard-pressed for time you might appreciate a city tour, lasting two to three hours. These range in price from 4800Ft to 6000Ft (or 8000Ft if combined with a visit to the parliament building) and can be booked through Budapest Tourist (☏318-6600), Ibusz (☏317-7767) or Buda Tours (☏302-6278; VI, Andrássy út 2). Ibusz and Budapest Tourist also organize guided tours of the parliament building, combined with visits to the Ethnographic Museum or the National Gallery. Few of the walking tours on offer are worth the money, with the exception of those around the old Jewish area behind the Dohány utca synagogue (see p.115).

If you are doing a lot of sightseeing you might consider buying a Budapest Card. For 3700Ft (48 hours) or 4500Ft (72 hours), you get free travel in most of the city, free entry to over sixty museums, and discounts of up to fifty percent in some shops and restaurants and on some sightseeing programmes and cultural and folklore events. The card is available from tourist offices, hotels, central metro stations and at the airport, and it comes with a booklet explaining where it can be used. However, the price means you'll have to work hard to save money on it, especially since the card is not valid for two of the most popular attractions – the parliament building and the funicular that goes up to the castle. Note, too, that although the card allows entry into the Liszt Memorial Museum, it's not valid for the Sunday concerts held there – which are free if you pay to go into the museum. The card does give discounts on the Airport Minibus service (normally 1800Ft each way; see p.3), but oddly you get a larger reduction buying two singles (1500Ft each way) than if you get a return ticket (1650Ft each way).

City transport

Budapest is an easy city to get around. The best way to see its historic quarters is on foot, and the cheap and efficient public transport system run by BKV ensures that few parts of the city are more than thirty minutes' journey from the centre, and many can be reached in half that time. The language and local geography may be unfamiliar, but it doesn't take long to pick up the basics. The website of the Budapest Transport Company (BKV) has more information, though it's in Hungarian only: ⓦ www.bkv.hu.

One thing to beware of while travelling around are **pickpockets**, especially on the M1 metro line. Gangs distract their victims by pushing them or blocking their way, while emptying their pockets and bags at the same time.

TICKETS AND PASSES

There's a whole array of **tickets** available for travelling on public transport, but since validating your ticket can be complex and is easy to forget – and ticket inspections are much stricter than they used to be – the best advice if you are staying for more than half a day is to get a **pass** (see below).

Single **tickets** valid for the metro, buses, trams, trolley buses, the Cogwheel Railway and suburban HÉV lines (to the edge of the city) cost 110Ft and are sold at metro stations, newspaper kiosks and tobacconists. Tickets valid only on the **metro** come in a variety of types, depending on how many lines you want to use and how many stops you want to go: a metro section ticket (75Ft) takes you three stops on the same line; a metro transfer ticket (170Ft) is valid for as many stops as you like with one line change; and a metro section transfer ticket (120Ft) takes you five stops with one line change. Tickets must be validated when you use them: on the metro and HÉV you punch them in the machines at the entrance (remember to validate a new ticket if you change lines); on trams, trolley buses and buses you punch the tickets on board in the small red or orange machines. Books of ten and twenty tickets are also available for 1000Ft and 1950Ft respectively – but note that if a ticket is separated from the book it will become invalid.

Day passes (*napijegy*) cost 850Ft and are valid for unlimited travel – on the metro, buses, trams, trolley buses, the Cogwheel Railway and suburban HÉV lines – until midnight; three-day passes cost 1750Ft. **Season tickets** cost around 2150Ft for a week, 2700Ft for two weeks and 4000Ft for a month, and are available from metro stations, but you'll need a passport photo for the accompanying photocard.

There is a 1500Ft **fine**, strictly enforced, for travelling without a valid ticket. If you have a season ticket but are not carrying it, the fine is higher, though most of it is refunded upon presentation of the season ticket within three days at the BKV office at VII, Akácfa utca 15, near Blaha Lujza tér metro. **Children** up to the age of 6 travel free.

THE METRO

Running at two- to twelve-minute intervals between 4.30am and 11.10pm, Budapest's **metro** reaches most areas of interest to tourists, its three lines intersecting at Deák tér in downtown Pest. From nearby Vörösmarty tér, the **yellow line** (line 1) runs out beneath Andrássy út to Mexikoi út, beyond the Városliget. The **red line** (line 2) connects Déli Station in Buda with Keleti Station and Örs vezér tere in Pest; and the **blue line** (line 3) describes an arc from Kőbánya-Kispest to Újpest-Központ, via Ferenciek tere and Nyugati Station. There's little risk of going astray once you've learned to recognize the signs *bejárat* (entrance), *kijárat* (exit), *vonal* (line) and *felé* (towards). Drivers announce the next stop between stations and the train's direction is indicated by the name of the station at the end of the line.

See map 1 for a plan of the metro.

BUSES, TRAMS AND TROLLEY BUSES

Buses (*autóbusz*) are useful for journeys that can't be made by metro – especially around Buda, where Moszkva tér (on the red line) and Móricz Zsigmond körtér (southwest of Gellért-hegy) are the main bus terminals. Bus stops are marked by a blue sign with the label "*autóbusz*" or with a picture of a bus in the centre, and have timetables underneath; most buses run every ten to twenty minutes from 5am to 11pm (*Utolsó kocsi indul . . .* means "the last one leaves . . ."). Regular services are numbered in black, buses with red numbers make fewer stops en route, and those with a red "E" suffix run non-stop between terminals. You should punch your own ticket on board; to get the bus to stop, push the button above

USEFUL ROUTES

Buses

#7 Bosnyák tér–Keleti Station–Móricz Zsigmond körtér (via Rákóczi út, Ferenciek tere, the *Hotel Gellért*, Rác and Rudas Baths). Red #7–173 continues on to Kelenföld Station.

#16 Erzsébet tér–Dísz tér (Castle District).

#22 Moszkva tér–Budakeszi.

#26 Nyugati tér–Szent István körút–Margit sziget–Árpád híd metro station.

#27 Móricz Zsigmond körtér–near the top of Gellért-hegy.

#56 Moszkva tér–Szilágyi Erzsébet fasor–Hűvösvölgy, with the red #56E operating a virtually non-stop service.

#65 Kolosy tér–Pálvölgyi Caves–halfway up Hármashatár-hegy.

#86 Southern Buda–Gellért tér–the Víziváros–Flórián tér (Óbuda).

#105 Apor Vilmos tér–Lánchíd–Deák tér.

Várbusz Minibus Moszkva tér–Dísz tér and back.

Night buses

#6É Moszkva tér–Margit sziget–Nyugati Station–Nagykörút–Móricz Zsigmond körtér.

#78É Örs vezér tere–Bosnyák tér–Keleti Station–Buda side of Erzsébet Bridge.

the door or on the handrail beside the door. Busy routes are also served by **night buses** (up to four every hour), with black numbers and an "É" suffix.

Yellow **trams** (*villamos*) are chiefly good for travelling around the Nagykörút or along the embankments. Services run from early in the morning to 11pm. **Trolley buses** (*trolibusz*) mostly operate northeast of the centre near the Városliget. The reason route numbers start at 70 is that the first trolley bus line was inaugurated on Stalin's seventieth birthday in 1949. Trolley bus #83 was started in 1961, when Stalin would have been 83.

#14É and #50É both run along Kispest (Határ út metro station)–Deák tér–Lehel tér along the route of the blue metro and on to the north and south.

#49É Moszkva tér–Erzsébet Bridge–Hotel Gellért–Móricz Zsigmond körtér.

Trams

#2 Margit Bridge–Petőfi Bridge along embankment–HÉV station at Közvágóhíd.

#4 Moszkva tér–Margit sziget–Nyugati Station–Nagykörút–Petőfi Bridge–Október 23 utca.

#6 Moszkva tér–Margit sziget–Nyugati Station–Nagykörút–Petőfi Bridge–Móricz Zsigmond körtér.

#19 Batthyány tér–Víziváros–Kelenföld Station.

#47 Deák tér–Szabadság Bridge–Hotel Gellért–Móricz Zsigmond körtér–Budafok.

#49 Deák tér–Szabadság Bridge–Hotel Gellért–Móricz Zsigmond körtér–Kelenföld Station.

#56 Moszkva tér–Szilágyi Erzsébet fasor–Hűvösvölgy.

Trolley buses

#72 Arany János utca metro station–Nyugati Station–Zoo–Széchenyi Baths–Petőfi Csarnok–Thököly út.

#74 Dohány utca (outside the Main Synagogue)–Városliget.

TAXIS

Budapest's **taxis** have gained themselves a reputation for ripping off foreigners – the best advice is to use one of the following established companies: Főtaxi (☎ 222-2222) or Citytaxi (☎ 211-1111) are the most reliable and the latter also has an English-speaking service; Tele-5-taxi (☎ 355-5555); Buda-taxi (☎ 233-3333); and Volántaxi (☎ 466-6666). Avoid unmarked private cars and those hanging around the stations and airport – the "airport" taxis often charge a far higher rate than the normal taxis from the air-

TAXIS

15

port into town. Beware also of fake Fő and City taxis, sporting copies of the red-and-white chequerboard or yellow shield logos, which will charge you a vastly inflated price.

Taxis can be flagged down on the street or, for a cheaper rate, ordered by phone. There are ranks throughout the city and you can hop into whichever cab you choose – don't feel you have to opt for the one at the front of the line if it looks at all dodgy. Be sure your taxi has a meter that is visible, and that it is switched on when you get in; rates should also be clearly displayed. **Fares** begin at 200Ft, and the price per kilometre is around 250Ft.

SUBURBAN TRAINS

Overground **HÉV trains** provide easy access to Budapest's suburbs, running at least four times an hour between 6.30am and 11pm. As far as most visitors are concerned, the most useful line is the one from **Batthyány tér** (on the red metro line) out to **Szentendre** (see p.139) north of Budapest, which passes through Óbuda, Aquincum and RómaiFürdő. The other lines originate in Pest, with one running northeast from **Örs vezér tere** (also on the red metro line) to **Gödöllő** via the Formula One racing track at Mogyoród; the other southwards from **Soroksári út** (bus #23 or #54 from Boráros tér) to **Ráckeve**, on Csepel sziget. On all these routes, a normal city transport ticket will take you to the city limits, beyond which you must punch additional tickets according to the distance travelled. Alternatively, you can purchase a ticket that covers the whole journey at the ticket office in the station or from the conductor on board.

FERRIES AND OTHER RIDES

Although **ferries** play little useful part in the transport system, they do offer an enjoyable ride. From May to September there are boats between Boráros tér (by Petőfi híd) and Batthyány tér up to Jászai Mari tér and Rómaifürdő – running every fifteen to thirty minutes between 7am and 7pm and costing 200–450Ft. From May to August there is also a boat from the Jászai Mari tér dock to Pünkösdfürdő in northern Buda (1hr; check times on the board at the main dock), though you might prefer to disembark at Margit sziget, before the boat reaches dismal Békásmegyer. Ferry tickets can be obtained from kiosks (where timetables are posted) or machines at the docks.

Other pleasure rides can be found in the Buda Hills, on the **Cogwheel Railway** (*Fogaskerekű vasút*), the **Children's Railway** (*Gyermekvasút*, largely staffed by kids) and the **Chairlift** (*Libegő*) between Zugliget and János-hegy, all of which are detailed on p.65. An experience not to be missed is a ride in the vintage **funicular** (*Sikló*) that ascends from Clark Ádám tér to the Buda Palace on Várhegy (see p.53).

THE GUIDE

Várhegy

Várhegy (Castle Hill), often referred to simply as the Vár, is Buda's most prominent feature. A mile-long plateau encrusted with bastions, mansions and a huge palace, it dominates both the Víziváros below and Pest, over the river, making this stretch of the river one of the grandest, loveliest urban waterfronts in Europe. The hill's striking location and its strategic utility have long gone hand in hand: Hungarian kings built their palaces here because it was easy to defend, a fact appreciated by the Turks, Habsburgs and other occupiers. **Buda Palace** serves as a reminder of this past, rising like a house of cards at the southern end of the hill, as proud yet insubstantial as those who ruled there while Hungary's fate was determined by mightier forces.

Várhegy's buildings have been almost wholly reconstructed from the rubble of 1945, when the Wehrmacht and the Red Army battled over the hill while Buda's inhabitants cowered underground. It was the eighty-sixth time that Várhegy had been ravaged and rebuilt over seven centuries, rivalling the devastation caused by the recapture of Buda from the Turks in 1686. It was this repeated destruction that caused the melange of styles that characterizes the hill. While the palace is a faithful postwar reconstruction of the Habsburg behemoth that bestrode the ruins of earlier

APPROACHES TO VÁRHEGY

The simplest and most novel approach to Várhegy is to ride up to the palace by Sikló (see p.53), a renovated nineteenth-century funicular that runs from Clark Ádám tér by the Lánchíd (see p.51). From Moszkva tér (on metro line 2) you can either take the Várbusz, a minibus that leaves from the raised side of Moszkva tér and terminates by the palace, or walk uphill to the Vienna Gate at the northern end of the Castle District. Walking from Batthyány tér via the steep flights of steps (*lépcső*) off Fő utca involves more effort, but the dramatic stairway up to the Fishermen's Bastion is worth the sweat. The most direct approach from Pest is to ride bus #16 from Erzsébet tér across the Lánchíd to the lower terminal of the Sikló, or to the end of the line on Dísz tér, near Buda Palace.

palaces, the neo-Gothic **Mátyás Church** and **Fishermen's Bastion** are romantic nineteenth-century evocations of medieval glories, interweaving past and present national fixations.

However, the streets of the **Castle District** (*Várnegyed*), the residential area to the north of the palace, still follow their medieval courses, with Gothic arches and stone carvings half-concealed in the courtyards and passages of eighteenth-century Baroque houses, whose facades are embellished with fancy ironwork grilles. For many centuries, residence here was a privilege granted to religious or ethnic groups, each occupying a specific street. This pattern persisted through the 145-year-long Turkish occupation, when Armenians, Circassians and Sephardic Jews established themselves under the relatively tolerant Ottomans. The liberation of Buda by a multinational Christian army under Habsburg command was followed by a pogrom and ordinances restricting the right of residence to Catholics and

VÁRHEGY

Germans, a law that remained in force for nearly a century. Almost every building here displays a *műemlék* (listed) plaque giving details of its history (in Hungarian), and a surprising number are still homes rather than embassies or boutiques – there are even a couple of schools and corner shops. At dusk, when most of the tourists have left, pensioners walk their dogs and toddlers play in the long shadows of Hungarian history.

SZENTHÁROMSÁG TÉR

Map 5, D3.
The obvious starting point is **Szentháromság tér** (Holy Trinity Square), the historic heart of the district, named after an ornate **Trinity Column** erected in 1713 in thanksgiving for the abatement of a plague; a scene showing people dying from the Black Death appears on the plinth. To the southwest stands the former **Town Hall** of Buda, which functioned as a municipality until the unification of Buda, Pest and Óbuda in 1873; notice the corner statue of Pallas Athene, bearing Buda's coat of arms on her shield. Down the road at Szentháromság utca 7, the tiny **Ruszwurm patisserie** has been a pastry shop and café since 1827, and was a gingerbread shop in the Middle Ages. Its Empire-style decor looks much the same as it would have done under Vilmos Ruszwurm, who ran the patisserie for nearly four decades from 1884.

Mátyás Church

Map 5, D3. Mon–Sat 9am–5pm, Sun 1pm–5pm; 200Ft, crypt and treasures 200Ft; audioguide 200Ft.
The square's most prominent feature is the neo-Gothic **Mátyás Church** (*Mátyás templom*), with its wildly asymmetrical diamond-patterned roofs and toothy spires.

Officially dedicated to Our Lady but popularly named after "Good King Mátyás", the building is a late nineteenth-century re-creation by architect Frigyes Schulek, grafted onto those portions of the original thirteenth-century church that survived the siege of 1686. Ravaged yet again in World War II, the church was laboriously restored by a Communist regime keen to show its patriotic credentials, and the historic "Change of Systems" in 1990 saw the sanctity of this "ancient shrine of the Hungarian people" reaffirmed – which means that visitors are expected to be properly dressed and respectfully behaved.

As you enter the church through its twin-spired **Mary Portal**, the richness of the interior is overwhelming. Painted leaves and geometric motifs run up columns and under vaulting, while shafts of light fall through rose windows onto gilded altars and statues with stunning effect. Most of the **frescoes** were executed by Károly Lotz or Bertalan Székely, the foremost historical painters of the nineteenth century. The **coat of arms of King Mátyás** can be seen on the wall to your left, just inside; his family name, Corvinus, comes from the raven (*corvus* in Latin) that appeared on his heraldry and on every volume in the famous Corvin Library.

Around the corner, beneath the south tower, is the **Loreto Chapel**, containing a Baroque Madonna, while in the bay beneath the Béla Tower you can see two medieval capitals, one carved with monsters fighting a dragon, the other with two bearded figures reading a book. The tower is named after Béla IV, who founded the church, rather than his predecessor in the second chapel along, who shares a double sarcophagus with Anne of Chatillon. Originally located in the old capital, Székesfehérvár, the **tomb of Béla III** and his queen was moved here after its discovery in 1848. Although Hungary's medieval kings were crowned at Székesfehérvár, it was customary to make a prior appearance in Buda – hence the sobriquet, the "Coronation Church".

By paying extra to visit the **crypt** you can see the red-marble tombstone of a nameless Árpád prince, and a small collection of **ecclesiastical treasures** and relics, including the right foot of St János. Otherwise, climb a spiral staircase to the **Royal Oratory** (included in price of main ticket) overlooking the stained-glass windows and embossed vaulting of the nave; here votive figures and vestments prepare the way for a **replica of the Coronation Regalia**, whose attached exhibition is more informative about the provenance of St Stephen's Crown than that accompanying the originals, on display in Parliament (see p.92).

Mass is celebrated in the Mátyás Church (daily 7am, 8.30am & 6pm, plus 10am & noon on Sundays and public holidays) in Latin or Hungarian (from noon onwards), with a choir and organ music. It is also a superb venue for concerts during the festival seasons, and evening organ recitals throughout the year. Details appear in listings magazines and on the church's own website Ⓦwww.matyas-templom.hu. Tickets are available on the spot or from any booking agency (see p.267).

FISHERMEN'S BASTION

Map 5, E3.

After the Mátyás Church, the most impressive sight in Várhegy is the **Fishermen's Bastion** (*Halászbástya*) just beyond, which frames the view of Pest across the river. Although fishermen from the Víziváros reputedly defended this part of the hill during the Middle Ages, the existing bastion is purely decorative. An undulating white rampart of cloisters and stairways intersecting at seven tent-like turrets (symbolizing the Magyar tribes that conquered the

FISHERMEN'S BASTION

KING STEPHEN

If you commit just one figure from Hungarian history to memory, make it King Stephen, for it was he who welded the tribal Magyar fiefdoms into a state and won recognition from Christendom. Born Vajk, son of Grand Duke Géza, he emulated his father's policy of trying to convert the pagan Magyars and develop Hungary with the help of foreign preachers, craftsmen and merchants. By marrying Gizella of Bavaria in 996, he was able to use her father's knights to crush a pagan revolt after Géza's death, and subsequently received an apostolic cross and crown from Pope Sylvester II for his coronation on Christmas Day, 1000 AD, when he took the name Stephen (István in Hungarian).

Though noted for his enlightened views (such as the need for tolerance and the desirability of multiracial nations), he could act ruthlessly when necessary. After his only son Imre died in an accident and a pagan seemed likely to inherit, Stephen had the man blinded and poured molten lead into his ears. Naming his successor, he symbolically offered his crown to the Virgin Mary rather than the Holy Roman Emperor or the pope; she has since been considered the Patroness of Hungary. Swiftly canonized after his death in 1038, Saint Stephen became a national talisman, his mummified right hand a holy relic, and his coronation regalia the symbol of statehood. Despite playing down his cult for decades, even the Communists eventually embraced it in a bid for some legitimacy, while nobody in post-Communist Hungary thinks it odd that the symbol of the republic should be the crown and cross of King Stephen.

Carpathian Basin), it looks as though it was dreamt up by the illusionist artist Escher, but was actually designed by Schulek as a foil to the Mátyás Church. The **view** of Pest across the river is only surpassed by the vistas from the terrace of Buda Palace, and the Citadella on Gellért-hegy.

Between the bastion and the church, an equestrian **stat-ue of King Stephen** honours the founder of the Hungarian nation, whose conversion to Christianity and coronation with a crown sent by the pope presaged the Magyars' integration into European civilization (see box opposite). The relief at the back of the plinth depicts Schulek offering a model of the Mátyás Church to Stephen. Like the church and the bastion, his statue is reflected in the copper-glass facade of the **Budapest Hilton**, incorporating chunks of a medieval Dominican church and monastery on the side facing the river, and an eighteenth-century Jesuit college on the other, which bears a copy of the **Mátyás Relief** from Bautzen in Germany that's regarded as the only true likeness of Hungary's Renaissance monarch.

MUSEUM OF COMMERCE AND CATERING

Map 5, D2. Wed–Fri 10am–5pm, Sat & Sun 10am–6pm; 100Ft, student 50Ft.

Be sure to visit the fascinating **Museum of Commerce and Catering** (*Kereskedelmi és Vendéglátóipari Múzeum*) at Fortuna utca 4, where the *Fortuna Inn* was once located. The commerce section contains antique shopfronts and interiors and an early twentieth-century illuminated sign advertising beer, and, as a finale, its curator activates a model dog that raps on the glass with its paws, which was meant to attract passers-by into stores. The catering part pays homage to the restaurateur Károly Gundel, the confec-tioner Emil Gerbeaud, and Alfred Dobos, who became a celebrity when his *dobostorta*, a caramel-topped layered sponge cake, won a prize at the Vienna Exhibition. Another section called "Hospitable Budapest" covers tourism, nightlife and spas, featuring furnishings from old coffee houses and a reconstructed bedroom from the *Gellért*

Hotel. Waiters used such specialized items of cutlery as asparagus clippers, produced by the Budapest instrument-makers Ignácz Dreher & Son, whose 25-bladed pocket knife (anticipating the Swiss Army version) is also on display.

THE MUSIC HISTORY MUSEUM

Map 5, E2. Tues–Sun: April–Oct 10am–6pm; Nov–March 10am–5pm; 300Ft, student 150Ft.

The **Music History Museum** (*Zenetörténeti Múzeum*) at Táncsics Mihály utca 7 occupies the Baroque Erdödy Palace where Beethoven was a guest in 1800 and Bartók once had a workshop before he emigrated. Though its postwar interior is a let-down after the courtyard, it focuses attention on the splendid instruments that represent three centuries of music, from a Holczman harp made for Marie Antoinette and a unique tongue-shaped violin in the classical section to hurdy-gurdies, zithers, cowhorns and bagpipes in the folk part. You can also see the Schunda pedal-cimbalom, a factory product which began to replace home-made folk instruments by the 1900s. There's also an exhibition of Bartók's scores and jottings, including bits of *The Wooden Prince* and *Violin Rhapsody No.2*.

On your way out, have a look at no. 9 next door, which was once the Joseph Barracks where the Habsburgs jailed Hungarian radicals such as Mihály Táncsics, after whom the street is named. In an earlier age the street was known as Zsidó utca (Jewish Street), when both Ashkenazi and Sephardic Jews lived here.

THE MEDIEVAL JEWISH PRAYER HOUSE

Map 5, D2. May–Oct Tues–Sun 10am–5pm; 200Ft, student 80Ft.
Buda's Ashkenazi community was established in the reign of

Béla IV and encouraged by King Mátyás, who let the Jews build a synagogue and appointed a Jewish council led by Jacobus Mendel. Part of Mendel's house survives in the entrance to Táncsics Mihály utca 26, which contains a **Medieval Jewish Prayer House** (*Középkori Zsidó Imaház*), once used by the Sephardis. All that remains of its original decor are two Cabbalistic symbols painted on a wall, and, though the museum does its best to flesh out the history of the community with maps and prints, all the real treasures are in the Jewish Museum in Pest (see p.116).

KAPISZTRÁN TÉR

At the end of Táncsics Mihály utca lies **Bécsi kapu tér**, named after the **Vienna Gate** (*Bécsi kapu*) that was erected on the 250th anniversary of the recapture of Buda. Beside it, the forbidding-looking neo-Romanesque **National Archives** (no admission) guard the way to **Kapisztrán tér**, a larger square centred on the **Mary Magdalene Tower** (*Magdolna-torony*), whose accompanying church was wrecked in World War II. In medieval times this was where Hungarian residents worshipped; Germans used the Mátyás Church. Today the tower boasts a peal of ornamental bells that jingles through a medley composed by the jazz pianist György Szabados that includes Hungarian folk tunes, Chopin *Études* and the theme from *Bridge Over the River Kwai*.

Beyond the tower is a **statue of Friar John Capistranus**, who exhorted the Hungarians to victory at the siege of Belgrade in 1456; the pope hailed it by ordering church bells to be rung at noon throughout Europe. It shows Capistranus bestriding a dead Turk and is aptly sited outside the Military History Museum.

The Military History Museum

Map 5, C1. April–Sept 10am–6pm; Oct–March 10am–4pm; closed Mon; 250Ft, student 80Ft.

The **Military History Museum** (*Hadtörténeti Múzeum*), in a former barracks on the north side of the square, has gung-ho exhibitions on the history of hand weapons from ancient times till the advent of firearms, and the birth and campaigns of the Honvéd (national army) during the 1848–49 War of Independence. However, what sticks in the memory are the sections on the Hungarian Second Army that was decimated at Stalingrad, and the "Thirteen Days" of the 1956 Uprising (accompanied by newsreel footage at 11am & 2pm). In the courtyard are post-Communist memorials to the POWs who never returned from the Gulag.

The entrance to the museum is on the Tóth Árpád sétány, a promenade lined with cannons and chestnut trees, overlooking the Buda Hills, which leads past a giant **flagpole** striped in Hungarian colours to the symbolic **grave of Abdurrahman**, the last Turkish Pasha of Buda, who died on the walls in 1686 – a "valiant foe", according to the inscription.

ORSZÁGHÁZ UTCA

Back towards Szentháromság tér, there's more to be seen on **Országház utca**, which was the district's main thoroughfare in the Middle Ages and known as the "street of baths" during Turkish times. Its present name, Parliament Street, recalls the sessions of the Diet held in the 1790s in a former Poor Clares' cloister at no. 28, where the Gestapo imprisoned 350 Hungarians and foreigners in 1945. No. 17, over the road, consists of two medieval houses joined together and has a relief of a croissant on its keystone, from the time when it was a bakery. A few doors down from the old parliament building, Renaissance sgraffiti survive on the underside of the bay window of no. 22 and a Gothic trefoil-arched cornice on the house next door, while the one beyond has been rebuilt in its original fifteenth-century form.

ÚRI UTCA

Úri utca (Gentleman Street) also boasts historic associations, for it was at the former Franciscan monastery at no. 51 that the five Hungarian Jacobins were held before being beheaded on the "Blood Meadow" below the hill in 1795. Next door is a wing of the Poor Clares' cloister that served as a postwar telephone exchange before being turned into a **Telephone Museum** (*Telefónia Múzeum*; Tues–Sun 10am–4pm; 100Ft, student 50Ft). The museum's curator strives to explain the development of telephone exchanges since Tivadar Puuskás introduced them to Budapest in the early 1900s – activating a noisy rotary one that's stood here since the 1930s – and you're invited to dial up commentaries in English or songs in Hungarian, check out the webcam and internet facilities, and admire the personal phones of Emperor Franz Josef, Admiral Horthy and the Communist leader Kádár.

Further down the street, on either side, notice the statues of the four seasons in the first floor niches at nos. 54–56, Gothic sedilia in the gateway of nos. 48–50, and three arched windows and two diamond-shaped ones from the fourteenth and fifteenth centuries at no. 31.

The Labyrinth of Buda Castle

Map 5, C4. Daily 9.30am–7.30pm; guided tours every half hour; 900Ft, student 700Ft.

An unusual attraction is the **Labyrinth of Buda Castle** (*Budavári Labirintus*), better known as the *Várbarlang* (Castle caves), whose main entrance is at Úri utca 9. Cavities formed by hot springs and cellars dug since medieval times form 10km of galleries that were converted into an air-raid shelter for up to 10,000 people in the 1930s and used as such in World War II. The labyrinth remained in military hands till the 1980s, when it opened as a waxworks; refurbished in 1997, it is now marketed as a New Age experience of shamanism and history. One section features copies of the cave paintings of Lascaux (Buda's caves also sheltered prehistoric hunters), while masked figures and a giant head sunken into the floor enliven other dank chambers. There's another entrance beyond the castle walls at Lovas út 4, which is wheelchair-accessible for some of the way; contact ©labirint@elender.hu for details.

THE GOLDEN EAGLE PHARMACY

Map 5, D4. Tues–Sun 10.30am–6.30pm; 100Ft, student 50Ft.

Heading south from Szentháromság tér towards the palace, check out the **Golden Eagle Pharmacy Museum** (*Arany Sas Patikamúzeum*) at Tárnok utca 18. The Golden Eagle was the first pharmacy in Buda, established after the expulsion of the Turks, and moved to its present site in the eighteenth century. Its original murals and furnishings lend authenticity to dubious nostrums, including the skull of a mummy used to make "Mumia" powder to treat epilepsy, and a reconstruction of an alchemist's laboratory complete with dried bats and crocodiles. Notice the portrait of the Dominican nun who is also a pharmacist – common practice for nuns and monks in the Middle Ages. The *Tárnok* coffee house, next door but one, occupies a medieval building with a Renaissance sgraffiti facade of red and yellow checks and roundels, and, like the street, is named after the royal treasurers who once lived there.

DÍSZ TÉR

Map 5, D5.

Both Tárnok utca and Úri utca end in **Dísz tér** (Parade Square), whose cobbled expanses are guarded by a mournful Honvéd memorial to the dead of 1848–49. Straight ahead lies the scarred hulk of the old **Ministry of Defence**, while to your left stands the **Castle Theatre** (*Várszínház*). A Carmelite church until the order was dissolved by Josef II, its conversion was supervised by Farkas Kempelen, inventor of a chess-playing automaton. It was here that the first-ever play in Hungarian was staged in 1790, and where Beethoven performed in 1808. The last building in the row is the **Sándor Palace** (*Sándor Palota*), formerly the prime minister's residence, where Premier Teleki shot himself in protest at Hungary joining the Nazi invasion of Yugoslavia. It is currently being restored.

The Turul statue

Next door to Sándor Palace, the upper terminal of the **Sikló** funicular is separated from the terrace of Buda Palace by stately railings and the ferocious-looking **Turul statue** – a giant bronze eagle clasping a sword in its talons, which is visible from across the river. In Magyar mythology the Turul sired the first dynasty of Hungarian kings by raping the grandmother of Prince Árpád, who led the tribes into the Carpathian Basin. The Turul also accompanied their raids on Europe bearing the sword of Attila the Hun in its talons. During the nineteenth century it became a symbol of Hungarian identity in the face of Austrian culture, but wound up being co-opted by the Habsburgs, who cast Emperor Franz Josef as a latter-day Árpád, founder of the Dual Monarchy for the next millennium. Today, the Turul has been adopted as an emblem by Hungary's skinheads.

DÍSZ TÉR

From here, you a descend a staircase to the **terrace** of the palace, commanding a sweeping **view** of Pest. Beyond the souvenir stalls prances an **equestrian statue of Prince Eugene of Savoy**, the liberator of Buda. The bronze statues nearby represent **Csongor** and **Tünde**, the lovers of Vörösmarty's drama of the same name.

BUDA PALACE

Map 5, D7–D8. Sikló, Várbusz or bus #16.

As befits a former royal residence, the lineage of **Buda Palace** (*Budavári palota*) can be traced back to medieval times, the rise and fall of various palaces on the hill reflecting the changing fortunes of the Hungarian state. The first fortifications and dwellings, hastily erected by Béla IV after the Mongol invasion of 1241–42, were replaced by the grander palaces of the Angevin kings, who ruled in more prosperous and stable times. This process of rebuilding reached its zenith in the reign of Mátyás Corvinus (1458–90), whose palace was a Renaissance extravaganza to which artists and scholars from all over Europe were drawn by the blandishments of Queen Beatrice and the prospect of lavish hospitality. The rooms had hot and cold running water and during celebrations the fountains and gargoyles flowed with wine. After the Turkish occupation and the long siege that ended it, only ruins were left – which the Habsburgs, Hungary's new rulers, levelled to build a palace of their own.

From Empress Maria Theresa's modest beginnings (a mere 203 rooms, which she never saw completed), the palace expanded inexorably throughout the nineteenth century, though no monarch ever dwelt here, only the Habsburg Palatine (viceroy). After the collapse of the empire following World War I, Admiral Horthy inhabited the building with all the pomp of monarchy until he was deposed by a German coup in October 1944. The palace was left unoccupied, and it wasn't long before the siege of Buda once again resulted in total devastation. Reconstruction work began in the 1950s in tandem with excavations of the medieval substrata beneath the rubble. The medieval section was incorporated into the new building, whose interior is far less elegant than the prewar version, being designed to accommodate cultural institutions.

The complex houses the **Museum of Contemporary Art** (Wing A), the **Hungarian National Gallery** (Wings B, C and D), the **Budapest History Museum** (E) and the **National Széchenyi Library** (F) – of which the first three are definitely worth seeing and could easily take an afternoon. There are separate entrances for each.

The Hungarian National Gallery

Map 5, D7. Tues–Sun 10am–6pm; 500Ft, student 250Ft, disabled free; Habsburg crypt 300Ft. Guided tours in English 1300Ft for up to five persons; ☎0660/559-955. Audioguide 950Ft.

Most people's first port of call is the **Hungarian National Gallery** (*Magyar Nemzeti Galéria*), devoted to Hungarian art from the Middle Ages to the present. It contains much that's superb, but the vastness of the collection and the confusing layout can be fatiguing. The main entrance is on the eastern side of Wing C, overlooking the river, behind the statue of Eugene of Savoy. It's not worth buying a special ticket to see the separate **Habsburg crypt** until you've checked that a tour is scheduled, as they require at least 25 people. The crypt contains the tombs of several Habsburgs who ruled as Palatine, or viceroy, of Hungary up until 1849.

Ground floor

On the ground floor of the museum, marble reliefs of Beatrice and Mátyás and a lovely **wooden ceiling** from a

BUDA PALACE

sixteenth-century church are the highlights of a **Medieval and Renaissance Lapidarium**, which you need to pass through to reach the fantastic collection of fifteenth-century **Gothic altarpieces** and panels at the rear of Wing D. Salvaged from churches great and small that escaped destruction by the Turks, some are artful and others rustic, but all are full of character and detail. Notice the varied reactions to the *Death of the Virgin* from Kassa (a centre of altar-painting) and the gloating spectators in the Jánosrét *Passion*. From the same church comes a *St Nicholas* altar as long as a limo and lurid as a comic strip, whose final scene shows cripples being cured by the saint's corpse. Also strange to modern eyes are *The Expulsion of St Adalbert*, who seems blithely oblivious to the burning of his church, and the woodcarving of *St Anthony the Hermit*, carrying a hill upon his back. The pointed finials on the high altar from Liptószentmária anticipate the winged altarpieces of the sixteenth century on the floor above. To get there without returning to the foyer, use the small staircase nearby and turn left, left and left again at the top.

First floor

The first floor covers the widest range of art and is likely to engage you the longest. It picks up where the ground floor left off in the former Throne Room, where **late Gothic altarpieces** with soaring pinnacles and carved surrounds are displayed. Most of them come from churches that are now in Slovakia or Romania, such as the altarpiece of the Virgin from Csíkmenaság or the homely St Anne altarpiece from Kisszeben, which looks like a medieval playgroup. On an altar from Berki, Mary Magdalene is raptured by angels as bishops are impaled, while another piece from Lipótszentandrás shows St Andrew clutching the poles for his crucifixion. Also look out for *The Visitation* by the anonymous "Master MS", in the anteroom, and the coffered ceiling from Gogánváralija, in the room behind the Kisszeben altarpiece.

Many of the works in the adjacent section on **Baroque art** once belonged to Prince Miklós Esterházy (including his portrait), or were confiscated from private owners in the 1950s. The prolific Austrian, **Anton Maulbertsch**, who executed scores of altars and murals reminiscent of Caravaggio, is represented here by smaller works such as *Christ Carrying His Cross*. In the central block, don't miss **Ádám Mányoki**'s portrait of Ferenc Rákóczi II from 1712, a sober study of a national hero that foreshadowed a new artistic genre of **National Historical art** in the nineteenth century.

People coming up the staircase to the central block are confronted by *Zrínyi's Sortie*, a vast canvas by Peter Krafft depicting the suicidal sally by the defenders of Szigetvár against a Turkish army fifty times their number. Not a drop of blood spatters the melee, as Count Zrínyi leads the charge across the bridge. On the upper landing hangs **Gyula Benczúr**'s *Reoccupying of Buda Castle*, whose portrayal of Eugene of Savoy and Karl of Lotharingia suggests a mere exchange of Turkish rulers for Habsburg ones, while *The Bewailing of László Hunyadi* by **Viktor Madarász**, in Wing D, would have been read as an allusion to the execution of Hungarian patriots after the War of Independence. In Wing B, notice Benczúr's *The Baptism of Vajk*, depicting the future St Stephen's conversion to Christianity, and two disparate battle scenes by **Bertalan Székely**: *Recovering the Corpse of Louis II* after the catastrophic Hungarian defeat at Mohács in 1526, and *The Women of Eger*, exalting their defiance of the Turks in 1552.

The rest of Wing B covers other trends in **nineteenth-century art**, namely genre painting, rural romanticism and Impressionism. Though best known as a historical painter, **Károly Lotz** also excelled at scenes like *Thunderstorm on the*

Puszta and *Horses at the Watering Place*, evoking the hazy skies and manly world of the Hungarian "Wild West". A section is devoted to works by **Mihály Munkácsy** and **László Paál**, exhibited together since both painted landscapes – though Paál did little else, whereas Munkácsy was internationally renowned for pictures with a social message (*The Condemned Cell*, *Tramps of the Night*) and bravura historical works like *The Conquest* (in the Parliament building). Many canvases have suffered from his use of bitumen in mixing paint, which has caused them to darken and crack – a problem that hasn't affected **László Mednyánszky's** moonlit *Fishing on the Tisza*. Another section displays works by **Pál Szinyei Merse**, the "father of Hungarian Impressionism", whose models and subjects were cheerfully bourgeois, for example *A Picnic in May*.

Second and third floors

Walking upstairs to the second floor, you come face to face with three huge canvases by the visionary artist **Tivadar Kosztka Csontváry**, whose obsession with the Holy Land and the "path of the sun" inspired scenes like *Look Down on the Dead Sea* and *Ruins of the Greek Theatre at Taormina*. When Picasso saw an exhibition of his works years later, he remarked: "And I thought I was the only great painter of our century." Six more, smaller Csontvárys can be found in Wing D.

Discerning the main trends in **twentieth-century art** up until the Communist era isn't made any easier by the juxtaposition of Post Impressionists like János Kmetty and Károly Ferenczy with exponents of Constructivism such as Béla Uitz, in Wing C, which splits up what should be a unified exhibition on **Symbolism** and **Art Nouveau** – two movements that were so entwined in Hungary that the distinction is moot. Wing D focuses on members of the Gödöllő and Nagybánya artists' colonies (whose influences were as diverse as William Morris, Klimt and Cézanne) – with fey nymphs by Simon Hollósy and enigmatic tapestries by János Vaszary – whilst a remote part of Wing B showcases work by **József Rippl-Rónai**, a pupil of Munkácsy's whose portraits went mostly unrecognized in his lifetime but are now regarded as Art Nouveau classics. The genre was more rewarding for contemporary applied artists like Miksa Róth, Károly Kernstok and the architect Ödön Lechner.

At the top of the stairs to the third floor, a *Throne of Fire* portraying the awful fate of the peasant rebel leader Dózsa is the sole survivor of the Socialist art that filled the third floor until its eviction in the 1990s. The space now hosts **temporary exhibitions** of graphics or photos by contemporary Hungarian artists.

Museum of Contemporary Art

Map 5, D7. Tues–Sun 10am–6pm; 400Ft, student 200Ft.
The **Museum of Contemporary Art** (*Kortárs Művészti Múzeum*) is a stylish joint venture by the Ministry of Culture and corporate sponsors, established in 1996 to build upon an earlier bequest by the German industrialist Peter Ludwig, in the year of Hungary's transition to democracy. Before then, Wing A of the palace had contained the Museum of the Working Class Movement, whose staff made amends for decades of misinformation by organizing an exhibition on the Stalinist era before moving out – hence the lavish use of red marble in the cloistered atrium, which is now used for **temporary exhibitions**, usually of installation art.

The **Ludwig Collection** includes US pop art such as Warhol's *Single Elvis*, Lichtenstein's *Vicky* and Rauschenberg's *Hedge*, Picasso's *Musketeer with a Sword*, and a felt-and-fat *Sealed Letter* by Beuys, but most of the museum's acquisitions are work by lesser-known Europeans, in veins from Hyper-Realism to neo-Primitivism.

The Museum of Contemporary Art has a pleasant *café* that's seldom crowded, with a view of the Buda Hills.

The Mátyás Fountain and Lion Courtyard

The square outside the museum is flanked on three sides by the palace and overlooks Buda to the west, though the **view** is marred by the MTI (Hungarian News Agency) building on Nap-hegy (Sun Hill). By the far wall stands the flamboyant **Mátyás Fountain**, whose bronze figures recall the legend of Szép Ilonka. This beautiful peasant girl met the king while he was hunting incognito, fell in love with him, and died of a broken heart after discovering his identity and realizing the futility of her hopes. The man with a falcon is the king's Italian chronicler, who recorded the story for posterity (it is also enshrined in a poem by Vörösmarty).

A gateway guarded by lions leads into the **Lion Courtyard**, totally enclosed by further wings. To your right is the **National Széchenyi Library** (*Országos Széchenyi Könyvtár*), occupying the nineteenth-century Ybl block, whose full size is only apparent from the far side of the hill, where it looms over Dózsa tér like a mountain. The library was founded in 1802 on the initiative of Count Ferenc Széchenyi, the father of István, who spearheaded the Reform era. A repository for publications in Hungarian and material relating to the country from around the world, by law it receives a copy of every book, newspaper and magazine that is published in Hungary. Its central reading room is open to the public (Mon 1–9pm, Tues–Sat 9am–9pm; free) and there are temporary exhibitions on diverse subjects. During library hours, a passenger **lift** in the adjacent building by the Lion Gateway provides direct access to and from Dózsa tér, at the foot of Várhegy.

The Budapest History Museum

Map 5, D8. Mid-May to mid-Sept daily 10am–6pm; Nov–Feb 10am–4pm, March & Oct 10am–6pm, closed Tues; 500Ft, student 200Ft.

On the far side of the Lion Courtyard, the **Budapest History Museum** (*Budapest Történeti Múzeum*) covers two millennia of history on three floors, before descending into original vaulted, flagstoned halls from the Renaissance and medieval palaces unearthed during excavations. It's worth starting with **prehistory**, on the top floor, to find out about the ancient Magyars. Here you can see the artefacts of their nomadic precursors, who overran the Pannonian Plain after the Romans left, such as a gold bridle and stirrup fastenings in a zoomorphic style from Avar burial mounds. Due to the ravages inflicted by the Mongols and the Turks there's little to show from the time of the Conquest or Hungary's medieval civilization, so most of the second floor is occupied by **Budapest in Modern Times**, an exhibition giving insight into urban planning, fashions, trade and vices, from 1686 onwards. At either end of the section, two lifesize replicas of the lions on the Lánchíd bracket the last century, starting with the hopes of the Reform era and ending with the devastated city of 1945. Other items range from an 1880s barrel organ to one of the Swedish Red Cross notices affixed to Jewish safe houses by Wallenberg (see p.117).

The **remains of the medieval palace** are reached from the basement via an eighteenth-century cellar spanning two medieval yards on a lower level. A wing of the ground floor of King Sigismund's palace and the cellars beneath the Corvin Library form an intermediate stratum overlaying the

BUDA PALACE

cross-vaulted crypt of the **Royal Chapel** and a **Gothic Hall** displaying statues from later in the fourteenth century, which were found in 1974. In another chamber are portions of red marble fireplaces and a massive portal carved with cherubs and flowers from the palace of King Mátyás. Emerging into daylight, bear left and up the stairs to reach another imposing hall, with a view over the castle ramparts.

Gellért-hegy, Tabán and the Víziváros

Gellért-hegy is as much a feature of the city's waterfront panorama as Várhegy and the Parliament building: a craggy dolomite cliff rearing 130m above the embankment, offering a fabulous view of the city. At its foot, the Gellért Hotel is famous for its Art Nouveau thermal baths and summer terrace. This is one area you'd be foolish to miss.

North of Gellért-hegy, **Tabán**, once Buda's artisan quarter, now has more roads than buildings and makes an incongruous setting for two of Budapest's most historic and magical Turkish baths. Further north again, between the castle and the river, the **Víziváros** is something of a quiet residential backwater in the heart of Buda, with a distinctive atmosphere, but few specific sights other than the Parish Church on Batthyány tér, and the Lánchíd and Sikló, 800m south.

The area to the **north of Várhegy** has a few attractions in the backstreets off Margit körút, and is best approached from the transport hub of Moszkva tér. Its slightly seedy streetlife and surprisingly wide range of eating and drinking places is a world apart from the affluent Rózsadomb, just uphill, while beyond are the Buda Hills.

GELLÉRT-HEGY

Map 3, G13. Bus #86 or tram #19 from Batthyány tér; tram #47 or #49 from the Kiskörút in Pest.

Surmounted by the Liberation Monument and the Citadella, **Gellért-hegy** makes a distinctive contribution to Budapest's skyline. The hill is named after the Italian missionary Ghirardus (Gellért in Hungarian), who converted pagan Magyars to Christianity at the behest of King Stephen. After his royal protector's demise, vengeful heathens strapped Gellért to a barrow and toppled him off the cliff, where a larger than life **statue of St Gellért** now stands astride an artificial waterfall facing the Erzsébet híd, his crucifix raised as if in admonition to motorists.

The Gellért Hotel and Baths

Pool: May–Sept daily 6am–7pm, July & Aug Fri & Sat also 8pm to midnight; Oct–April Mon–Fri 6am–7pm, Sat & Sun 6am–5pm. Baths: daily 6am–6pm. Pool & baths 1800Ft (800Ft after 5pm); baths only 1700Ft.

At the foot of the hill, the graceful wrought-iron **Szabadság híd** (Liberty Bridge) links the inner boulevard of Pest to Szent Gellért tér on the Buda side, dominated by the Art Nouveau **Gellért Hotel**. Opened in 1918, it was commandeered as a staff headquarters by the Reds, the Romanian army, and finally by Admiral Horthy, following his triumphal entry into "sinful Budapest" in 1920. During the 1930s and 40s, its balls were the highlight of Budapest's social calendar, when debutantes danced on a glass floor laid over its pool. The attached **Gellért Baths** (entered from Kelenhegyi út) are magnificently appointed with majolica

GELLÉRT-HEGY, TABÁN AND THE VÍZIVÁROS

tiles and mosaics, and so swanky that they charge sightseers
250Ft to espy the columned, Roman-style thermal pool,
with its lion-headed spouts and mixed-sex bathing. Stairs at
the far end descend to the separate thermal baths, with
ornate plunge pools and separate areas for men and women.
There is also a summer outdoor pool with a wave-machine
and terraces for nude sunbathing.

The Cave Church

Map 3, H13. Daily 8am–9pm; free.

On the hillside opposite the hotel you'll find the **Cave
Church** (*Sziklatemplom*), where masses are conducted by
white-robed monks of the Pauline order. The only order
indigenous to Hungary (founded in 1256), its monks served
as confessors to the Hungarian kings until Josef II dissolved
the order in 1773, though it was re-established 150 years
later. The Cave Church was created in the 1930s by monks
from the nearby Pauline monastery, and functioned until
the whole community was arrested by the ÁVO at midnight mass on Easter Monday, 1951, whereupon the chapel
was sealed up until 1989. Flickering candles and mournful
organ music create an eerie atmosphere during services
(daily 8.30–9.30am, 11am–noon, 4.30–6.30pm & 8–9pm),
but tourists are only allowed to enter between times.

From here, you can follow one of the footpaths to the summit – about a twenty-minute climb. The hillside, which still
bears fig trees planted by the Turks, was covered in vineyards
until a phylloxera epidemic struck in the nineteenth century.

The Liberation Monument and Citadella

Map 3, G13. Tram #16 or #19 from Szent Gellért tér to Móricz
Zsigmond körtér, then bus #27 to the end of the line followed by a
10-minute walk.

GELLÉRT-HEGY

45

Whether you walk up or get there by bus, the **summit** of Gellért-hegy affords a stunning **panoramic view**, drawing one's eye slowly along the curving river, past bridges and monumental landmarks, and then on to the Buda Hills and Pest's suburbs, merging hazily with the distant plain.

On the summit stands the **Liberation Monument** (*Felszabadulási emlékmű*) beside the citadel – a female figure brandishing the palm of victory over 30m aloft. There is a famous tale that the monument was originally commissioned by Admiral Horthy in memory of his son István (who was killed in a plane crash on the Eastern Front in 1942), but that, by substituting a palm branch for the propeller it was meant to hold and placing a statue of a Red Army soldier at the base, it was deftly recycled to commemorate the Soviet soldiers who died liberating Budapest from the Nazis. While the story may not be true, the monument's sculptor, Zsigmond Kisfaludi-Strobl, certainly succeeded in winning approval as a "Proletarian Artist", despite having previously specialized in busts of the aristocracy – and was henceforth known by his compatriots as "Kisfaludi-Strébel" (*strébel* meaning "to climb" or "step from side to side"). The monument survived calls for its removal following the end of Communism, but its inscription was rewritten to honour those who died for "Hungary's prosperity", and the Soviet soldier was banished to the Statue Park on the outskirts of Budapest (p.132).

The **Citadella** or fortress behind the monument was built by the Habsburgs to dominate the city in the aftermath of the 1848–49 Revolution; ironically, both its architects were Hungarians. When the historic Compromise was reached in 1867, citizens breached the walls to affirm that it no longer posed a threat to them – though in fact an SS regiment did later hole up in the citadel during World War II. Today it contains a tourist hostel and an informative outdoor museum relating the hill's history since the Celtic

Eravisci lived there two thousand years ago, but it's the stunning view from the ramparts that justifies the 300Ft admission charge.

TABÁN

The **Tabán** district, bordering the northern end of Gellért-hegy, chiefly consists of arterial roads built in Communist times on land left vacant by the prewar demolition of a quarter renowned for its drinking dens and open sewers. Traditionally this was inhabited by Serbs (*Rác* in Hungarian), who settled here en masse after the Turks were expelled, though, in a typically Balkan paradox, some were present earlier, working in the Ottoman gunpowder factories which may have been the origin of the name Tabán (from *tabahane*, the Turkish for "armoury"). Thankfully, the slum-clearance and motorway building spared Tabán's historic Turkish baths, and its traditions of lusty nightlife have been revived by outdoor bars like *Romkert*, open till 4am in the summer (see pp.202–203).

The Rudas Baths

Map 3, G12. Baths: men only, Mon–Fri 6am–7pm, Sat 6am–1pm; 700Ft. Pool: Mon–Fri 6am–6pm, Sat & Sun 6am–1pm; 600Ft.
The relaxing and curative effects of Buda's **mineral springs** have been appreciated for two thousand years. The Romans built splendid bathhouses at Aquincum and, while these declined with the empire, interest revived after the Knights of St John built a hospice on the site of the present Rudas Baths, near where St Elizabeth cured lepers in the springs below Gellért-hegy. However, it was the Turks who consolidated the habit of bathing (as Muslims, they were obliged to wash five times daily in preparation for prayer) and constructed proper bathhouses which function to this

TABÁN

day – though their surroundings and exteriors give little clue to what's inside.

The men-only **Rudas Baths** (*Rudas Gyógyfürdő*), in the shadow of Gellért-hegy, harbour a fantastic octagonal pool constructed in 1556 on the orders of Pasha Sokoli Mustapha. Bathers wallow amid shafts of light pouring in from the star-shaped apertures in the domed ceiling, surrounded by stone pillars with iron tie-beams and a nest of smaller pools for parboiling oneself or cooling down. There is also a modern swimming pool, open to both sexes, to the left of the entrance.

In the evening, the locality takes on a new dimension, as the outdoor *Romkert* bar around the corner fills up with smartly dressed people sipping cocktails and looking to pick somebody up.

The Király Baths (p.55) to the north of Batthyány tér are just as atmospheric as the Rudas. See p.228 for a rundown of the city's bathhouses, their practices and etiquette, and the relevant Hungarian terms.

The Rác Baths

Map 3, F11. Women: Mon, Wed & Fri 6.30am–7pm; men Tues, Thurs & Sat 6.30am–7pm; 600Ft.

Heading on to the Rác Baths, you'll pass the **Water Hall** (*Ivócsarnok*; Mon, Wed & Fri 11am–6pm, Tues & Thurs 7am–2pm) beneath the road to the bridge, which sells mineral water from three nearby springs by the tumbler. Regular imbibers bring bottles or jerrycans to fill.

The **Rác Baths** (*Rác Gyógyfürdő*), in a yellow building dating from the 1830s, are tucked away beneath Hegyalja út, leading uphill away from the bridgehead of the Erzsébet híd. The Turkish pool is less impressive than the ones in the

TABÁN

Rác and Király baths, and is frequented by those who find its sulphurous water at 40°C good for skin complaints and painful joints, or are attracted by the active gay scene.

The cuboid **memorial stone** outside the baths commemorates the 51st Esperanto Congress held in Budapest in 1966 – an event that would have been inconceivable in Stalin's day, when Esperanto was forbidden for conflicting with his thesis that the time for an international language had yet to come. Nearby, on one of the grassy areas that comprise Döbrentei tér, is a seated **statue of Empress Elizabeth** (1837–98), who endeared herself to Hungarians by learning their language and refusing to be stifled by her crusty husband, Franz Josef. Assassinated by an anarchist in Switzerland, she was widely mourned in Hungary and is still fondly known by her nickname, "Sissi". The Erzsébet híd (Elizabeth Bridge) is named after her.

The Semmelweis Medical Museum

Map 3, F10. Tues–Sun 10.30am–6pm; 150Ft, student 70Ft.

Often overlooked by tourists, the **Semmelweis Medical Museum** (*Semmelweis Orvostörténeti Múzeum*), at Apród utca 1–3, contains a fascinating collection of artefacts relating to the history of medicine, with mummified limbs from ancient Egypt and a shrunken head used by Borneo witch doctors giving an international dimension to the display. Other exhibits, including a medieval chastity belt, trepanning drills, a lifesize wax model of a dissected female cadaver, and a sewing machine for closing stomach incisions, all give an idea of the centuries of misconceptions and the slow progress of medicine through fatal errors.

The story of the museum's namesake, **Dr Ignác Semmelweis**, is also explained, though only in Hungarian. While serving in Vienna's public hospitals in the early nineteenth century, he discovered the cause of puerperal fever –

TABÁN

a form of blood poisoning contracted in childbirth that was usually fatal. He noticed that deaths were ten times lower on the wards where only midwives worked than on the ones attended by doctors and students, who went from dissecting corpses to delivering babies with only a perfunctory wash. His solution was simply to sterilize hands, clothes and instruments between operations, earning him the title of "saviour of mothers".

The museum also contains the 1876 **Holy Ghost Pharmacy**, transplanted here from Király utca, and a collection of portraits including one of Vilma Hugonai, Hungary's first woman doctor, and one of Kossuth's sister, Zsuzsanna, who founded the army medical corps during the War of Independence. The insignificant-looking stones in the park out back are actually Turkish gravestones.

The museum is just around the corner from **Szarvas tér** (Stag Square), named after the eighteenth-century *Stag House* inn at no. 1, which functions as a restaurant to this day.

THE VÍZIVÁROS

Inhabited by fishermen, craftsmen and their families in medieval times, the **Víziváros** or Watertown, between Várhegy and the Danube, became depopulated during the seventeenth century, and was resettled by Habsburg mercenaries and their camp followers after the Turks were driven out. The following century saw the neighbourhood gradually gentrified, with solid apartment blocks meeting at odd angles on the hillside, reached by alleys which mostly consist of steps rising from the main street, **Fő utca**. Some of these are still lit by gas lamps and look quite Dickensian on misty evenings. Although the Víziváros extends as far north as the Király Baths (see p.55), most visitors find the stretch between the Lánchíd and Batthyány tér quite sufficient.

GELLÉRT-HEGY, TABÁN AND THE VÍZIVÁROS

The Széchenyi Lánchíd

Map 3, F8. Bus #86 or tram #19 from Szent Gellért tér; bus #2 or #16 from Erzsébet tér in Pest.

The majestic **Lánchíd** (Chain Bridge) has a special place in the history of Budapest and in the hearts of its citizens. As the first permanent link between Buda and Pest (replacing seasonal pontoon bridges and ferries), it was a tremendous spur to the country's economic growth and eventual unification, linking the rural hinterland to European civilization so that Budapest became a commercial centre and transport hub. The bridge symbolized the abolition of feudal privilege, as nobles, hitherto exempt from taxes, were obliged to pay the toll to cross it. It also symbolized civic endurance, having been inaugurated only weeks after Hungary lost the 1849 War of Independence, when Austrian troops tried and failed to destroy it.

However, in 1945, the Wehrmacht dynamited all of Budapest's bridges in a bid to check the Red Army. Their reconstruction was one of the first tasks of the postwar era, and the reopening of the Lánchíd on the centenary of its inauguration (November 21) was heralded as proof that life was returning to normal, even as Hungary was becoming a Communist dictatorship. Today, the bridge is once again adorned with the national coat of arms, rather than Soviet symbols.

The idea for a bridge came to **Count István Széchenyi** (see box on p.52) after he was late for his father's funeral in 1820 because bad weather had made the Danube uncrossable. Turning his idea into reality was to preoccupy him for two decades, and it became the centrepiece of a grand plan to modernize Hungary's communications. Owing to Britain's industrial pre-eminence and Széchenyi's Anglophilia, the bridge was designed by **William Tierney Clark** (based on his earlier plan for Hammersmith Bridge)

51

COUNT SZÉCHENYI

Count István Széchenyi (1791–1860) was the outstanding figure of Hungary's Reform era. As a young aide-de-camp he cut a dash at the Congress of Vienna and did the rounds of stately homes across Europe. While in England, he steeplechased hell-for-leather, but still found time to examine factories and steam trains, providing Bernard Shaw with the inspiration for the "odious Zoltán Karpathy" of *Pygmalion* (and the musical *My Fair Lady*). Back in Hungary, he pondered solutions to his homeland's backwardness and offered a year's income from his estates towards the establishment of a Hungarian Academy. In 1830 he published *Hitel* (Credit), a hard-headed critique of the nation's feudal society.

Though politically conservative, Széchenyi was obsessed with modernization. A passionate convert to steam power after riding on the Manchester–Liverpool railway, he invited Britons to Hungary to build rail lines and the Lánchíd. He also imported steamships and dredgers, promoted horsebreeding and silk-making, and initiated the dredging of the River Tisza and the blasting of a road through the Iron Gates of the Danube. Alas, his achievements were rewarded by a melancholy end. The 1848 Revolution and the triumph of Kossuth triggered a nervous breakdown, and Széchenyi eventually shot himself.

and constructed under the supervision of a Scottish engineer, **Adam Clark** (no relation), from components cast in Britain. Besides the technical problems of erecting what was then the longest bridge in Europe (nearly 380m), there was also an attempt by the Austrians to blow it up – which Adam Clark personally thwarted by flooding its chain-lockers. He also dissuaded a Hungarian general from setting it alight in 1849.

Whereas Széchenyi later died in an asylum, having wit-
nessed the triumph and defeat of his *bête noire*, Kossuth,
Clark settled happily in Budapest with his Hungarian wife.
After his death, he was buried on the spot that now bears
his name, though his remains were subsequently moved to
Kerepesi Cemetery.

The Sikló and Kilometre Zero

Map 3, F8. Daily 7.30am–10pm; closed second & fourth Mon of
every month; 400Ft uphill, 300Ft downhill, under 10s 200Ft.
Budapest Card not valid on this route.

Clark also built the **tunnel** (*alagút*) under Várhegy, which
Budapesters joked could be used to store the new bridge
when it rained. Next to the tunnel entrance at the river end
is the lower terminal of the **Sikló**, a nineteenth-century
funicular running up to the palace. Constructed on the
initiative of Ödön, Széchenyi's son, it was only the second
funicular in the world when it was inaugurated in 1870,
and functioned without a hitch until wrecked by a shell in
1945. The yellow carriages are exact replicas of the originals, but are now lifted by an electric winch rather than a
steam engine. In the small park at its foot stands **Kilometre
Zero**, a zero-shaped monument from where all distances
from Budapest are measured.

Szilágyi Desző tér

Map 3, F6.
Beyond the **Institut Français** at Fő utca 17 – which sponsors a Bastille Day bash on the embankment – and a former
Capuchin church featuring Turkish window arches at no.
30, you'll emerge onto **Szilágyi Desző tér**, a square infamous for the events that occurred here in January 1945.
When Eichmann and the SS had already fled, members of

the Fascist Arrow Cross massacred hundreds of Budapest's Jews and dumped their bodies in the river; an inconspicuous plaque commemorates the victims. From here, you can make a brief detour up Vám utca, just north of the square, to see the **Iron Block**, a replica of a wooden block into which itinerant apprentices once hammered nails for good luck; the original is in a museum.

Batthyány tér

Map 3, E5. Batthyány tér metro (M2); bus #16 from Erzsébet tér in Pest.

The main square and social hub of the Víziváros, **Batthyány tér** is named after the nineteenth-century prime minister, Lajos Batthyány, but started out as Bomba tér (Bomb Square), after an ammunition depot sited here for the defence of the Danube. Today it is busy with shoppers visiting the supermarket in an old market hall on the western side of the square, and commuters using the underground interchange between the metro and the HÉV suburban line to Szentendre. The sunken, two-storey building to the right of the market used to be the *White Cross Inn*, where Casanova reputedly once stayed. Many of the older buildings in this area are sunken in this way, owing to the ground level being raised several feet in the nineteenth century to combat flooding.

The twin-towered **Church of St Anne** (*Szent Anna templom*) on the corner of Fő utca is one of the finest Baroque buildings in Budapest. Commissioned by the Jesuits in 1740, it wasn't consecrated until 1805, owing to financial problems, the abolition of the Jesuit order in 1773, and an earthquake. During Communist times there were plans to demolish the building, as it was feared that the metro would undermine its foundations, but these, fortunately, came to nothing. Figures of Faith, Hope and Charity hover above the entrance, and in the middle of the facade St Anne cherishes the child Mary, while God's eye surmounts the Buda coat of arms on its tympanum. The interior is ornate yet homely, its high altar festooned with statues of St Anne presenting Mary to the Temple in Jerusalem, accompanied by a host of cherubim and angels, while chintzy bouquets and potted trees welcome shoppers dropping in to say their prayers.

In the northern corner of the square, the **Church of the St Elizabeth Nuns** is worth a look inside for its fresco of St Florian protecting the faithful during the 1810 fire of Tabán.

The Király Baths

Map 3, E3. Men, Mon, Wed & Fri 9am–8pm; women, Tues & Thurs 6.30am–7pm, Sat 6.30am–noon; 600Ft.

You can identify the **Király Baths** (*Király gyógyfürdő*) by the four copper cupolas, shaped like tortoise shells, poking from its eighteenth-century facade. Together with the Rudas, this is the finest of Budapest's Turkish baths, whose octagonal pool, lit by star-shaped apertures in the dome, was built in 1570 for the Buda garrison. The baths' name, meaning "king", comes from that of the König family who owned them in the eighteenth century. Since the baths became a major meeting place for gay men in the mid-1990s, bathers have been obliged to wear swimming trunks.

On the way to the baths you'll pass the hulking Fascist-style **Military Court of Justice** at Fő utca 70–72, where Imre Nagy and other leaders of the 1956 Uprising were secretly tried and executed in 1958. The square outside has now been renamed after Nagy, whose body lay in an unmarked grave in the New Public Cemetery for over thirty years (see p.137), and makes a suitably emollient site for the new Foreign Ministry building.

Bem tér

Map 3, F3.

Fő utca terminates at **Bem tér**, named after the Polish general Joseph Bem, who fought for the Hungarians in the War of Independence, and was revered by his men as "Father". A **statue of Bem** with his arm in a sling recalls him leading them into battle at Piski, crying "I shall recapture the bridge or die! Forward Hungarians! If we do not have the bridge we do not have the country." Traditionally a site for demonstrations, it was here that the crowds assembled prior to marching on parliament at the beginning of the 1956 Uprising.

A century ago, the surrounding neighbourhood was dominated by a foundry established by the Swiss ironworker Abrahám Ganz, which grew into the mighty Ganz Machine Works. The original ironworks only ceased operation in 1964, when it was turned into a **Foundry Museum** (*Öntödei Múzeum*; Tues–Sun 9am–4pm; 150Ft, student 70Ft). You can still see the old wooden structure and the huge ladles and jib-cranes *in situ*, together with a collection of cast-iron stoves, tram wheels, lamp posts and other exhibits. The museum is located at Bem utca 20, 200m from Bem tér, or barely a block from Margit körút (see p.57).

MOSZKVA TÉR TO RÓZSADOMB

Map 3, B4. Moszkva tér metro (M2); tram #4 or #6 from the Nagykörút in Pest.

The area immediately north of Várhegy is defined by the transport hub of **Moszkva tér** (Moscow Square), which has kept its name owing to the sheer cost of renaming all the vehicles, maps and signs on which it appears. The new **Mammut mall** (fronted by a statue of the woolly beast) is a magnet for shoppers, while the recently opened Millenarium Park provides a cultural focal point, augumenting the long-standing tourist attraction of Gül Baba's tomb, on the lower slopes of Rózsadomb. Otherwise, Moszkva tér is the place to catch buses to such destinations as the Cogwheel Railway (#56) or Budakeszi Game Park (#22), and trams to Pest (#4 & #6) or the Wolf's Meadow Cemetery (#59) – as covered in later chapters.

The Millenarium Park

Daily 8am–8pm (later depending on events); free. For details of events ☎438-5335.

The main attraction lies behind the mall, where the site of the former Ganz Machine Works has been transformed into a **Millenarium Park** (*Millenáris Park*) with water features, vineyards and plots of corn to represent different regions of Hungary. Kids can be let loose on the fantastic **playground**, where the Péter Zöld troupe provides entertainment from 8am to sundown, while visitors of all ages can enjoy the performances at the outdoor theatre (1000Ft) and the diverse, ever-changing rota of events and exhibitions (mostly free) in the converted factory buildings. The **Sensational Hungarians exhibition** promises to dazzle visitors with the creativity and ingenuity of the nation's sons and daughters over the ages, while an "inn" by the Lovöház utca entrance hosts an internet café.

Gül Baba's tomb and Rózsadomb

Map 3, D1. Tram #4 or #6 from Moszkva tér or the Nagykörút in Pest.

The smoggy arc of **Margit körút** underlines the gulf between the polluted inner city and the breeze-freshened heights of Budapest's most affluent neighbourhood,

MOSZKVA TÉR TO RÓZSADOMB

Rózsadomb (Rose Hill). The hill is named after the flowers that were reputedly introduced to Hungary by a revered Sufi dervish, Gül Baba, the "Father of the Roses", who participated in the Turkish capture of Buda but died during the thanksgiving service afterwards. The **Tomb of Gül Baba** (May–Oct Tues–Sun 10am–6pm; 300Ft, student 200Ft) is fittingly located on Mecset utca (Mosque Street), five minutes' walk uphill from Margit körút via Margit utca. Having been restored with funds donated by the Turkish government, it is surrounded by a colonnaded parapet with fine views, set in a pristine park with rose-bushes and marble fountains decorated with ceramic tiles. The octagonal shrine is adorned with Arabic calligraphy and Turkish carpets.

The **Rózsadomb** itself is as much a social category as a neighbourhood, for a list of residents would read like a Hungarian *Who's Who*. During the Communist era this included the top Party *funcionárusok*, whose homes featured secret exits that enabled several ÁVO chiefs to escape lynching during the Uprising. Nowadays, wealthy film directors and entrepreneurs predominate, and the sloping streets are lined with spacious villas and flashy cars.

Óbuda, Római Fürdő and Margit sziget

Óbuda is the oldest part of Budapest, though that's hardly the impression given by the factories and high-rises that dominate the district today, hiding such ancient ruins as remain. Nonetheless, it was here that the Romans built a legionary camp and a civilian town, later taken over by the Huns. Under the Hungarian Árpád dynasty this developed into an important town, but in the fifteenth century it was eclipsed by Várhegy. The original settlement became known as Óbuda (Old Buda) and was incorporated into the newly formed Budapest in 1873. The old town centre is as pretty as Várhegy, but to find the best-preserved Roman ruins you'll have to go to the Római Fürdő district, further out. Both are accessible by HÉV train from Batthyány tér or the Margit híd.

ÓBUDA

Map 7. HÉV train to the Árpád híd stop.

After its incorporation within the city, **Óbuda** became a

popular place to eat, drink and make merry, with dozens of garden restaurants and taverns serving fish and wine from the locality. Some of the most famous establishments still exist around **Fő tér**, the heart of eighteenth-century Óbuda, but, while there's no denying the charm of their Baroque facades and wrought-iron lamps, in many cases they are simply trading on past glories and you'd do better eating elsewhere (see p.180).

There's more to enjoy from a cultural standpoint, with three museums in the vicinity. Directly opposite the HÉV exit at Szentlélek tér 1, the **Vasarely Museum** (Map 7, H2; Tues–Sun 10am–5.30pm; 200Ft) displays eyeball-throbbing Op Art works by Viktor Vasarely, one of the founders of the genre, who was born in Pécs in southern Hungary and emigrated to Paris in 1930.

Just around the corner from the museum, at Fő tér 1, the Baroque Zichy mansion contains a courtyard seemingly unchanged since Habsburg times, at the back of which you'll find the upstairs **Kassák Museum** (Map 7, H2; Tues–Sun 10am–6pm; 150Ft) dedicated to the Hungarian Constructivist Lajos Kassák, and a **Local History Exhibition** (Tues–Sun 10am–6pm; 100Ft), with rooms in the Sváb (German) and Art Nouveau styles, and a cute collection of antique toys.

Whatever the weather, you'll see several figures sheltering beneath umbrellas on Fő tér: life-sized sculptures by Imre Varga, whose *oeuvre* is the subject of the **Varga Museum** at Laktanya utca 7 (Map 7, H1; Tues–Sun 10am–6pm; 250Ft, student 150Ft). While a sense of humour pervades his sheet-metal, iron and bronze effigies of famous personages (including the one of Béla Kun addressing a crowd that's now in the Statue Park), Varga was also responsible for the sobering Holocaust Memorial in Pest.

ÓBUDA

Óbuda's Roman remains

Map 7. Bus #86 from Batthyány tér or Flórián tér.

Although the largest site lies further out in Római Fürdő district (see overleaf), Óbuda does have several excavated ruins to show for its past. On modern-day Flórián tér, 500m west of Fő tér, graceful columns stand amid a shopping plaza, while the old **military baths** and other finds lurk beneath the Szentendrei út flyover, running off Flórián tér. The largest ruin is the weed-choked, crumbling **amphitheatre** (*amfiteátrum*) at the junction of Pacsirtamező and Nagyszombat utca, 800m further south, which can be reached by bus #86 or by walking 400m north from Kolosy tér, near the Szépvölgyi út HÉV stop. The amphitheatre once seated up to 16,000 spectators.

> While you're in the Óbuda area, check out a couple of good patisseries renowned for their ice creams: the *Veress*, on the corner of Bok utca, leading south from the amphitheatre, and the *Daubner*, up on Szépvölgyi út, leading towards the caves in the Buda Hills (see Chapter 4).

The most intriguing relic, however, is fifteen minutes' walk northwest of Flórián tér, where three canopies behind the high-rise block at Meggyfa utca 19–21 shelter the remains of the **Hercules Villa** (Tues–Sun: May–Sept 10am–6pm; late April & Oct 10am–5pm; 100Ft), whose name derives from the third-century AD **mosaic floor** beneath the largest canopy. This mosaic, originally composed of 60,000 stones carefully selected and arranged in Alexandria, depicts Hercules about to vomit at a wine festival. Another mosaic portrays the centaur Nessus abducting Deianeira, whom Hercules had to rescue as one of his twelve labours.

ÓBUDA

61

RÓMAI FÜRDŐ

Map 2, E3. Access by HÉV to Aquincum for the ruins, or Római
Fürdő for the campsite and lido.

North of Óbuda, the riverside factory belt merges into the
Római Fürdő (Roman Bath) district, a prelude to the
leafy suburb of Csillaghegy that could be ignored but for its
campsite and **lido** and the ruins of Aquincum. Originally
a settlement of camp followers spawned by the legionary
garrison, Aquincum eventually became a *municipium* and
then a *colonia*, the provincial capital of Pannonia Inferior.
The **ruins of Aquincum** (Map 2, E3; Tues–Sun:
May–Sept 9am–6pm; Oct & late April 9am–5pm; 400Ft)
are visible from the Aquincum HÉV stop, as is a small
amphitheatre on the other side of the tracks. Enough of the
foundation walls and underground piping survives to give a
fair idea of the layout of Aquincum, with its forum and law
courts, its sanctuaries of the goddesses Epona and Fortuna
Augusta, and the collegia and bathhouses where fraternal
societies met. Its bare bones are given substance by an
excellent **museum** (same hours; 300Ft) and smaller exhibitions around the site, whose star exhibits are a mummy pre-
served in natron, a cult-relief of the god Mithras and a
reconstructed water-organ.

MARGIT SZIGET

Map 2, E4. Bus #26 from Nyugati tér or the Árpád híd metro in Pest
runs the length of the island; trams #4 and #6 from Moszkva tér or
the Nagykörút stop halfway across the Margit híd, at the southern
end of the island.

There's a saying that "love begins and ends on **Margit
sziget**", for this verdant island has been a favourite meeting
place for lovers since the nineteenth century (though before

1945 a stiff admission charge deterred the poor). It remains one of Budapest's most popular parks, with two public baths fed by thermal springs, an outdoor theatre and other amenities. At a refreshing distance from the noise and pollution of the city centre, it's still sufficiently close to feature in its waterfront panorama.

Motorists can only approach from the north of the island, via the Árpád híd, at which point they must leave their vehicles at a paying car park. Trams stop at the southern entrance to the island. On the left-hand side here you can rent **bikes**; they tend to be rather battered, but are good enough to get you around the five-kilometre circuit from one end to the other.

A royal game reserve under the Árpáds and a monastic colony until the Turkish conquest, the island was named at the end of the nineteenth century after Princess **Margit** (Margaret), the daughter of Béla IV. Legend has it that he vowed to bring her up as a nun if Hungary survived the Mongol invasion, and duly confined the 9-year-old in a convent when it did. She apparently made the best of it, acquiring a reputation for curing lepers and other saintly deeds, as well as for never washing above her ankles. Beatification came after her death in 1271, and a belated canonization in 1943. Her name had already been bestowed on the **Margit híd**, which was built by a French company in the 1870s and linked Margit sziget to Buda and Pest. It is an unusual bridge in the form of a splayed-out V, with a short arm joined to the southern tip of the island. In November 1944 it was blown up by the Nazis, killing hundreds of people including the German sappers who had detonated the explosives by mistake. Photos of the result can be seen in the underpass at the Pest end.

The southern part of the island features a huge circular concrete fountain, a millennial monument and the **Hajós Alfréd** swimming pools (known as the "Sport"; daily

MARGIT SZIGET

6am–6pm; 500Ft), named after the winner of the 100m and 1200m **swimming baths** at the 1896 Olympics. Hajós was also an architect and designed the indoor pool, but the main attractions here are the all-season outdoor 50m pool and the fresh pastries at the buffet. Two hundred metres further north lies the **Palatinus Strand** (May–mid-Sept daily 8am–7pm; 600Ft), which can hold as many as ten thousand people at a time in seven open-air thermal pools, complete with a water chute, wave machine and segregated terraces for nude sunbathing.

Off to the east of the road between the two pools are the **ruins of a Franciscan church** from the late thirteenth century, while a **ruined Dominican church and convent** stands in the vicinity of the **Outdoor Theatre** (*Szabadtéri Színpad*) further north along the main road, which hosts plays, operas, fashion shows and concerts during summer. The café here makes a convenient stop for a beer and a snack, being easily located by the **water tower** that rises above the complex.

A short way northeast of the tower is a **Premonstratensian Chapel**, whose Romanesque tower dates back to the twelfth century when the order first established a monastery on the island. The tower's fifteenth-century bell is one of the oldest in Hungary. Further north lie two luxury **spa hotels**, the refurbished *fin-de-siècle Ramada Grand* and the modern *Thermal*, the latter beside a rock garden with warm springs that sustain tropical fish and giant water lilies.

The Buda Hills

T he **Buda Hills** are as close to nature as you can get within the city limits: a densely wooded arc around a sixth of Budapest's circumference. It's a favourite place for walking in all seasons, with many trails all marked with the distance or the duration (ó stands for hour; p for minutes). While some parts can be crowded with walkers and mountain-bikers at the weekend, during the week it's possible to ramble for hours and see hardly a soul. If your time is limited, the most rewarding destinations are the "railway circuit" using the Cogwheel and Children's railways and the chairlift, or a visit to the caves near the valley of Szépvölgy, perhaps followed by the Kiscelli Museum or Bartók's house. You could also combine the railway circuit with a visit to Budakeszi Game Park, on the city limits (see Chapter 11).

THE "RAILWAY CIRCUIT"

Map 2.

This is an easy and enjoyable way to visit the hills that will especially appeal to kids. The whole return trip can take under two hours if connections click and you don't dawdle, or an afternoon if the opposite applies. You begin at Moszkva tér (see p.56) by boarding tram #18 or #56 or bus

#56, and alighting opposite the cylindrical *Budapest Hotel*, beside the lower terminal of the **Cogwheel Railway** (*Fogaskerekűvasút*). The third such railway in the world when it was inaugurated in 1874, the system was steam-powered until 1929 when it was electrified. It runs every ten minutes or so (daily 5am–11pm; 100Ft), rising slowly through the villa-suburb of Svábhegy; for the best view take a window seat on the right-hand side, facing backwards.

From the upper terminal on **Széchenyi-hegy** it's a minute's walk to the **Children's Railway** (*Gyermekvasút*). A narrow-gauge line built by youth brigades in 1948, it's almost entirely run by 13- to 17-year-olds, enabling them to get hands-on experience if they fancy a career with MÁV, the Hungarian Railways company. Watching them wave flags, collect tickets and salute departures with great solemnity, you can see why it appealed to the Communists. Until 1990 it was known as the Pioneers' Railway after the organization that replaced the disbanded Scouts and Guides movements (now re-formed). Trains depart for the eleven-kilometre, 45-minute journey to Hűvösvölgy every 45–60 minutes (June–Aug daily 9am–5pm; Sept–May Tues–Sun same hours; 150Ft).

The first stop, **Normafa**, is a popular excursion centre with a modest **ski-run**. Its name comes from a performance of the aria from Bellini's *Norma* given here by the actress Rozália Klein in 1840. Across the road, the humble *Rétes büfé* serves delicious strudel and coffee every day of the year including holidays. **János-hegy**, three stops on, is the highest point in Budapest. On the 527-metre-high summit, fifteen minutes' climb from the station, the **Erzsébet lookout tower** offers a panoramic view of the city and the Buda Hills. By the buffet below the summit is the upper terminal of the **chairlift** or *Libegő*, meaning "floater" in Hungarian (May–Sept 9.30am–5pm; Oct–April

9.30am–4pm; closed every other Mon; 300Ft), down to **Zugliget**, from where #158 buses return to Moszkva tér.

From the main road by **Szépjuhászné**, the next stop after János-hegy, you can catch bus #22 to the Budakeszi Game Park (see p.135). Wild boar, which prefer to roam during the evening and sleep by day, are occasionally sighted in the forests above **Hárshegy**, one stop before Hűvösvölgy, both in the Buda Hills. Also linked directly to Moszkva tér by #56 and #56E (nonstop) buses, **Hűvösvölgy** (Cool Valley) is the site of the popular *Náncsi Néni* restaurant (see p.181).

THE CAVES

Map 7, A5 & C7.
In the hills to the north of Hűvösvölgy are caves that are unique for having been formed by thermal waters rising up from below, rather than by rainwater. Two of the sites have been accessible to the public since the 1980s, with guided tours (some English spoken) every hour on the hour, whenever there are five people. In both cases the starting point is Kolosy tér in Óbuda (accessible by bus #86 from Flórián tér or Batthyány tér, or bus #6 from Nyugati tér in Pest), from where you catch bus #65 five stops to the Pálvölgy Cave, or bus #29 four stops to the Szemlő-hegy Cave. As the two caves are ten minutes' walk apart, it's possible to dash from one to the other and catch both tours within two hours; if you're planning to do this, it's worth buying a combined ticket.

The **Pálvölgy Stalactite Cave** (*Pálvölgyi cseppkő barlang*; Tues–Sun guided tours 10am–4pm; 400Ft, student 300Ft), at Szépvölgyi út 162, is the larger and more spectacular labyrinth. Tours of the stalactites and stalagmites last about half an hour and involve lots of steps and constricted passages. Discovered in the 1900s, the Pálvölgy is the longest

THE CAVES

67

of the cave systems in the Buda Hills and is still being explored by speleologists.

The **Szemlőhegy Cave** (*Szemlőhegyi barlang*; April–Oct Mon & Wed–Fri 10am–3pm, Sat & Sun 10am–4pm; 300Ft, student 200Ft), at Pusztaszeri út 35, is quite different, with less convoluted and claustrophobic passages and no stalactites. Instead, the walls are encrusted with cauliflower- or popcorn-textured precipitates formed by warm water dissolving mineral salts. The cave was found in 1930 by Maria Kesslerné. Its air is exceptionally clean and the lowest level is used as a respiratory sanatorium. Afterwards you can view a museum of cave finds and plans from all over Hungary.

If you're into caving, the Hungarian Association of Speleologists in Budapest (☎346-0494) can put you in touch with groups exploring caves in the Buda Hills and elsewhere in Hungary.

THE KISCELLI MUSEUM

Map 7, D3. Bus #165 from Kolosy tér and a short walk. Tues–Sun: April–Oct 10am–6pm; Nov–March 10am–4pm; 300Ft.

Fifteen minutes' walk from the Szemlő-hegy Cave, the **Kiscelli Museum**, on a hilltop to the northwest of the caves, occupies a former Trinitarian monastery in a beautiful wooded setting at Kiscelli utca 108. The museum's collection includes antique printing presses and the 1830 Biedermeier furnishings of the Golden Lion pharmacy, which used to stand on Kálvin tér. Also on show are carved shop signs, sculptures and graphics by twentieth-century Hungarian artists, and antique furniture exhibited in the blackened shell of the monastery's Gothic church, which makes a dramatic backdrop for operas, performances and fashion shows (☎388-8560 for details).

THE BARTÓK MEMORIAL HOUSE AND NAPRAFORGÓ UTCA

Map 2, C4. Bus #29 from Szemlőhegy Cave to the Nagybányai út stop, or bus #5 from Március 15 tér or Moszkva tér to the Pasaréti terminus. Tues–Sun 10am–5pm; 300Ft.

Music lovers can make a pilgrimage to the **Bartók Memorial House** (*Bartók Béla Emlékház*) at Csalán utca 29, in a leafy suburb below Láto-hegy. The villa was the residence of Béla Bartók, his wife and two sons from 1932 until their emigration to America in 1940, by which time Bartók despaired of Hungary's right-wing regime. Besides an extensive range of Bartók memorabilia you can see some of his original furniture and possessions, including folk handicrafts collected during his ethno-musical research trips to Transylvania with Zoltán Kodály, and the shirt cuff on which Bartók wiped his pen-nibs when composing scores. Chamber music **concerts** are held here from September until May (⊤394-2100 for information).

Before returning to Moszkva tér, it's worth a brief detour to see the delightful **Napraforgó utca housing estate**, built in 1931. Its 22 houses embody different trends in Modernist architecture, from severe Bauhaus to folksy Arts and Crafts style. The estate is signposted on Pasaréti tér, near the #5 bus terminus; follow Pasaréti út till you reach a playing field and cross the bridge on the left.

The Belváros

Abuzz with pavement cafés, street artists, vendors, boutiques and nightclubs, the Belváros, or Inner City, is the hub of Pest and, for tourists at least, the epicentre of what's happening. Commerce and pleasure have been its lifeblood as long as Pest has existed, first as a medieval market town and later as the kernel of a city whose *belle époque* rivalled Vienna's. Since their fates diverged, the Belváros has lagged far behind Vienna's Centrum in prosperity, but the gap is fast being narrowed, at least superficially. It's now increasingly like any Western city in its consumer culture, but you can still get a sense of the old atmosphere, especially in the quieter backstreets south of Kossuth utca.

APPROACHES TO THE BELVÁROS

Most people walk into the Belváros from Deák tér (see p.81), whose metro station is near the terminus of trams #47 and #49 from Buda, and the Erzsébet tér bus station. Any of the side streets to the west will bring you to Váci utca or Vörösmarty tér in a few minutes. Two other approaches by metro are M1 to Vörösmarty tér, exiting outside the *Gerbeaud* patisserie, or M3 to Ferenciek tere, midway down Váci utca.

The **Kiskörút** (Small Boulevard) that surrounds the Belváros follows the course of the medieval walls of Pest, showing how compact it was before the phenomenal expansion of the nineteenth century. However, little remains from further back than the eighteenth century, as the "liberation" of Pest by the Habsburgs in 1686 left the town in ruins. Some Baroque churches and the former Greek and Serbian quarters attest to its revival by settlers from other parts of the Habsburg empire, but most of the **architecture** dates from the era when Budapest asserted its right to be an imperial capital, between 1860 and 1918. Today, first-time visitors are struck by the statues, domes and mosaics on the Neoclassical and Art Nouveau piles, which are reflected in the mirrored banks and luxury hotels that symbolize the new order.

After a stroll along **Váci utca** from **Vörösmarty tér** and a look at the splendid view of Várhegy from the **embankment**, the best way to appreciate the Belváros is by simply wandering around. People-watching and window-shopping are the most enjoyable activities, and though prices are above average any visitor should be able to afford to sample the **cafés**. Shops are another matter – there are few bargains – and nightclubs a trap for the unwary, but there's nothing to stop you from enjoying the **cultural life**, from jazz musicians and violinists on Vörösmarty tér to world-class conductors and soloists at the **Vigadó** concert hall, around the corner.

VÖRÖSMARTY TÉR

Map 6, C3. Vörösmarty tér metro (M1).

Vörösmarty tér, the leafy centre of the Belváros, is a good starting point for exploring the area. Crowds eddy around the portraitists, conjurers and saxophonists, and the craft stalls that are set up over summer, Christmas and the wine festival. While children play in the fountains, teenagers lounge around the **statue of Mihály Vörösmarty** (1800–50), a poet and translator whose hymn to Magyar identity, *Szózat* (Appeal), is publicly declaimed at moments of national crisis. Its opening line "Be faithful to your land forever, Oh Hungarians" is carved on the statue's pedestal. Made of Carrara marble, the statue has to be wrapped in plastic sheeting each winter to prevent it from cracking. The black spot above the inscription is reputedly a "lucky" coin donated by a beggar towards the cost of the monument.

On the north side of the square is the **Gerbeaud patisserie**, Budapest's most famous confectioner. Founded in 1858 by Henrik Kugler, it was bought in 1884 by the Swiss confectioner Emile Gerbeaud, who invented the *konyakos meggy* (cognac-cherry bonbon). He sold top-class cakes at reasonable prices, making *Gerbeaud* a popular rendezvous for the middle classes. His portrait hangs in one of the rooms, whose gilded ceilings and china recall the *belle époque*. The smaller *Kis-Gerbeaud* salon is no longer a haunt of octogenarian "Gerbeaud ladies" wearing furs and lace gloves, having been turned into a cake shop.

From the terrace outside you can observe the entrance to the **Underground Railway** (*Földalatti Vasút*), whose vaguely Art Nouveau cast-iron fixtures and elegant tilework stamp it as decades older than the other metro lines. Indeed, it was the first on the European continent and second in the world (after London's Metropolitan line) when it was inaugurated in 1896, and ran from Vörösmarty tér to the Millennial Exhibition grounds at Hősök tere. For its centenary, the line was equipped with the latest technology and its stations restored to their original decor. If you're curious to know more about its history, visit the Underground Railway Museum at Deák tér (see p.81).

The Underground Railway's route along Andrássy út is covered in Chapter 7, with Hősök tere described in Chapter 8.

At the lower end of the square, the **Bank Palace** was built between 1913 and 1915, in the heyday of Hungarian self-confidence, by Ignác Alpár, who also designed the pre-war Stock Exchange on Szabadság tér (see p.87). It now houses the **Budapest Stock Exchange**, which was reborn in 1990, 42 years after the Communists suppressed its predecessor, and allows visitors to observe its trading floor (Mon–Fri 10.30am–1.30pm; free). Count Mihály Károlyi, the radical liberal who became Prime Minister in 1918, had an office in the building across the street and used to address crowds from its balcony.

VÁCI UTCA

Deák tér, Vörösmarty tér or Ferenciek tere metro.

Váci utca has been famous for its shops and **korzó** (promenade) since the eighteenth century. During the 1980s, its vivid streetlife became a symbol of the "consumer socialism" that distinguished Hungary from other Eastern Bloc states, but Budapesters today are rather less enamoured of Váci: dressed-to-kill babes and their sugar daddies would rather pose in malls, and teenagers can find *McDonald's* anywhere, leaving Váci utterly dependent on tourists for its livelihood and bustle.

The downside of this is apparent along the stretch between Vörösmarty tér and Ferenciek tere, where overpriced souvenir shops and cafés compete with hustlers (see box on p.74), buskers and exchange bureaux for a share of the trade. Though people-watching is still a major diversion, **shopping** is less rewarding than it was when there were all kinds of small shops in the yards off the street, now driven out by

CLASSIC STINGS ON VÁCI

The northern half of Váci is notorious for its *konzum lány*, or "consume girls", who lure male tourists into bars or clubs where two drinks cost $350 and goons ensure that the tab is settled. Disregard pickups and avoid places offering the "companionship of lovely ladies" and the problem won't arise – but even then there's a risk of gross overcharging at restaurants or bars which don't list their prices. The most notorious case was in 1997, when four Danes had to pay 1,300,000Ft ($6000) for a meal at the *Halászcsárda* on Ferenciek tere, whose owner said, "As far as I'm concerned, we can charge tourists anything we like". While the worst offenders are out of business, it's still wise to be cautious and check prices before ordering. If you get stung, try insisting that you'll only pay in the presence of the police. Tourinform (V, Vigadó utca 6) has a conference line with the police (☎438-8080), on which they'll translate from English or German. You might still have to pay in front of the cops, but at least you'll get a receipt, which is vital for filing a complaint at the Bureau of Consumer Affairs (VIII, József körút 6 ☎459-4800; Mon–Thurs 8am–6pm, Fri 9am–2pm).

soaring rents. A few landmarks along the way might catch your eye, such as the scantily-clad **fisher-girl statue** on **Kristóf tér** (Map 6, C3), or the **Pest Theatre** (no. 9) on the site of the *Inn of the Seven Electors*, where the 12-year-old Liszt performed in 1823.

Váci's looks improve beyond Ferenciek tere: since the southern stretch was also pedestrianized in 1997, it has leapfrogged over its northern sibling to become more stylish and *korzó*-friendly, with some funky boutiques and specialist shops, and lots of restaurants and cafés. The old buildings have been tastefully facelifted, even ones down towards the

VÁCI UTCA

Great Market Hall (p.129); these are quite humble compared to edifices like the prewar **Officers' Casino** on the
corner of Ferenciek tere (now a bank's headquarters), or the
nineteenth-century hulk of the **Old Budapest City Hall**
at nos. 62–64, where the city council still meets. Look out
for the sculptural **plaque** on the wall of no. 47, commemorating the fact that the Swedish King Carl XII stayed here
during his lightning fourteen-day horse-ride from Turkey
to Sweden, in 1714.

SZERVITA TÉR AND PETŐFI UTCA

If the hustle on Váci utca deters you, head down Kristóf tér
towards **Szervita tér** – named after the eighteenth-century
Servite Church, whose facade bears a relief of an angel
cradling a dying horseman, in memory of the VII Kaiser
Wilhelm Hussars killed in World War I. Across the way are
two remarkable buildings from the golden age of Hungarian
architecture. No. 3 has a gable aglow with a superb
Secessionist mosaic of *Patrona Hungariae* (Our Lady of
Hungary) flanked by shepherds and angels, one of the finest
works of Miksa Róth. The **Rózsavölgyi building**, next
door, was built a few years later between 1910 and 1913 by
the "father" of Hungarian Modernism, Béla Lajta, whose
earlier association with the National Romantic school is evi-
dent from the majolica decorations on its upper storeys, typical of the style. On the ground floor is the Rózsavölgyi
music shop, one of the oldest and best in the city.

Behind the church, the Brutalist-style **MATÁV** phone,
fax and email centre is equally striking, but a rather less
attractive presence on **Petőfi utca**, the street running parallel to Váci utca between Vörösmarty and Ferenciek tere.
Though it has none of Váci's glamour and all of its traffic, it
still draws crowds with its array of **music shops** and the
central post office (no. 13).

FERENCIEK TERE

Map 6, C6. Ferenciek tere (M3) or Astoria (M2) metro.

Ferenciek tere is named after the **Franciscan Church** on the corner of Kossuth utca, whose facade bears a relief recalling the great flood of 1838, in which over four hundred citizens were killed. More would have died had not Baron Miklós Wesselényi personally rescued scores of people in his boat; his efforts are depicted on a plaque outside the church.

However, the square is chiefly notable for the **Párizsi Udvar**, a flamboyantly eclectic shopping arcade. Completed by Henrik Schmal in 1915, its fifty naked statues above the third floor were deemed incompatible with its intended role as a savings bank, symbolized by images of bees throughout the building. The old deposit hall now houses an Ibusz office, while the arcade is as dark as an Andalucian mosque and twice as ornate; its dome was designed by Róth.

As Ferenciek tere runs on towards the Kiskörút, it becomes Kossuth Lajos utca, which is the main east-west axis of the city, connecting Buda with the hinterland of Pest. Its junction with the Kiskörút is named after the **Astoria Hotel** on the corner, a prewar haunt of spies and journalists that was commandeered as an HQ by the Nazis in 1944 and the Soviets after the 1956 Uprising. Today, its Neoclassical coffee lounge is redolent of Stalinist chic gone to seed.

KÁROLYI MIHÁLY UTCA

Walking southwards from the Franciscan Church, you'll come to another thoroughfare, initially named after Count Mihály Károlyi, the liberal politician whose birthplace at no. 16 houses the **Petőfi Literary Museum** (*Petőfi Irodalmi Múzeum*; Tues–Sun 10am–6pm; 250Ft), showcasing the personal effects of Petőfi and other Hungarian writers, but with little text in English. The street is subsequently called Kecskeméti utca, as it once led to a gate in the walls and thence to Kecskemét; its junction with the Kiskörút is bridged by the *Mercure Korona Hotel*, a flesh-pink creation of Finta's, with plainclothes guards lurking outside its shopping arcade.

The Serbian Orthodox Church

Map 6, C8.

Further along Kecskeméti utca, past the **ELTE law faculty** – the Hungarian equivalent of Oxbridge or Harvard for future highflyers – a right turn into Szerb utca will bring you to the **Serbian Orthodox Church**, built by the Serbian artisans and merchants who settled here after the Turks were driven out. Secluded in a high-walled garden, it is only open for High Mass on Sunday (10.30–11.45am), when the singing of the liturgy, the clouds of incense and flickering candles create an atmosphere that's quite unearthly. A block or so south, part of the **medieval wall** of Pest can be seen on the corner of Bástya utca and Veres Pálné utca.

ALONG THE EMBANKMENT

Ferenciek tere metro (M3) or tram #2.

The **Belgrád rakpart** (Belgrade Embankment) bore the brunt of the fighting in 1944–45, when the Nazis and the Red Army exchanged salvos across the Danube. Like the Várhegy in Buda, postwar clearances exposed historic sites and provided an opportunity to integrate them into the environment – but the magnificent **view** of Buda Palace and Gellért-hegy is hardly matched by two colossal eyesores on the Pest side. While such historic architecture as remains can be seen in a fifteen-minute stroll between the Erzsébet híd and the Lánchíd, **tram #2** enables you to see a longer stretch of the waterfront between Fővám tér and Kossuth tér, periodically interrupted by a tunnel that's the first to be flooded if the Danube overflows its embankments, as sometimes happens in the summer.

The bold white pylons and cables of the **Erzsébet híd** (Elizabeth Bridge) are as cherished a feature of the panorama as the stone Lánchíd or the wrought-iron Szabadság híd. Of all the Danube bridges blown up by the Germans as they retreated to Buda in January 1945, this was the only one not rebuilt in its original form. Its approach ramp starts beyond twin *fin-de-siècle* office buildings named the **Klotild and Matilde Palaces**, after two Habsburg princesses of that era.

Belváros Parish Church

Map 6, B5. Mon–Sat 7am–7pm, Sun 8am–7pm; free.

In the shadow of the approach ramp, the grimy facade of the **Belváros Parish Church** masks its origins as the oldest church in Pest. Founded in 1046 as the burial place of St Gellért (see p.44), it was rebuilt as a Gothic hall church in the fifteenth century, turned into a mosque by the Turks and then reconstructed as a church in the eighteenth century. This history is reflected in the church's interior, and by coming after Latin Mass at 10am on Sunday you can see the Gothic sedilia and Turkish *mihrab* (prayer niche) behind the high altar, which are otherwise out of bounds. The vaulted nave and side chapels are Baroque.

MÁRCIUS 15 TÉR AND PETŐFI TÉR

On the square beside the Belváros Parish Church, a sunken enclosure exposes the remains of **Contra–Aquincum**, a Roman fort that was an outpost of the settlement at Óbuda at the end of the third century. More pertinently to Hungarian history, the name of the square, **Március 15 tér**, refers to March 15, 1848, when the anti-Habsburg Revolution began, while the adjacent **Petőfi tér** is named after Sándor Petőfi, whose *National Song,* the anthem of 1848, and romantic death in battle the following year made him a patriotic icon (see box on p.80). Erected in 1882, the square's **Petőfi statue** has long been a focus for demonstrations as well as patriotic displays – especially on March 15, when the statue is bedecked with flags and flowers. Behind it looms the **Greek Orthodox Church**, built by the Greek community in the 1790s and currently the object of a tug-of-war between the Patriarchate of Moscow that gained control of it after 1945, and the Orthodox Church in Greece that previously owned it. Services (Sat 6pm & Sun 10am) are in Hungarian, but accompanied by singing in the Orthodox fashion.

Just north of Petőfi tér, the gigantic **Marriott Hotel** is situated between the embankment and the street running parallel, Apáczai Csere János utca. Inaugurated as the *Duna Intercontinental* in 1969, it was the first hotel in the Eastern Bloc managed in partnership with a Western firm and the model for others on the rakpart. Its architect József Finta has since built a dozen hotels and business centres in Pest. On the Danube side of the *Marriott*, the concrete esplanade is a sterile attempt at recreating the prewar **Duna-korzó**, the most informal of Budapest's promenades, where it was socially acceptable for strangers to approach celebrities and stroll beside them. The outdoor cafés here charge premium rates for the wonderful view.

SÁNDOR PETŐFI

Born on New Year's Eve, 1822, of a Slovak mother and a Southern Slav butcher-innkeeper father, Sándor Petőfi was to become obsessed by acting and by poetry, which he started to write at the age of fifteen. As a strolling player, soldier and labourer, he absorbed the language of working people and composed his lyrical poetry in the vernacular, to the outrage of critics. Moving to Budapest in 1844, he fell in with the young radical intellectuals who met at the *Pilvax Café* and embarked on his career as a revolutionary hero. He declaimed his *National Song* from the steps of the National Museum on the first day of the 1848 Revolution, and fought in the War of Independence with General Bem in Transylvania, where he disappeared during the battle of Segesvár in 1849. Though he was most likely trampled beyond recognition by the Cossacks' horses (as predicted in one of his poems), Petőfi was long rumoured to have survived as a prisoner. In 1990, a Hungarian entrepreneur sponsored an expedition to Siberia to uncover the putative grave, but it turned out to be that of a woman.

THE VIGADÓ

Map 6, B2. Vörösmarty tér metro (M1).

Vigadó tér is an elegant square full of stalls and buskers, named after the **Vigadó** concert hall, whose name translates as "having a ball" or "making merry". Inaugurated in 1865, this splendidly Romantic pile by Frigyes Feszl has hosted performances by Liszt, Mahler, Wagner, von Karajan and other renowned artists. Badly damaged in World War II, it didn't reopen until 1980, such was the care taken to recreate its sumptuous decor. The acoustics in the Large

Hall were also improved, though, like the grand staircase, this can only be seen by concert-goers. The foyer, however, is accessible from 1pm, when the box office opens.

Don't overlook the statue of the **Little Princess** on the railings by the embankment. After dusk, you'll hardly notice that she isn't a person, if you notice her at all. By day, she looks like a cross-dressing boy in a Tinkerbell hat.

From Vigadó tér, the Duna-korzó continues past the *Inter-Continental Hotel* to end in a swirl of traffic at Roosevelt tér, on the edge of the Lipótváros, described in Chapter 6.

DEÁK TÉR AND ERZSÉBET TÉR

Map 6, E3. Deák tér metro (M1/M2/M3).

Three metro lines, two segments of the Kiskörút and several important avenues meet at **Deák tér** and **Erzsébet tér** – two squares that merge into one another (making local addresses extremely confusing) to form a jumping-off point for the Belváros and Lipótváros. You'll recognize the area by two landmarks: the enormous mustard-coloured **Anker Palace** on the Kiskörút, and the **Lutheran Church** by the metro pavilion on the edge of the Belváros, which hosts some excellent concerts, including Bach's *St John Passion* over the fortnight before Easter. Next door, the **Lutheran Museum** (*Evangélikus Múzeum*; Tues–Sun 10am–6pm; 300Ft) displays a facsimile of Martin Luther's last will and testament, and a copy of the first book printed in Hungarian, a New Testament from 1541.

Underground Railway Museum

Map 6, E3. Tues–Sun 10am–6pm. 100Ft or one BKV ticket.

Accessible via the upper sub-level of Deák tér metro, the **Underground Railway Museum** (*Földalattivasút Múzeum*) extols the history of Budapest's original metro. Its genesis was a treatise by Mór Balazs, proposing a steam-driven tram network starting with a route along Andrássy út, an underground line being suggested as a fallback in case the overground option was rejected. Completed in under two years, in time for the Millennial Exhibition, the metro was inaugurated by Emperor Franz Josef, who agreed to allow it to bear his name, which it kept until 1918. The exhibits include two elegant wooden carriages (one used up until 1973) and period fixtures and posters, which enhance the museum's nostalgic appeal.

More recent excavations have been less successful. Just north of Deák tér, workers toil in a vast pit that was intended for the foundations of a new National Theatre, until the project was blocked by the prime minister to spite Budapest's mayor. Dubbed the "**National Hole**", it is now set to become an underground car park and conference centre, with a park on the surface.

A Tourinform office (see p.8) is conveniently located just off Deák tér, on Sütő utca.

DEÁK TÉR AND ERZSÉBET TÉR

The Lipótváros

The **Lipótváros** (Leopold Town), lying to the north of the Belváros, started to develop in the late eighteenth century, first as a financial centre and later as the seat of government and bureaucracy. Several institutions of national significance are found here, including Parliament, St Stephen's Basilica, the National Bank and the Television headquarters. Though part of the V district, its ambience is quite different from that of the Belváros, with sombre streets of Neoclassical buildings interrupted by squares flanked by monumental Art Nouveau or neo-Renaissance piles. It's busy with office workers by day, but used to be dead in the evenings and at weekends until *Cafe Kor*, *Gandhi* and *Lou Lou* brought some life to the area. Another source of vitality is the Central European University (CEU), funded by the Hungarian-born billionaire financier George Soros.

Depending on where you're coming from, it makes sense to start either with Roosevelt tér, just inland of the Lánchíd, or St Stephen's Basilica, two minutes' walk from Erzsébet tér. Most of the streets between them lead towards the set-piece expanse of Szabadság tér, whence you can head on towards Parliament – though the Kossuth metro station or tram #2 from the Belgrád rakpart will provide quicker access.

ROOSEVELT TÉR

Map 4, A8. Kossuth tér (M2) or Arany János utca (M3) metro.

At the Pest end of the Lánchíd, **Roosevelt tér** is blitzed by traffic, making it difficult to stand back and admire **Gresham Palace** on the eastern side of the square. This splendid but decrepit example of Art Nouveau was commissioned by a British insurance company in 1904, and is named after the financier Sir Thomas Gresham, the originator of Gresham's law, that bad money drives out good. His bust high up on the facade, and the interior arcade and stained-glass windows by Miksa Róth, are unlikely to be visible until renovation work on the building has finished, and it begins a new lease of life as a hotel.

Statues of Count Széchenyi and Ferenc Deák stand at opposite ends of the square, the former not far from the **Hungarian Academy of Sciences** (*Magyar Tudományos Akadémia*) that was founded after Széchenyi pledged a year's income from his estates towards its establishment in 1825 – as depicted on a relief on the wall facing Akadémia utca. The Nobel Prize-winning scientist György Hevesy, discoverer of the element hafnium, was born at Akadémia utca 3, across the road.

While the Academy and the Lánchíd are tangible reminders of Széchenyi's enterprise, there is nothing to remind us of Deák's achievement in forging an *Ausgleich* (Compromise) with the Habsburgs. This was symbolized by the crowning of Emperor Franz Josef as King of Hungary in 1867, when soil from every corner of the nation was piled into a Coronation Hill, on the site of the present square. Here the emperor flourished the sword of St Stephen and promised to defend Hungary against all its enemies – a pledge that proved almost as ephemeral as the hill itself. Eighty years later, the square was renamed Roosevelt tér in honour of the late US president – a rare example of Cold War courtesy that was never revoked.

ST STEPHEN'S BASILICA

Map 4, C7. Arany János utca (M3) or Bajcsy-Zsilinszky út (M1) metro. Mon–Sat 9am–noon, Sun 1–4pm; free. Panorama Tower April & May 10am–5pm, June–Aug 10am–6.30pm, Sept & Oct 10am–6pm; 500Ft, student 400Ft.

St Stephen's Basilica (*Szent István-bazilika*) took so long to build that Budapesters used to joke, "I'll pay you back when the basilica is finished". Work began in 1851 under the supervision of József Hild, continued after his death under Miklós Ybl, and was finally completed by Joseph Krauser in 1905. At the inaugural ceremony Franz Josef was seen to glance anxiously at the dome, whose collapse during a storm in 1868 had naturally set progress back. At 96m, it is exactly the same height as the dome of the Parliament building – both allude to the putative date of the Magyars' arrival in Hungary (896 AD).

The Basilica is best visited when its interior is open for sightseeing, as its beauty lies in the carvings, frescoes and chapels, the variegated marble, gilded stucco and bronze mouldings, and the splendid **organ** above the doorway. In the second chapel to the right is a painting of King Stephen offering the Crown of Hungary to the Virgin (see p.26), while a statue of him haloed as a saint (but with a sword at his side) forms the centrepiece of the altar. In a chapel to the left at the back is the gnarled **mummified hand of St Stephen**, Hungary's holiest relic, whose custodian solicits coins to illuminate the casket holding the *Szent Jobb* (literally, "holy right"), paraded through the streets on August 20, the anniversary of his death. Although the **treasury** (200Ft extra) is paltry compared to that at Esztergom's Basilica, you shouldn't miss the so-called **Panorama Tower**; save the 302 steps for the return and take the lift up. Besides offering a grand **view** over Pest, you can also see the framework of girders and ladders inside the cupola, which is 25m higher than the Basilica's inner, acoustic dome.

Mass is held on Sundays & holidays at 8.30am, 9.30am, 10am & noon, and on other days at 7am & 8am. From July to October, there are organ concerts on Mondays at 7pm.

BAJCSY-ZSILINSZKY ÚT

While Stephen is revered as the founder and patron saint of Hungary, the pantheon of national heroes includes a niche for Endre Bajcsy-Zsilinszky (1866–1944), after whom the avenue that runs past the Basilica is named. Originally a right-winger, he ended up an outspoken critic of Fascism, was arrested in Parliament (a statue on Deák tér captures the moment) and shot as the Russians approached. **Bajcsy-Zsilinszky út** runs northwards to **Nyugati tér**, dominated by **Nyugati Station**, an elegant, iron-beamed terminal built in 1874–77 by the Eiffel Company of Paris. The **Westend City Centre**, beside the station, is Budapest's largest mall, boasting four hundred outlets and an artificial waterfall three storeys high. The avenue is also the demarcation line between the V (Lipótváros) and VI (Terézváros) districts.

During the summer, "nostalgia" steam trains run from Nyugati Station to the Rail Heritage Park; see p.134 for details.

SZABADSÁG TÉR

Map 4, B6. Arany János utca metro (M3).

For over a century the Lipótváros was dominated by a gigantic barracks where scores of Hungarians were imprisoned or executed, until this symbol of Habsburg tyranny was demolished in 1897 and the site redeveloped as **Szabadság tér** (Liberty Square). Invested with significance from the outset, it became a kind of record of the vicissitudes of modern Hungarian history, where each regime added or removed monuments, according to their political complexion.

The Stock Exchange and National Bank

In the early years of the last century, Hungary's burgeoning prosperity was expressed by two monumental temples to capitalism on opposite sides of the square. To the west stood the **Stock Exchange**, one of the grandest buildings in Budapest. Designed by Ignác Alpár, it has blended motifs from Greek and Assyrian architecture and is crowned with twin towers resembling Khmer temples. After the Communists closed down the Stock Exchange in 1948, it became the headquarters of Hungarian Television (*Magyar Televízió*, or *MTV*).

Alpár also designed the **National Bank** (*Nemzeti Bank*), which still functions as such and is notable for the reliefs on its exterior, representing such diverse aspects of wealth creation as Magyars ploughing and herding, ancient Egyptians harvesting wheat, and Vikings loading their longships with loot. The building, entered at Szabadság tér 8, contains a small **Museum of Banknotes** (Thurs 9am–2pm; free) featuring curiosities like the "Kossuth" banknotes that were issued in America during the politician's exile after the failed War of Independence, and notes denominated in billions of forints from the period of hyperinflation in 1946. The mirrored-glass and granite **International Bank Centre** at the southern end of the square is a triumphant affirmation that Hungary has rejoined the capitalist system.

SZABADSÁG TÉR

Szabadság tér's monuments

Turning from money to politics, notice the **statue of General Harry Bandholtz** of the US Army, who intervened with a dogwhip to stop Romanian troops from looting the Hungarian National Museum in 1919. The statue was erected in the 1930s, when Hungary was still smarting from the 1920 Treaty of Trianon that gave away two-thirds of its territory and a third of its Magyar population to the "Successor States" of Romania, Czechoslovakia and Yugoslavia. This deeply felt injustice inspired several other monuments on Szabadság tér, namely the Monument to Hungarian Grief – featuring a flag at half mast and a quotation from Lord Rothermere (the proprietor of the *Daily Mail*, whose campaign against Trianon was so appreciated that he was offered the Hungarian crown) – and four statues called North, South, East and West, whose inauguration in 1921 was attended by 50,000 people.

At the end of World War II all of these monuments were removed by the Communists, who converted the base of the Monument to Hungarian Grief into the **Soviet Army Memorial**, commemorating the liberation of Budapest from the Nazis, with reliefs of Red Army troops and tanks advancing on Ferenciek tere and Parliament. When the Socialists got the boot in 1990, there were calls to remove the Soviet memorial and restore all the old nationalist ones (the Communists had already reinstated Bandholtz prior to President Bush's visit in 1989), but wiser counsels prevailed.

To compound the irony, the Soviet memorial stands near the former headquarters of the Fascist Arrow Cross, and directly in front of the **US Embassy**, which for fifteen years gave shelter to Cardinal Mindszenty, the Primate of Hungary's Catholic Church, in the aftermath of the 1956 Uprising. Later, however, the US became embarrassed by his presence, as did the Vatican, who finally persuaded him to leave for Austria in 1971 (see box on p.149).

THE FORMER POST OFFICE SAVINGS BANK

Map 4, B6.

Behind the US Embassy, the **former Post Office Savings Bank** on Hold utca is a classic example of Hungarian Art Nouveau – its tiled facade patterned like a quilt, with swarms of bees (symbolizing savings) ascending to the poly-chromatic roof, which is the wildest part of the building. Its architect, Ödön Lechner, once asked why birds shouldn't enjoy his buildings too, and amazing roofs are also a feature of his other masterpieces in Budapest, the Applied Arts Museum and Geological Institute. You can see the foyer during bank hours, but the rest of the interior is open to the public on only one day a year – European Heritage Day, in September (ask Tourinform for details; see p.8). Diagonally across the street is a wrought-iron **market hall**, one of five opened on a single day in 1896, which continue to serve the centre of Budapest to this day.

THE BATTHYÁNY AND NAGY MONUMENTS

At the junction of Hold and Báthory utca, a lantern on a plinth flickers with an **Eternal Flame** commemorating Count Lajos Batthyány, the Prime Minister of the short-lived republic declared after the 1848 War of Independence, whom the Habsburgs executed on this spot on October 6, 1849. As a staunch patriot – but not a revolutionary – Batthyány is a hero for conservative nationalists, and his monument the destination of annual marches on October 6 and public holidays.

The refrains and paradoxes of Hungarian history are echoed on Vértanuk tér (Martyrs' Square), between

Szabadság tér and Kossuth tér, where a **statue of Imre Nagy** – the reform Communist who became Prime Minister during the 1956 Uprising and was shot in secret two years afterwards – stands on a footbridge, gazing towards Parliament. With his raincoat, trilby and umbrella hooked over his arm, Nagy cuts an all-too-human, flawed figure – and is scorned by those who pay homage to Batthyány.

KOSSUTH TÉR

Map 4, A4. Kossuth tér metro (M2).

The apotheosis of the government district and Hungary's romantic self-image comes at **Kossuth tér**, with its colossal Parliament building and memorials to national heroes and epic moments in Hungarian history. The square is named after Lajos Kossuth, the leader of the 1848 Revolution against the Habsburgs (see box opposite), who was originally represented by a sculptural tableau showing him and his ministers downcast by their defeat in 1849. However, the Communists replaced it with a more "heroic" one of Kossuth rousing the nation to arms, by Kisfaludy-Strobl. The other main statue is of Prince Ferenc Rákóczi II, an earlier hero of the struggle for Hungarian independence, whose plinth is inscribed with the words "The wounds of the noble Hungarian nation burst open!" This is a reference to the anti-Habsburg war of 1703–11, but also perfectly describes the evening of October 23, 1956, when crowds filled the square, chanting anti-Stalinist slogans at Parliament – the prelude to the Uprising that night. An **eternal flame** burns in memory of those who died on Kossuth tér on October 25, when ÁVO snipers opened fire on a peaceful crowd that was fraternizing with Soviet tank-crews.

LAJOS KOSSUTH

Lajos Kossuth was the incarnation of post-Napoleonic bourgeois nationalism. Born into landless gentry in 1802, he began his career as a lawyer, representing absentee magnates in Parliament. His Parliamentary reports, which advocated greater liberalism than the Habsburgs would tolerate, became widely influential during the Reform era, and he was jailed for sedition. While in prison, Kossuth taught himself English by reading Shakespeare. Released in 1840, he became editor of the radical *Pesti Hírlap*, was elected to Parliament and took the helm during the 1848 Revolution.

After Serbs, Croats and Romanians rebelled against Magyar rule and the Habsburgs invaded Hungary, the Debrecen Parliament proclaimed a republic with Kossuth as de facto dictator. However, after the Hungarians surrendered in August 1849, Kossuth escaped to Turkey, later touring Britain and America, espousing liberty. So eloquent were his denunciations of Habsburg tyranny that London brewery workers attacked General Haynau, the "Butcher of Vienna", when he visited the city. Karl Marx loathed Kossuth as a bourgeois radical, and tried to undermine his reputation with articles published in the New York *Herald Tribune* and the London *Times*. As a friend of the Italian patriot Mazzini, Kossuth spent his last years in Turin, where he died in 1894. His remains now lie in the Kerepesi Cemetery (p.126).

PARLIAMENT

Map 4, A5. Kossuth tér metro (M2). Guided tours in English: daily 10am & 2pm, but confirm when you buy a ticket from Gate X (from 8am), signposted on Kossuth tér; 1500Ft, student 750Ft. Budapest Card not valid.

The Hungarian **Parliament** building (*Országház*) makes the Houses of Parliament in London look humble, its architect Imre Steindl having larded Pugin's Gothic Revival style with Renaissance and Baroque flourishes. Sprawling for 268m along the embankment, its symmetrical wings bristle with finials and 88 statues of Hungarian rulers, surmounted by a dome 96m high (alluding to the date of the Magyar conquest; see p.272). Though most people are impressed by the building, the writer Gyula Illyés once famously dismissed it as "no more than a Turkish bath crossed with a Gothic chapel" – albeit one that cost 38,000,000 gold forints.

For centuries, Hungarian assemblies convened wherever they could, and it wasn't until 1843 that the Diet of Pozsony resolved to build a permanent "House of the Motherland" in Pest-Buda (as it was then called). By the time work began in 1885, the concept of Parliament had changed in so far as the middle classes were now represented as well, though over ninety percent of the population still lacked the right to vote. Gains were made in 1918, but they were soon curtailed under the Horthy regime, just as the attainment of universal adult suffrage in 1945 was rendered meaningless after 1948 by a Communist dictatorship. Happily, the wheel turned full circle eventually, as creeping liberalization in the late 1980s paved the way for the introduction of a multi-party democracy in 1990 – a watershed symbolized by the removal of the red star from Parliament's dome and the replacement of Communist emblems by the traditional coat of arms featuring the double cross of King Stephen – whose Coronation Regalia is now on show in the building's Cupola Hall.

The interior – and the Coronation Regalia

How much you see on the **tours** of the interior depends on Parliament's activities, but you can be sure of seeing the main staircase, the Cupola Hall and the Lords' Chamber, if nothing else (flash photography is not allowed). Statues, carvings, gilding and mosaics are ten a penny, lit by lamps worthy of the Winter Palace – but there are also cosy touches such as the individually numbered brass ashtrays where peers left their cigars smouldering in the lounge while they popped back into the chamber to hear someone speak; a good speaker was said to be "worth a Havana".

Guards holding drawn sabres flank the **Coronation Regalia**, whose centrepiece, **St Stephen's Crown**, has symbolized Hungarian statehood for over a thousand years. It consists of two crowns joined together: the cruciform crown that was sent as a gift by Pope Sylvester II to Stephen for his coronation in 1000; and a circlet given by the Byzantine monarch to King Géza I. The distinctive bent cross was caused by the crown being squashed as it was smuggled out of a palace in a baby's cradle; at other times it has been hidden in a hay-cart or buried in Transylvania, abducted to Germany by Hungarian fascists and thence taken to the US, where it reposed in Fort Knox until its return home in 1978, together with Stephen's crystal-headed sceptre, a fourteenth-century gold-plated orb and a sixteenth-century sword made in Vienna, used by his successors. Under the Dual Monarchy, Habsburg emperors ruled Hungary in the name of St Stephen, and travelled to Budapest for a special coronation ceremony, traditionally held in the Mátyás Church on Várhegy.

On a humbler note, there's a **scale model** of Parliament made of 100,000 matchsticks, built by a patriotic family over three years.

MUSEUM OF ETHNOGRAPHY

Map 4, A4. Kossuth tér metro (M2). Tues–Sun 10am–6pm; 500Ft, student 200Ft. Photo permit 200Ft, video 8000Ft; pre-arranged guided tours 3000Ft (☎473-2406).

Across the road from Kossuth's statue stands a neo-Renaissance building housing the **Museum of Ethnography** (*Néprajzi Múzeum*), one of the finest museums in Budapest, though it's little visited by tourists. Originally built as the Palace of the Supreme Court, petitioners would have been overawed by its lofty, gilded main hall, whose ceiling bears a fresco of the goddess Justitia surrounded by allegories of Justice, Peace, Revenge and Sin.

The museum's permanent exhibition on **Hungarian folk culture** occupies thirteen rooms on the first floor (off the left-hand staircase) and is fully captioned in English; there's also an excellent catalogue. Habsburg-ruled Hungary comprised a dozen ethnic groups, represented by exhibits arranged under headings such as "Institutions" and "Peasant Work"; the only groups not represented are the Jews and the gypsies. Though the beautiful costumes and objects on display are no longer part of everyday life in Hungary, you can still see them in parts of Romania, such as Maramureş and the Kalotaszeg, which belonged to Hungary before 1920.

Temporary exhibitions (on the second floor) cover anything from Bedouin life to Hindu rituals, while over Easter and Christmas there are **concerts** of Hungarian folk music and dancing, and **craft fairs**.

PALACE OF MIRACLES

Map 4, D1. Lehel tér metro (M3). Jan–mid-April Tues–Fri 9am–5pm, Sat & Sun 10am–6pm; mid-April–Dec Mon–Fri 10am–5pm, Sat & Sun 10am–6pm; 500Ft, children 450Ft.

Although it lies beyond the Lipótváros (which ends at Szent István körút, running from Nyugati Station to the Danube), visitors with kids or an interest in science should enjoy the **Palace of Miracles** (*Csodák palotája*) at Váci út 19. This interactive playhouse was the brainchild of two Hungarian physicists and aims to explain scientific principles to 6- to 12-year-olds, using optical illusions, a bed of nails, a simulated low-gravity "moonwalk" and a "miracle bicycle" on a tightrope – though the scarcity of explanations in English may leave you none the wiser.

The Terézváros

The **Terézváros** (Theresa Town), or VI district, is home to the State Opera House, the Academy of Music and the Hungarian equivalent of Broadway, making it one of the most vibrant parts of the city. Trams and buses circle the Nagykörút (Great Boulevard) 24-hourly, making it especially popular at night. Laid out in the late nineteenth century, this district was heavily influenced by Haussmann's redevelopment of Paris. At that time it was one of the smartest districts in the city, but later much of the area became run-down and deprived. While the villas near the park have recovered their value and café society flourishes around Liszt Ferenc tér, winos and drug addicts beg in the shadows of "Broadway".

Andrássy út, the main thoroughfare, is Budapest's longest, grandest avenue, marking the border between the Lipótváros and Terézváros. It runs in a perfect straight line for two and a half kilometres up to Hősök tere on the edge of the Városliget (City Park) – both of which are covered in the next chapter. Inaugurated in 1884 as the Sugár (Radial) út, it was soon renamed Andrássy út after the statesman Count Gyula Andrássy – the name that stayed in popular use throughout the years when this was officially Stalin Avenue (1949–56) or the Avenue of the People's Republic (1957–89), until it was formally restored in 1990. With its greystone edifices laden with dryads, its Opera House and coffee houses, the avenue retains something of the style that made it so fashionable in the 1890s, when "Bertie" the Prince of Wales drove its length in a landau, offering flowers to women as he passed.

The initial stretch up to the Oktogon is within walking distance of Erzsébet tér, but if you're going any further it's best to travel from sight to sight by the metro beneath the avenue, or bus #4.

THE POST OFFICE MUSEUM

Map 4, C7. Tues–Sun 10am–6pm; 100Ft, student 50Ft.

At Andrássy út 3 the **Post Office Museum** (*Posta Múzeum*) occupies a fabulous old apartment complete with parquet floors, marble fireplaces, Venetian mirrors and frescoes by Károly Lotz; its owners fled to the US in 1938. Exhibits include a compressed-air mail tube, vintage delivery vehicles, and a display on the inventor Tivadar Puskás, a colleague of Thomas Edison who set up the world's first switchboard and telephonic news service in Budapest in the early 1900s.

THE STATE OPERA HOUSE AND NEW THEATRE

Map 4, D6. Opera metro (M1). Tours daily at 3 & 4pm; 1200Ft. Use the entrance on Hajó utca.

The **State Opera** (*Állami Operaház*) was founded by Ferenc Erkel, the composer of Hungary's national anthem, and occupies a magnificent neo-Renaissance pile built in 1875–84 by Miklós Ybl. It can boast of being directed by Mahler (who complained about the anti-Semitism in the city), hosting performances conducted by Otto Klemperer and Antal Doráti, and sheltering two hundred local residents (including Kodály) in its cellars during the siege of

THE POST OFFICE MUSEUM

Budapest. The 1260-seat auditorium was the first in Europe to feature an iron fire curtain (after a fire at the Vienna Opera House), underfloor heating and air-conditioning. Its chandelier weighs three tonnes, and 2.7 kilos of gold were used to gild the fixtures. To the left of the stage is the box used by Emperor Franz Josef's wife, Sissi, who loved Hungarian opera as much as he detested it. The upstairs reception rooms and downstairs foyer are equally lavish, festooned with portraits and busts of Hungarian divas and composers.

In a similar vein, on Paulay Ede utca, off the other side of Andrássy, stands the **New Theatre** (*Új Színház*), whose blue and gold Art Nouveau facade and foyer (by Béla Lajta) look superb. Continuing north along Andrássy, you'll pass the stylish new **Goethe Institut** at no. 24 (a good place to stop for coffee), followed by a pharmacy that retains its original fixtures from 1889.

"BROADWAY" AND LISZT FERENC TÉR

Map 4, D6.
One block beyond the Opera, Andrássy is crossed by **Nagymező utca** – nicknamed "**Broadway**" because of the clubs and theatres on either side of the street, whose pavement features bronze impressions of the hand- or footprints of Hungarian entertainers. During the interwar years the best known club was the *Arizona,* run by Sándor Rozsnyai and his wife Miss Arizona (which inspired Pal Sándor's film of the same name, starring Hanna Schygulla and Marcello Mastroianni); the Rozsnyais were murdered by the Arrow Cross in 1944. Their club was at Nagymező utca 20, in the former home of the Habsburg court photographer who lends his name to the **Mai Manó Photography Museum** (Mon–Fri 2–7pm, Sat, Sun &

holidays 11am–7pm; 200Ft, student 100Ft), occupying two floors of the building and worth a visit for its fine exhibitions and photographic bookshop.

Further up Andrássy, past the *Fashion Cafe* (no. 36) where the Hungarian version of *Big Brother* is filmed, two elongated squares lined with pavement **cafés** provide a vibrant interlude. On the left is **Jókai tér**, with a large statue of the novelist Mór Jókai; while across the road on **Liszt Ferenc tér**, the composer hammers an imaginary keyboard with his vast hands, blind to the strolling crowds and the Music Academy that bears his name, further along.

See Chapter 15 for details of the cafés on Liszt Ferenc tér.

THE OKTOGON AND BEYOND

Map 4, E5. Oktogon metro (M1) or any tram or bus along the Nagykörút.

Shortly afterwards, Andrássy út meets the Nagykörút at the **Oktogon**, an eight-sided square flanked by eclectic buildings. With 24-hour fast-food chains ensconced in two of them, and buses and taxis running along the Nagykörút through to the small hours, the Oktogon never sleeps. During the Horthy period it rejoiced in the name of Mussolini tér, while under the Communists it was called November 7 tér after the date of the Bolshevik revolution.

A minute's walk past the Oktogon on the left-hand side, Andrássy út 60 was once the most terrifying address in Budapest – the **headquarters of the secret police**, recently turned into a **Museum of Terror**. Jews and other victims of the Arrow Cross were tortured here during World War II, after which the ÁVO (see box overleaf) commandeered the building and used it for the same purposes.

THE ÁVO

The Communist secret police began as the party's private security section during the Horthy era, when its chief, Gábor Péter, betrayed Trotskyites to the police to take the heat off their Stalinist comrades. After World War II it became the *Államvédelmi Osztály* or ÁVO (State Security Department), its growing power implicit in a change of name in 1948 – to the State Security Authority or ÁVH (though the old acronym stuck). Ex-Nazi torturers were easily persuaded to apply their skills on its behalf, and its network of spies permeated society. So hated was the ÁVO that any members caught during the Uprising were summarily killed, and their mouths stuffed with banknotes (secret policemen earned more than anyone else).

Prisoners were brought in by the side entrance on Csengery utca. When it was captured by insurgents in 1956, no trace was found of the giant meat-grinder rumoured to have been used to dispose of corpses. The new museum, opened in 2002, documents the building's grisly past, though it concentrates more on the activities of the ÁVO than on the Holocaust. Opening times were unavailable as this book went to press.

A little further on the opposite side, the Old Music Academy at no. 67 harbours the **Liszt Memorial Museum** (*Liszt Ferenc Emlékmúzeum*; Mon–Fri 10am–6pm, Sat 9am–5pm; closed Aug; 250Ft), entered from around the corner at Vörösmarty utca 35, where the composer – who was the first president of the Academy – lived from 1881 until his death in 1886. His glass piano and travelling keyboard are the highlights of an extensive collection of memorabilia and scores. Concerts are performed here by young pianists every Saturday at 11am (250Ft).

KODÁLY KÖRÖND TO HŐSÖK TERE

Kodály körönd, named after the composer Zoltán Kodály, is one of Budapest's most elegant squares, flanked by four neo-Renaissance mansions. At no. 1 on the northeast corner, the flat where he lived until his death in 1967 is a **Kodály Memorial Museum** (Wed 10am–4pm, Thurs–Sat 10am–6pm, Sun 10am–2pm; 80Ft), preserving his library, salon, dining room and folk art collection. During World War II the körönd was named Hitler tér, prompting the émigré Bartók to vow that he would not be buried in Hungary so long as anywhere in the country was named after Hitler or Mussolini.

Two fine collections of Asian art lurk just beyond the körönd. The **György Ráth Museum** (Tues–Sun: April–Oct 10am–6pm; Nov–March 10am–4pm; 300Ft, student 150Ft) displays lovely artefacts from all the great eastern civilizations in an Art Nouveau villa at Városligeti fasor 12 – reached by Bajza utca. The garden contains a statue of the Hungarian Orientalist Körösi-Csoma, shown as a Buddhist monk. By contrast, the **Ferenc Hopp Museum** (same hours and price; disabled free), at Andrássy út 103, is devoted to whimsical Japanese *netsuke* figures carved in wood and ivory. From here, the final stretch of Andrássy út up to Hősök tere is lined with spacious villas set back from the avenue, mostly housing embassies.

Hősök tere and the Városliget

A ndrássy út culminates in Budapest's two grandest public spaces, **Hősök tere** (Heroes' Square) and the **Városliget** (City Park). Both were created for the nationwide celebrations of the millennium of the Magyar conquest of Hungary, but as neither was ready on time the anniversary was rescheduled for the following year; historians revised the date of the conquest accordingly and have stuck to 896 ever since. The millennial celebrations were unashamedly nationalistic, but full of contradictions, as the Dual Monarchy tried to flatter Hungarians without alienating other ethnic groups that resented Magyar chauvinism, so each was represented at the exhibition.

Today the chief attractions are the **Museum of Fine Arts** and the romantic **Vajdahunyad Castle**, followed by a wallow in the **Széchenyi Baths**. Budapest's **Zoo**, **circus** and amusement park are also located in the vicinity, together with two of the city's classiest restaurants, and a handful of other museums.

HŐSÖK TERE

Map 4, H2. Hősök tere metro (M1) or bus #4.

The enormous ceremonial plaza of **Hősök tere** is flanked by two galleries resembling Greek temples, while at its centre is the **Millenary Monument** – Budapest's answer to Nelson's Column in London. It consists of a 36-metre-high column topped by the figure of the Archangel Gabriel who, according to legend, appeared to Stephen in a dream and offered him the crown of Hungary. Around the base are figures of Prince Árpád and his chieftains, who led the seven Magyar tribes into the Carpathian Basin. They look like a wild bunch; Huba even has stag's antlers strapped to his horse's head. As a backdrop to this, a semicircular colonnade displays statues of Hungary's most illustrious leaders, from King Stephen to Kossuth.

During the brief Republic of Councils in 1919, when the country was governed by revolutionary Soviets, the square was decked out in red banners and the column enclosed in a red obelisk bearing a relief of Marx. More recently, in June 1989, it was the setting for the ceremonial reburial of Imre Nagy and other murdered leaders of the Uprising (plus an empty coffin representing the "unknown insurgent") – an event which symbolized the dawning of a new era in Hungary. Today it's more likely to be filled with coach parties of tourists, and rollerbladers and skateboarders, for whom the smooth surface is ideal. The square was originally laid out as a garden, but paved over for the Eucharistic Congress of 1932.

Museum of Fine Arts

Map 4, H1. Tues–Sun 10am–5.30pm; 500Ft, student 200Ft; audioguide 950Ft, student 600Ft.

To the left of the square stands the **Museum of Fine Arts**

(*Szépművészeti Múzeum*), the international equivalent of the Hungarian National Gallery (see p.35), housed in an imposing Neoclassical building completed in 1906. Although the majority of exhibits are now labelled in English, explanatory captions are few, so art lovers should invest in an audioguide or a catalogue. On the lower ground floor there's an excellent **shop** for art books, posters and contemporary ceramics, a decent **café**, and the most stylish toilets in Budapest.

Lower ground floor: the Egyptian and twentieth-century art collections

To the right of the stairs is a small but choice **Egyptian Collection**, chiefly from the Late Period and Greco-Roman eras of Egyptian civilization. The highlights of the first room are four huge painted coffins and a child-sized one from Gamhud in Middle Egypt; *shabiti* figures, intended to perform menial tasks in the afterlife; and a mummified crocodile, cat and ibis from the Late Period, when animal cults reached their apogee. In the second room, look out for the sculpted heads of a nameless pharaoh and a bewigged youth from the New Kingdom, the painted coffin of a priestess of Amun bearing an uncanny resemblance to Julia Roberts, and a tautly poised bronze of the cat goddess Bastet.

On the other side of the foyer, the **Twentieth-Century Art Collection** features relatively few artists that you're likely to have heard of, but is nonetheless stimulating. In the Majovszky Hall, a scumbled Expressionist portrait by **Oskar Kokoschka** faces **Maurice Utrillo**'s *Street Scene*. There's a wonderfully simple Fauvist landscape by János Máttis, and two realist portraits in violet and green impasto by Gino Severini. **Marc Chagall**'s *Village in Blue* is a typically lyrical composition of floating figures, while Roberto Guttuso's *Seizure of the Land in Sicily* speaks of the urgency of the land reform cause in terms of Cubism and Social Realism. In the other room are abstracts such as István Beóthy's *Nuclear Form Nr.2* – a Möbius Strip with an extra twist, carved from teak – and a two-tone canvas based on the pyramids of Giza by the Op Artist **Victor Vasarely**.

In the corridor beyond the shop are Miróesque collages in sand, rope and chipboard by **Zoltán Kemény**, and the dangling wooden figures of Andras Böröcz's sculpture *The Hanged*. The **Ionic Pyramid** room is notable for its hanging, dismembered cloth figures by Gustav Troger and the slumped, hollowed-out figure in Magdalena Abakanowicz's *Cage No. 2*, while the **Doric Pyramid** room contains a superb collection of **Gothic sculptures**.

Ground floor: antiquities and nineteenth-century art

To the right of the lobby are several rooms devoted to **ancient Mediterranean cultures** from Etruria to Athens, mainly represented by jugs and vases. Highlights include a pair of bronze shin guards decorated with rams' heads; terracotta tiles portraying bestial deities; a man's torso and head from the pediment of a Campanian temple; lifelike busts of Roman worthies; and an Attic marble sarcophagus carved with hunting scenes.

Across the hall, the **Nineteenth-Century Art Collection** opens with a fanfare of Barbizons and Impressionists. However, the drama of **Courbet**'s wild landscapes and lifesized *Wrestlers*, the delight of **Monet**'s *Plum Trees in Blossom* and **Corot**'s *Remembrance of Coubrou* aren't sustained by weaker pictures like Cézanne's *The Cupboard*, Toulouse-Lautrec's *Three Ladies in the Refectory* or Manet's *Lady with a Fan*, though *Eternal Springtime* and *The Kiss* by **Rodin** both deserve an honourable mention.

The long hall at the end displays **historical** paintings like the massive *Crowning of Emperor Francis as King of Hungary* by Johann Peter Krafft, and Karl Theodor von Piloty's

Grand Guignol *Nero on the Ruins of Rome*. Sex pervades the **Symbolist and Decadent** works in the final room, notably Franz von Stuck's *The Kiss of the Sphinx*, John Quincey Adams's vampish *Lilli* and Hans Makart's *Nessus Raptures Deianeira*.

There are also two halls displaying large allegorical or religious works on loan from other European museums, notably Artemesia Gentileschi's *Salome with the Head of St John the Baptist*. To the rear, on the right, the **Prints and Drawings Room** exhibits rotating displays from the museum's extensive holdings of works by Raphael, Leonardo, Rembrandt, Rubens, Dürer, Picasso and Chagall, with solo restrospectives by lesser-known artists.

First floor: old masters

The museum's forte is its hoard of **Old Masters**, based on the collection of Count Miklós Esterházy, which he sold to the state in 1871. As a notice explains, this section has been re-hung in what is allegedly the once-again fashionable style of stacking one painting above another, which, though it may facilitate comparisons, doesn't allow visitors to appreciate the pictures well above eye level. The room numbering is also baffling, but the quality of the art transcends all these failings.

The **Spanish Collection** of seventy works is perhaps the best in the world outside Spain. Among the vivid altarpieces by unknown Catalonians in Room XIV, notice *A Bishop-Saint Enthroned*, whose obvious bewilderment belies his magnificent attire. Room XV is dominated by seven **El Grecos**, most notably *Christ Stripped of His Garments*, *The Agony in the Garden*, *The Apostle St Andrew* and *The Penitent Magdalene*; though Eugenio Cajes's *Adoration of the Magi* is equally awe-inspiring. In Room XVI hang several **Murillos**, of which *Ecce Homo* and *The Holy Family with the Infant St John and Christ* are superlative. You'll also find the moving *Martyrdom of St Andrew* by **Ribera**, five **Goyas**, ranging from war scenes (*2nd of May*) to portraits of the rich (*Señora Ceán Bermudez*) and humble (*The Knife-Grinder*), plus **Velázquez**'s *Peasant's Repast*.

The **Italian Collection** is also impressive, especially rooms XVIII and XXIII. The former contains **Raphael**'s small but exquisite *Esterházy Madonna* – a Virgin and Child with the infant St John – and a picture of a youth with a Mona Lisa-esque mystique. The latter's psychological depth is matched by portraits by **Giorgione** (whose own self-portrait exhudes sensitivity) and **Titian** (of a Venetian Doge, stern and watchful in his cloth-of-gold). Tintoretto's self-portrait is less focused, while Bellini's pig-eyed *Queen of Cyprus* verges on caricature. **Tintoretto** steals the show next door with *Hercules Expelling the Faun from Omphade's Bed* and a *Supper at Emmaus*. Unfortunately, **Veronese**'s *Allegory of Venice* is too high up to appreciate properly, though his *Crucifixion* is easier to admire. In Room XIII you'll find **Boccacio**'s *Adoration of the Infant Christ*, and in Room XX, the cheerfully gory *Judith with the Head of Holoferenes* and the cruel *Mocking of Job*.

Though less glamorous, the **German Collection** amply rewards a visit. Every emotion from awe to jealousy appears on the faces in **Holbein**'s *Dormition of the Virgin* in Room XVIII, while Room XIX has a dazzling array of works by **Altdorfer** and by **Cranach** the Elder. The suppressed violence of the latter's Crucifixions seem like presentiments of the Thirty Years' War a century ahead, while in his *Salome with the Head of St John the Baptist* Salome displays a platter with St John's head on it with the nonchalance of a hostess bringing out the roast. Finally, **Kauffmann**'s depiction of *The Wife of Count Esterházy as Venus* shows a strumpet with her jewellery box, while **Dürer**'s *Young Man* has an enigmatic smile.

Acknowledging that art transcends nationality, Room

XXI exhibits works by well-travelled artists such as **Canaletto**, who died in Warsaw after painting *The Palace of Kaunitz in Vienna*; Kauffmann (see p.107), whose career took her all over Europe; and **Tiepolo**, whose *St James the Great Conquering the Moors* once served as an icon for the Habsburgs.

Travel scenes and still lifes in Room XXII mark the start of the **Dutch Collection**, which leapfrogs over Room A into the rooms beyond. In Room B, the serenity of **Van Dyck**'s *St John the Evangelist* contrasts with the melodrama of **Rubens'** *Mucius Scaevola before Porsenna*, and Jordeans' *The Satyr and the Peasant*, while Room C is largely given over to **Brueghels**, from Pieter the Elder's *Sermon of St John the Baptist* to Pieter the Younger's *Blind Hurdy Gurdy Player* and Jan's *The Garden of Eden with the Fall of Man*. Also look out for *The Way to Calvary*, showing Christ being beaten through a fairy-tale medieval landscape, by the mysteriously named "Master of the Ausburg *Ecce Homo*".

The single room devoted to **English art** (A) can only muster a dullish portrait apiece by Hogarth, Reynolds and Gainsborough, and a melodramatic *Theatre Scene* by Zoffany.

The Palace of Arts and Dózsa György út

Map 4, I2. Tues–Sun 10am–6pm; 150Ft.

Across the square from the museum is the **Palace of Arts** (*Műcsarnok*), a Grecian pile with gilded columns and a mosaic of St Stephen as patron of the arts. Its magnificent facade and foyer are in contrast to the four austere rooms used for **temporary exhibitions** (two or three at a time), which are often first-rate, while another part currently houses the **Countryrama** – an overpriced 3D travelogue of Hungary, screened every half hour in different languages (10am–5pm; 1900Ft). Since the palace was inaugurated in

1896, its steps have been a stage for the state funeral of the painter Munkácsy, the reburial of Nagy, and other public ceremonies.

Before heading into the Városliget, take a glance down **Dózsa György út**, the wide avenue running off alongside the park, where domes and tents serve as **circus** and **concert** venues. In Communist times it was here that Party leaders reviewed parades from a grandstand, beneath a 25-metre-high statue of Stalin that was torn down during the Uprising, dragged to the Nagykörút and hammered into bits for souvenirs. A statue of Lenin was erected in its place, which remained until it was taken away "for structural repairs" in 1989 and finally ended up in the Statue Park (see p.132).

THE VÁROSLIGET

Map 4, I1. Hősök tere or Széchenyi Fürdő (Metro M1).

The **Városliget** starts just behind Hősök tere, where the fairy-tale towers of **Vajdahunyad Castle** rear above an island girdled by an artificial lake that's used for boating in the summer and, during winter, is transformed into the most splendid outdoor ice rink in Europe. Like the park, the castle was created for the Millenary Anniversary celebrations of 1896, and proved so popular that the temporary structures were replaced by permanent ones. The castle is a catalogue in stone of architectural styles from the kingdom of Hungary, incorporating parts of two Transylvanian castles and a replica of the chapel at Ják, enclosing a Renaissance courtyard that makes a romantic setting for evening **concerts** from July to mid-August.

In the main wing of the castle, the **Agriculture Museum** (*Mezőgazdasági Múzeum*; March–mid-Nov Tues–Fri & Sun 10am–5pm, Sat 10am–6pm; mid-Nov–Feb Tues–Fri & Sun 10am–4pm, Sat 10am–5pm; 300Ft) traces the history of hunting and farming in Hungary. Its most interesting sections relate to the early Magyars and such typically Hungarian breeds of livestock as longhorned grey cattle (favoured for their draught power rather than their milk) and woolly pigs. Upstairs, the hunting section is notable for a prehistoric dugout boat carved from a single piece of oak, which was found at Lake Balaton, and antique crossbows and rifles exquisitely inlaid with leaping hares and other prey. There is some fine pottery in the gift **shop**.

Even if you decide to skip the museum, don't miss the hooded **statue of Anonymous** outside. This nameless chronicler to King Béla is the prime source of information about early medieval Hungary, though the existence of several monarchs of that name during the twelfth and thirteenth centuries makes it hard to date him (or his chronicles) with any accuracy.

The Petőfi Csarnok and Transport Museum

Leaving Vajdahunyad island by the causeway at the rear, you'll be on course for the **Petőfi Csarnok**, a shabby 1970s "Metropolitan Youth Centre" about ten minutes away that regularly hosts concerts (outdoors in summer), films and parties, and a fine **flea market** at weekends (☎343-4327 or ⊛www.petoficsarnok.hu for information in English). At the back of the building is a stairway leading to the **Aviation and Space Flight Exhibition** (*Repüléstörténeti és Űrhajózási kiállítás*; April–Nov Tues–Fri 10am–5pm, Sat & Sun 10am–6pm; 300Ft, student 150Ft), which, among other items, contains the space capsule used by Hungary's first astronaut, Bertalan Farkas, and his Soviet colleague on the Soyuz-35 mission of 1980; and an L-2 monoplane sporting an Italian Fascist symbol, which broke world speed records in the Budapest–Rome races of 1927 and 1930. Alas, there seems to be nothing about Count László Almássy, Hungary's foremost aviator of that time, who is now better known abroad as the hero of the book and film *The English Patient*. Information is in Hungarian only.

Not far away you'll come to the **Transport Museum** (*Közlekedési Múzeum*; Tues–Fri 10am–5pm, Sat & Sun 10am–6pm; 300Ft, student 150Ft) on the edge of the park, of which the aviation exhibition above is an outgrowth. Try to time your visit for the running of the model train set on the floor above the foyer – switched on for fifteen minutes every hour, on the hour. Captions in English explain that the Hungarian transport network of the 1890s was among the most sophisticated in Europe; starting from a low technological base, railways, canals, trams and a metro had all been created within fifty years. You can also see vintage locomotives and scale models of steamboats, and a wonderful collection of Hungarian Railways posters from 1900 to 1980. Collectors can buy Hungarian model trains in the museum shop. Outside the building are remnants of two of the Danube bridges that were wrecked in 1945: the cast-iron Erzsébet híd (replaced by a new bridge) and a few links of the original chains from the Lánchíd, which is now supported by cables. The outdoor wagon-bar is a quiet nightspot.

The Rail Heritage Park in the XVI district is even better for trainspotters and children – see p.134 for details.

The Széchenyi Baths

Map 2; F5. Széchenyi Fürdő metro (M1). Outdoor pool daily: summer 6am–7pm; winter 6am–4pm; 1500Ft. Turkish baths Mon–Sat 6am–7pm, Sun 6am–1pm; 1200Ft.

On the far side of the park's main axis, Kós Károly sétány, the **Széchenyi Baths** (*Széchenyi Gyógyfürdő*) could be mistaken for a palace, so grand is its facade. Outside is a statue of the geologist Zsigmondy Vilmos, who discovered the thermal spring that feeds its outdoor pool and Turkish baths. In the huge mixed-sex pool you can enjoy the surreal spectacle of people playing **chess** while immersed up to their chests in steaming water – so hot that you shouldn't stay in for more than twenty minutes. The best players sit at tables around the pool's edge, the former world champion **Bobby Fischer** amongst them. Bring your own set if you wish to participate. A cosy private cubicle is included in the price. Tickets to each section cost 200Ft less after 3pm.

The Circus, Vidám Park and the Zoo

Map 2, F5. Széchenyi Fürdő metro (M1) or tram #72 from Arany János metro.

Beyond the baths, on the far side of Állatkerti körút, the **Municipal Circus** (*Fővárosi Nagycirkusz*) traces its origins back to 1783, when the Hetz Theatre played to spectators on what is now Deák tér (performances mid-April–Aug Wed, Fri & Sun 3pm & 7pm, Thurs 3pm, Sat 10am, 3pm & 7pm; 600–1000Ft). To the right is **Vidám Park**, an old-fashioned fairground known as the "English Park" before the war (daily 10am–8pm; 300Ft, free for children under 120cm in height); the funfair was the setting for Ferenc Molnár's play *Liliom*, which inspired the musical *Carousel*. The gilded merry-go-round to the left of the entrance and the wooden switchback at the back of the fairground both predate World War II. **Kis Vidám**, next door, is for kids under two years old (Mon–Fri 10am–6pm, Sat, Sun & holidays 9.30am–7pm; free).

Further down towards Hősök tere you'll find the delightful Elephant Gates of Budapest's **Zoo** (*Állatkert*; daily:

THE VÁROSLIGET

May–Aug 9am–7pm; April & Sept 9am–6pm; March & Oct 9am–5pm; Nov–Feb 9am–4pm; 800Ft, child 600Ft, family 2400Ft). When opened in 1866, its Art Nouveau pavilions by Károly Kós seemed the last word in zoological architecture, but it slowly stagnated until the 1990s, when a new director aided by private sponsors began long overdue improvements to give the animals better habitats and make the zoo more visitor-friendly. Don't miss the exotic Elephant House resembling a Central Asian mosque, the Palm House (180Ft) or the Bonsai garden. The children's corner is signposted "Állatóvoda". Besides the zoo stands *Gundel's*, one of the grandest restaurants in Budapest (see "Listings", p.186).

The Erzsébetváros

The mainly residential **Erzsébetváros** is composed of nineteenth-century buildings whose bullet-scarred facades, adorned with fancy wrought-ironwork, conceal a warren of dwellings and leafy courtyards. It is also traditionally the Jewish quarter of the city, which was transformed into a ghetto during the Nazi occupation and almost wiped out in 1944–45, but has miraculously retained its cultural identity. Its current resurgence owes much to increased contacts with international Jewry, and a revival of interest in their religion and roots among the 80,000-strong Jewish community of Budapest, which had previously tended towards assimilation, reluctant to proclaim itself in a country where anti-Semitic prejudices linger. There is no better part of Pest to wander around, soaking up the atmosphere.

KIRÁLY UTCA

The official boundary between the Terézváros and Erzsébetváros runs down the middle of **Király utca**, which used to be a main thoroughfare before Andrássy út was built. In the 1870s the street contained 14 of the 58 licensed brothels in Budapest, and as late as 1934 Patrick Leigh Fermor was told that "any man could be a cavalier for five pengöes" here. After decades of shabby respectability under Communism, the street has become quite fashionable, with new furniture shops, patisseries and restaurants. Though not the most logical place to start exploring the Jewish quarter, it makes a wonderful approach from the direction of Andrássy út, as you can walk through the Gozsdu udvar (see p.118), entering the passage at Király utca 11 and emerging on Dob utca in the Jewish quarter.

However, approaching the area from the **Kiskörút**, as most people do, the Dohány utca (Tobacco Street) Synagogue is the obvious first objective, located only five minutes' walk from Deák tér, just off Károly körút.

THE DOHÁNY UTCA SYNAGOGUE

Map 4, D9. Astoria or Deák tér metro (M2). Mon–Thurs 10am–5pm, Fri 10am–3pm, Sun 10am–2pm; 600Ft, student 200Ft, under-14s free. Guided tours daily except Sat 10.30am–3.30pm; 1900Ft (including admission); audioguide 850Ft.

The splendid **Dohány utca Synagogue** (*Dohány utcai Zsinagóga*), which also contains the **Jewish Museum**, is one of the landmarks of Pest. Europe's largest synagogue and the second biggest in the world after the Temple Emmanuel in New York, it can hold three thousand worshippers, members of the **Neolog** community, a Hungarian denomination combining elements of Reform and Orthodox Judaism. Designed by a Viennese Gentile, Lajos Förster, the building epitomizes the so-called Byzantine-Moorish style that was popular in the 1850s, and attests to the patriotism of Hungarian Jewry – the colours of its brickwork (yellow, red and blue) being those of Budapest's coat of arms. In the 1990s the synagogue was restored at a cost of over $40 million, funded by the Hungarian government and the Hungarian-Jewish diaspora, notably the Emmanuel Foundation, fronted by the Hollywood actor Tony Curtis, born of 1920s emigrants.

Having admired its gilded onion-domed towers and passed through a security check, you can marvel at the **interior** by Frigyes Feszl, the architect of the Vigadó concert hall. The layout reflects the synagogue's Neolog identity, with the *bemah*, or Ark of the Torah, at one end, in the Reform fashion, but with men and women seated apart, according to Orthodox tradition. The ceiling is decorated with arabesques and Stars of David, the balconies for female worshippers are surmounted by gilded arches, and the floor is inset with eight-pointed stars. On Jewish festivals, it is filled to the rafters with Jews from all over Hungary, whose chattering disturbs their more devout co-religionists. At other times, the hall is used for concerts of classical or klezmer music, as advertised outside.

Next, visitors cross a courtyard full of simple headstones, marking the **mass grave** of 2281 Jews who died here during the icy winter of 1944. You can also see part of the brick wall that surrounded the ghetto, with a plaque commemorating its liberation by the Red Army on January 18, 1945. Behind the courtyard looms the cuboid, domed **Heroes' Temple**, erected in 1929–31 in honour of the 10,000 Jewish soldiers who died fighting for Hungary during World War I. These days it serves as a synagogue for everyday use and is not open to tourists.

The Jewish Museum

Heading upstairs to the **Jewish Museum** (*Zsidó Múzeum*), on the left-hand side of the main synagogue, notice a relief of Tivadar (Theodor) Herzl, the founder of modern Zionism, who was born and taught here. In the foyer is a gravestone inscribed with a *menora* (seven-branched candlestick) from the third century AD – proof that there were Jews living in Hungary six hundred years before the Magyars arrived. The first three rooms are devoted to

Jewish festivals, with beautifully crafted objects such as Sabbath lamps and Seder bowls, some from medieval times. The final room covers the Holocaust in Hungary, with chilling photos and examples of anti-Semitic propaganda. Oddly, the museum says nothing about the huge contribution that Jews have made to Hungarian society, in every field from medicine to poetry.

Upon leaving, turn the corner onto Wesselényi utca and enter the **Raoul Wallenberg Memorial Garden**, named after the Swedish consul who saved 20,000 Jews by lodging them in safe houses or, failing that, by plucking them from trains bound for Auschwitz. He was last seen alive the day before the Red Army liberated the ghetto; arrested by the Soviets on suspicion of espionage, he died in the Gulag. The park's centrepiece is a **Holocaust Memorial** by Imre Varga, shaped like a weeping willow, each leaf engraved with the names of a family killed by the Nazis. On the plinth are testimonials from their relatives living in Israel, America and Russia. Also within the grounds is the Goldmark Hall, named after Károly Goldmark, the composer of the opera *The Queen of Sheba*.

Walking tours of the quarter (daily except Sat noon & 3pm; 1600Ft; ☎317-2754 for tickets and information) reveal local colour and historical details you might otherwise miss; you can sign up at the main synagogue.

AROUND THE BACKSTREETS

Fanning out behind the synagogue is what was once the Jewish **ghetto**, created by the Nazis in April 1944. Initially, the Hungarian government feared that concentrating all the Jews within one area would expose the rest of Budapest to Allied bombing raids, but by November such considerations were forgotten, and all Jews living outside the ghetto were compelled to move there. As their menfolk had already been conscripted into labour battalions intended to kill them from overwork, the 70,000 inhabitants of the ghetto were largely women, children and old folk, crammed into 162 blocks of flats, with over 50,000 of them (in buildings meant for 15,000) around Klauzál tér alone.

Directly across the road from the Wallenberg Memorial Garden, **Rumbach Sebestyén utca** leads northwards to the **synagogue** of the so-called "Status Quo" or middling-conservative Jews (not open to the public). Though outwardly akin to the Dohány utca synagogue – with a Moorish-style facade in yellow and red brick, inset with blue crosses – its interior conforms to conservative prescriptions, with a detached gallery for women, and the *bemah* in the centre of the hall. As a plaque outside notes, the building served as a detention barracks in August 1941, from where up to 1800 Slovak and Polish refugees were deported to the Nazi death camps.

En route to the Status Quo synagogue, as you cross Dob utca, you'll see a **monument to Carl Lutz**, the Swiss Consul who began issuing *Schutzpasses* to Jews, attesting that they were Swiss or Swedish citizens – a ruse subsequently used by Wallenberg. Lutz was a more ambiguous figure, who ceased issuing passes and tried to prevent others from doing so after being threatened by the Gestapo. After the war he was criticized for abusing Swiss law and, feeling slighted, proposed himself for the Nobel Peace Prize. His monument – a gilded angel swooping down to help a prostrate victim – is locally known as "the figure jumping out of a window".

Just beyond Lutz's memorial, a grey stone portal at no. 16 leads into the **Gozsdu udvar**, an eerie 200-metre-long passageway connecting seven courtyards that runs through to Király utca 11. A hive of life and activity before the Holocaust, it is now scheduled for redevelopment, which the remaining residents fear will mean becoming an adjunct to the Madách tér business centre. However, Romanian claims to the property, arising from an unsettled prewar compensation deal, have stalled further action and left the udvar in limbo.

The kosher *Frölich* patisserie at Dob utca 22 is one of several Jewish businesses on **Kazinczy utca**, the centre of the 3000-strong Orthodox community, where one can still hear Yiddish spoken. There's a butcher's in the yard of no. 41, up to the left of Dob utca, while down to the right is a kosher baker (no. 28), and the non-kosher Jewish *Carmel* restaurant (no. 31). Almost next door to the last stands the **Orthodox Synagogue**, an Art Nouveau edifice that melds into the curve of the street, its pediment bearing a Hebrew inscription asserting: "This place is none other than the house of God and the gate to heaven." Though its interior is off-limits to the public, the gate to the right leads into an L-shaped courtyard containing a Jewish school and the *Hanna* Orthodox kosher restaurant – also accessible via an arcade on Dob utca.

MUSEUM OF ELECTROTECHNOLOGY

Map 4 E9. Tues–Sat 11am–5pm; guided tours as posted outside; free. For something quite different, visit the **Museum of Electrotechnology** (*Magyar Elektrotechnikai Múzeum*) in a former electricity substation at Kazinczy utca 21. Its curators demonstrate the world's first dynamo (invented in 1859 by Áynos Jedlik, a Benedictine monk) and other devices in rooms devoted to such topics as the history of light bulbs and the Hungarian section of the Iron Curtain; though the current was too weak to kill and the minefields were removed in 1965, patrols kept it inviolate until 1989, when the Hungarians ceased shooting escapees, thereby spelling the end of the Iron Curtain as a whole.

THE "GARMENT DISTRICT"

Beyond the Nagykörút, the VII district changes, becoming more working-class and tinged with Arab and Chinese influences as one nears the **"Garment District"** around **Garay tér**, whose bustling **market** hall is a lunch-spot for workers from the sweatshops in a neighbourhood where wholesalers do business in a dozen languages and travel agents offer trips to Mecca. While it's easier to get there from Keleti Station (see p.5), the transition is best appreciated by starting at **Blaha Lujza tér** (take M2, or any bus along Rákóczi út) and walking up Dohány utca past the hulk of the once-renowned **New York Coffeehouse** on the corner of the Nagykörút. While its Beaux Arts facade survived being rammed by a tank in 1956, its Art Nouveau interior has been rotting away ever since competing claims of ownership were filed in the 1990s, and there are fears that the whole building may collapse.

The Józsefváros and Ferencváros

S eparated from the Erzsébetváros by Rákóczi út, which runs out to Keleti Station, the **Józsefváros** is an amalgam of high and low life. Although it boasts several prestigious institutions around the Kiskörút, including the Hungarian National Museum, Eötvös Loránd University and the Erkel Theatre, the hinterland beyond the Nagykörút was nicknamed "Chicago" during the 1920s and 1930s, and is still associated with prostitution and criminal activities. While the area between the Kiskörút and Nagykörút is nothing to worry about, caution is warranted elsewhere, especially after dark.

Bordering the Józsefváros to the south is the **Ferencváros**, the most solidly working-class of the inner-city districts, whose tenements are swelteringly hot in the summer. It is chiefly of interest for the wonderful market hall on Vámház körút and the Applied Arts Museum on Üllői út – but football fans will want to see "Fradi" in action at the FTC Stadium.

MÚZEUM KÖRÚT

Map 4, D10. Astoria (M2) or Kálvin tér (M3) metro; tram #47 or #49 along the Kiskörút.

Part of the Kiskörút, **Múzeum körút** separates the Belváros and Józsefváros. Aside from being curved rather than straight, it resembles Andrássy út in miniature, lined with trees, shops and grandiose buildings. Immediately beyond the East-West Business Centre by the Astoria junction stands the old faculty of the **Eötvös Loránd Science University** (known by its Hungarian initials as ELTE). It is named after the physicist Loránd Eötvös, whose pupils included many of the scientists who later developed the US atomic bombs at Los Alamos, including Edward Teller, "Father of the Hydrogen Bomb".

Further on and across the street, a large crenellated section of the **medieval wall of Pest** lurks in the courtyard of no. 21. Originally 2km long and 8m high, the walls gradually disappeared as the city was built up on either side, but fragments remain here and there.

Staying on the outer edge of Múzeum körút, you'll find the **Múzeum Kávéház** at no. 12, one of the earliest coffee houses in Pest, whose original frescoes and Zsolnay ceramic reliefs dating from 1885 still grace what has long since become a restaurant. Dining here is a must, but it's essential to reserve; see p.184 for details. At the next corner, just before the National Museum, you can wander off down Bródy Sándor utca to see the nondescript **Radio Building** (nos. 5–7), where ÁVO guards fired upon students demanding access to the airwaves, an act which turned the hitherto peaceful protests of October 23, 1956 into an uprising against the secret police and other manifestations of Stalinism.

Hungarian National Museum

Map 4, E11. Kálvin tér metro (M3). May–Sept Tues–Sun
10am–6pm, Oct–April Wed–Sun 10am–4pm; 600Ft, student 300Ft.

Like the National Library on Várhegy, the **Hungarian National Museum** (*Magyar Nemzeti Múzeum*) was the brainchild of Count Ferenc Széchenyi (father of István), who donated thousands of prints and manuscripts to form the basis of its collection. Housed in a Grecian-style edifice by Mihály Pollack, it was only the fourth such museum in the world when it opened in 1847, and soon afterwards became the stage for a famous event in the 1848 Revolution, when Sándor Petőfi first declaimed the *National Song* from its steps, with its rousing refrain – "Choose! Now is the time! Shall we be slaves or shall we be free?" ("Some noisy mob had their hurly-burly outside so I left for home," complained the director.) Ever since, March 15 has been commemorated here with flags and speeches.

By way of amends for losing the Coronation Regalia in 2000 (now on display in Parliament – see p.91), the National Museum is undergoing a major refit, set to finish in 2003. This has resulted in two new subterranean levels, devoted to **medieval and Roman sculptures** – the latter starring a third-century mosaic floor from a villa at Balácpuszta in western Hungary. Also accessible from the foyer is a darkened room displaying King Stephen's Byzantine silk **coronation robe**, which is far too fragile to be exhibited in the Parliament building.

Hungarian history exhibition

The main exhibition on the upper floor traces Hungarian history from the Árpád dynasty to the end of Communism. Room 1 contains Béla III's crown, sceptre and sword, and Room 2 the Anjou Fountain from the royal palace at Visegrád (see p.145). Don't miss the ivory saddles inlaid with

MÚZEUM KÖRÚT

hunting scenes in Room 3, the suit of armour of the child-king Sigismund III in Room 5, nor the huge Renaissance Báthory pew in Room 6. Turkish weaponry and the gold-embroidered tunic of Prince Gábor Bethlen of Transylvania in Room 7 speak of the 150 years when Hungary was divided and its destiny decided by intriguers and warlords, including the Forgáchs and Nádasdys depicted in the oldest **portraits** in Hungary, hung in Room 8 – except for the infamous "Blood Countess", whose picture is kept in storage. The Countess, widow of national hero Ferenc Nádasdy, was charged with torturing six hundred women to death and reputedly bathing in their blood to preserve her beauty; she was walled up in her castle and the atrocity hushed up.

The Reform era and the *belle époque* are covered in Rooms 11–18, followed by World War II and the Communist era in Room 20. The last features newsreel footage and such items as a radio set dedicated to Stalin's seventieth birthday, a fragment of the Stalin statue and the crest of Party headquarters torn down by crowds in 1956, and kitsch tributes to János Kádár, who reimposed Communist rule with a vengeance, but later liberalized it to the point that his successors felt able to abandon it entirely. Not to be missed are the **propaganda** films from the Horthy, Fascist and Stalinist eras, whose resemblance to one another makes the point.

KÁLVIN TÉR

Map 4, D12. Kálvin tér metro (M3).

Múzeum körút ends at **Kálvin tér**, a busy intersection above a metro underpass, straddled by the *Mercure Korona Hotel* (see p.77) on the Belváros side. With a little trial and error, you should find the exit that emerges near the **Szabó Ervin Library** (Mon, Tues & Thurs 9am–9pm, Sat & Sun 9am–1pm), whose ornate reading room miraculously sur-

vived the heavy streetfighting around Kálvin tér in 1944
and 1956, as did the Fountain of Justice, installed outside in
1929 as a reminder of the injustice inflicted on Hungary by
the Treaty of Trianon, which features a relief of Lord
Rothermere (see p.88).

**The continuation of the Kiskörút and the Applied
Arts Museum on Üllői út are covered on p.130.**

TO THE NAGYKÖRÚT AND KELETI STATION

Map 4. Blaha Lujza tér or Keleti pu. metro (M2); tram #4 or #6.

To stretch your legs, take a stroll through the atmospheric
quarter behind the library, with its crumbling churches and
parochial schools, wine cellars and workshops. Eventually
you'll emerge on the **József körút** – one of the sleazier
arcs of the Nagykörút – with *lezbiánus* shows that have survived the crackdown on **Rákóczi tér**, following a law in
1999 that restricted **prostitution** to "tolerated zones" (in
fact, only one for the whole country, in the city of
Miskolc), which merely drove the trade into brothels more
easily controlled by the Mafia. By day, however, the shabby
square is simply a place for locals to shop in the market hall
and Chinese wholesalers.

While theatre-goers bestow bourgeois respectability upon
Köztársaság tér – the home of Budapest's "second" opera
house, the **Erkel Theatre** (named after the composer of the
national anthem, Ferenc Erkel) – the grittier side of life pre-
vails at **Keleti Station** on Baross tér. As Budapest's "gateway
to the east", it's not surprising that Chinese takeaways and
Arab shops are a feature of the area – nor the incessant ID
checks by the **police**, who patrol here in threes ("One can
read, one can write, and the third one keeps an eye on the
two intellectuals", as the old joke has it).

Crime and Police History Museum

Map 4, I8. Keleti pu. metro (M2). Tues–Sun 10am–5pm; free.

Handily for the police, their precinct HQ is only two blocks from the station, at Mosonyi utca 6. Tourists who'd never go there otherwise can visit its bizarre **Crime and Police History Museum** (*Bűnügyi és Rendőrség-Történeti Múzeum*), accessed via a separate door guarded by a dummy sentry. Since the museum is captioned in Hungarian only, you can easily miss the ideological cast of the display of uniforms and memorabilia going back to Habsburg times, which harbours a tribute to the Communist border guards and militia. Be thankful you're not an exhibit in the other hall, where many displays depict murders and mutilations in horrific detail – unlike the staged crime scene with a sign listing key points for trainee investigators. Stuff on forgery and art theft in the 1980s begs the question why there's nothing about crime nowadays. The show ends with a fraternal display of police insignia and toy squad cars from around the world; look out for the laughing-skull patch of Haiti's notorious Tontons Macoutes hit squad.

KEREPESI CEMETERY

Map 2, F6. Keleti pu. metro (M2). Daily: April & Aug 7am–7pm; May–July 7am–8pm; Sept 7am–6pm; Oct 7am–5.30pm; Nov–March 7.30am–5pm; free.

Five minutes' walk from the museum, along Fiumei út, you'll find **Kerepesi Cemetery** (*Kerepesi temető*), the Père Lachaise of Budapest, where the famous, great and not-so-good are buried. Vintage hearses and mourning regalia in the **Funerary Museum** (Mon–Thurs 10am–3pm, Fri 10am–1pm; free) near the main gates illuminate the Hungarian way of death and set the stage for the necropolis. In Communist times, Party members killed during the

Uprising were buried in a prominent position near the entrance and government ministers in honourable proximity to Kossuth, while leaders and martyrs who "Lived for Communism and the People" were enshrined in a starkly ugly **Pantheon of the Working Class Movement**, which was so shoddily built that it's falling apart; some have been removed by their relatives since the demise of Communism. Party leader János Kádár – who ruled Hungary from 1956 to 1988 – rates a separate grave, heaped with wreaths from admirers; his reputation has risen in recent years, and there's even talk of a monument.

Further in lie the florid **nineteenth-century mausoleums** of Kossuth, Batthyány, Deák and Petőfi (whose family tomb is here though his own body was never found). Don't miss the Art Nouveau funerary arcades between

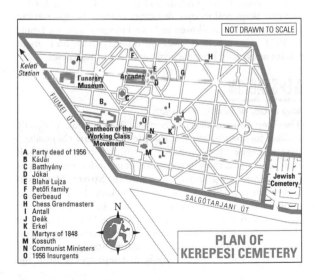

A Party dead of 1956
B Kádár
C Batthyány
D Jókai
E Blaha Lujza
F Petőfi family
G Gerbeaud
H Chess Grandmasters
I Antall
J Deák
K Erkel
L Martyrs of 1848
M Kossuth
N Communist Ministers
O 1956 Insurgents

PLAN OF KEREPESI CEMETERY

NOT DRAWN TO SCALE

Keleti Station

Funerary Museum

Arcades

Pantheon of the Working Class Movement

Jewish Cemetery

FIUMEI ÚT

SALGÓTARJANI ÚT

N

KEREPESI CEMETERY

Batthyány's and the novelist Jókai's mausoleums, nor the nearby tomb of the diva Lujza Blaha, the "Nation's Nightingale", whose effigy is surrounded by statues of serenading figures. Other notables include the composer Erkel, the confectioner Gerbeaud and three chess grandmasters whose tombs are engraved with the chess moves that won them their titles. A more recent addition is József Antall, the first post-Communist prime minister of Hungary, honoured by an allegorical monument with horses struggling to burst free of a sheet.

Beyond Kerepesi lies an overgrown **Jewish cemetery** (Mon–Fri & Sun 8am–2pm), with some beautiful Art Nouveau tombs of artists, politicians and industrialists, many designed by the brilliant architect Béla Lajta. That of Manfred Weiss, founder of the Csepel ironworks, is still maintained by Csepel's council, in gratitude and by way of apology for the fact that Weiss had to sign his factory over to the government in return for being allowed to leave Hungary with his family in 1944. The cemetery gates are on Salgótarján utca, about ten minutes' walk from the main entrance to Kerepesi.

NÉPSTADION

Map 2, G5. Népstadion metro (M2).

The **Népstadion** district, north of Kerepesi út, is chiefly notable for the 76,000-seat **People's Stadium** (*Népstadion*) where league championship and international **football** matches, concerts by foreign pop stars and events such as the national dog show are held. Its **Sport Museum** (*Sportmúzeum*; daily except Fri 10am–4pm; 100Ft) features temporary exhibitions on sports themes, in Hungarian only. The stadium itself was built in the early 1950s by 50,000 Budapesters who "volunteered" their labour, unpaid, on Soviet-style "free Saturdays". Stalinist statues of healthy proletarian youth line the court that separates it from the smaller **Kisstadion** and the indoor **Sportcsarnok**, which also hosts occasional concerts. The Népstadion **bus station** completes this concrete ensemble.

Otherwise, the only reason to come is to catch trolley bus #75 along Stefánia út, behind the Sportcsarnok, to admire the **Geological Institute** (no. 14). The last of the three edifices in Budapest designed by Ödön Lechner, its exterior is as striking as the Postal Savings Bank (p.89) and the Applied Arts Museum (see p.130), with a gingerbread facade, scrolled gables and steeply pitched Transylvanian roofs patterned in bright blue tiles, crowned by figures holding globes on their backs. By visiting its small geological **museum** (Jan 7–Dec 19 Thurs, Sat & Sun 10am–4pm; 150Ft), you can also see something of the interior.

From the Geological Institute, you can continue along Stefánia út by trolley bus #75 to reach the Városliget (see p.109).

FERENCVÁROS

Kálvin tér or Ferenc körút metro (M3).

Ferencváros (Franz Town), the IX district, was developed to house workers in the latter half of the nineteenth century, and remains the most working class of Budapest's inner suburbs. During the 1930s and 1940s, its population confounded Marxist orthodoxy by voting for the extreme right, who returned the favour by supporting the local football team **FTC** – popularly known as "**Fradi**" – which became the unofficial team of the opposition under Communism and is nowadays known for its hardcore hooligan supporters. The club's green and white colours can be seen throughout the district; for more on Fradi and the football scene in general, see p.224.

Initially, Ferencváros takes its tone from two institutions

FERENCVÁROS

on Vámház körút, the section of the Kiskörút that separates it from the Belváros. The wrought-iron **Great Market Hall** (*Nagycsarnok*; Mon 6am–5pm, Tues–Fri 6am–6pm, Sat 6am–2pm) is as famous for its ambience as for its produce, with tanks of live fish downstairs and stalls festooned with strings of paprika at the back, where former British prime minister Mrs Thatcher once endeared herself by haggling during a visit.

Nearer the Danube, the **Economics University** (named after Karl Marx during Communist times) makes a fine sight at night, reflected in the river, and adds to the liveliness of the area by day. The building was originally Budapest's main Customs House (*Vámház*) – hence the name of the körút. On the Belváros side, a free-standing section of the **medieval walls** of Pest can be found in the courtyard of no. 16. Everything else of interest in the district is too far away to walk to, but readily accessible by public transport.

Applied Arts Museum

Map 4, F13. Ferenc körút metro (M3). Tues–Sun: mid-March–Oct 10am–4pm; Nov–mid-March 10am–6pm; 500Ft, student 200Ft.

The **Applied Arts Museum** (*Iparművészeti Múzeum*) is worth a visit purely to see the building by Ödön Lechner, who strove to create a uniquely Hungarian form of architecture emphasizing the Magyars' Ugric roots, but was also influenced by Art Nouveau. Inaugurated by Emperor Franz Josef during the 1896 Millennial celebrations, it has an enormous dome tiled in green and yellow and a portico with ceramic Turkic motifs on a yolk-coloured background, from the Zsolnay porcelain factory in Pécs. By contrast, the all-white interior is reminiscent of Moghul architecture: at one time it was thought that the Magyars came from India.

THE JÓZSEFVÁROS AND FERENCVÁROS

The museum's fine show of **Arts and Crafts** since medieval times is surpassed by **Style 1900**, devoted to the movement known as Art Nouveau, Jugendstil or Secessionist, with a superb collection ranging from William Morris wallpaper and Tiffany vases to stained-glass panels by Hungarian masters like József Rippl-Rónai and Miksa Róth. Since the museum's hoard of furniture from other epochs was moved to the Nagytétény Castle Museum (see p.135) there's been plenty of space for temporary exhibitions, too.

The Kilián Barracks and Corvin Cinema

Map 4, F13. Ferenc körút metro (M3).

One block beyond the Applied Arts Museum, the underpass at the junction of the Nagykörút will bring you out on either side of Üllői út beside two buildings associated with the 1956 Uprising. On the right side stands the former **Kilián Barracks**, whose Hungarian garrison was the first to join the insurgents. As the Uprising spread, it became the headquarters of Colonel Pál Maléter and teams of teenage guerillas (some as young as 12) who sallied forth from the alleys surrounding the **Corvin Cinema**, to lob Molotov cocktails at Soviet tanks. Since the fall of Communism they have been honoured by a **statue of a young insurgent** outside the cinema. Its auditoria are named after illustrious Hungarian actors or directors such as Alexander Korda – one of many Magyars who made it in Hollywood (Béla Lugosi and Zsa Zsa Gabor being the most famous).

FERENCVÁROS

Further out

hile the centre of Budapest is hardly short of attractions, it would be a shame to overlook some of the ones further out towards the city limits. The Statue Park, with its exiled Communist memorials, is the prime destination for foreigners, and the Rail Heritage Park – where visitors can drive steam trains – is popular with Hungarian tourists. After that, it really depends on your inclinations whether you want to visit the Budakeszi Game Park or the Nagytétény Castle Museum on the outskirts of Buda, or the Wolf's Meadow and New District cemeteries that complete the roll-call of illustrious Hungarian dead begun at Kerepesi. You can reach any of them from the city centre within an hour.

STATUE PARK

Map 2, C9. Daily 10am–dusk; winter Sat, Sun & public holidays only; may be closed during bad weather – phone to check (☏424-7500); 300Ft, student 200Ft. Ⓦwww.szoborpark.hu.

Easily the most popular site on the outskirts, the **Statue Park** (*Szoborpark*) brings together 42 of the monuments that once glorified Communism in Budapest. The idea was suggested by a historian during the period of transition to democracy and put into practice following the municipal assembly's ruling that each district should decide the fate of its own statues, with the museum finally opening in 1993. The site is beside Balatoni út in the XXII district, 15km from the city centre. Getting there involves taking a red-numbered bus #7-713 from the Párizsi Udvar in Pest (p.14) to Etele tér in Buda, and then a yellow Volán bus from stand #2 towards Diósd, which takes twenty minutes to reach the park. You'll need to buy a ticket from the driver, as passes aren't valid on this route.

The Statue Park's outsized gate is clearly visible from the highway, its bogus Classical facade framing giant statues of Lenin, Marx and Engels. Lenin's once stood beside the Városliget, while Marx's and Engels' are carved from granite quarried at Mauthausen, the Nazi concentration camp later used by the Soviets. Inside the grounds you'll encounter the Red Army soldier that guarded the foot of the Liberation Monument on Gellért-hegy, and dozens of other statues and memorials, large and small. Here are prewar Hungarian Communists like Béla Kun (secretly shot in Moscow on Stalin's orders) and Jenő Landler (afforded a place in the Kremlin Wall); Dimitrov, hero of the Comintern; and the Lenin statue from outside the Csepel ironworks.

Artistically, the best statues are the Republic of Councils Monument – a giant charging sailor based on a 1919 revolutionary poster – and Imre Varga's Béla Kun Memorial, with Kun on a tribune surrounded by a surging crowd of workers and soldiers (plus a bystander with an umbrella). Budapesters fondly remember the statue of Captain Ostapenko that stood on the highway to the Balaton and Vienna, where hitch-hikers would arrange to meet their friends (a locality still known as "Ostapenko"), while the removal of the monument to the Hungarian contingent of the International Brigade in the Spanish Civil War (three robotic figures with fists clenched to their heads) provoked a heartfelt debate that few of the others engendered.

STATUE PARK

Among the **souvenirs** on sale are small Lenin and Stalin candles, cans of air from "the last breath of socialism", and selections of revolutionary songs, which can be heard playing from a 1950s' radio set. There's also an informative English-language brochure (400Ft).

RAIL HERITAGE PARK

Map 2, G2. Tues–Sun: May–Oct 10am–6pm; Nov–March 10am–3pm; 800Ft, student 600Ft, child 200Ft, family 1600Ft, cameras 200Ft, videocameras 800Ft.

Inaugurated in 2000, the **Rail Heritage Park** (*Magyar Vasúttörténeti Park*) is still evolving but already a popular attraction for Budapest families, that's bound to draw more foreigners as word gets out. Located in the freight yards of the XIV district, 6km beyond the Városliget, its sheds and sidings house over seventy kinds of locomotives and carriages from 1900 onwards, and at certain times of the day (10am–12.15pm & 1.30–5.30pm) you can even **drive** a steam train (1000Ft) or a luggage cart (300Ft) – wear old clothes. Many of the staff are ex-employees of MÁV (Hungarian State Railways), proud of a tradition inherited from the Royal Hungarian Railways, dating back to the 1840s. The museum above the visitors' centre displays information in Hungarian only, but all kinds of train books, videos and MÁV souvenirs are sold downstairs.

From April to October, you can travel to the museum **by steam train** (*különvonat*) from Nyugati Station (Tues–Sun 9.45am–3.45pm); tickets are available from MÁV Nosztalgia in the station, or Belgrád rakpart 26 in the Belváros (ⓦwww.mavnosztalgia.hu). Otherwise, the park gates at Tatai út 95 are a short walk from the Rokolya utca stop, a longish ride by bus #20 or #30 from Keleti Station or Dózsa György út.

NAGYTÉTÉNY CASTLE MUSEUM

Map 2, D9. March–April & Nov–Dec Tues–Sun 10am–4pm; May & Sept–Oct Tues–Sun 10am–6pm; June–Aug Tues–Fri 10am–6pm, Sat & Sun 10am–8pm; 300Ft, cameras 400Ft, videocameras 1000Ft.

At some distance from the city centre, the **Nagytétény Castle Museum** (*Nagytétényi Kastélymúzeum*) is strictly for lovers of antique furniture or stately homes – so think twice before undertaking the lengthy (30–45min) journey by bus #3 from Móricz Zsigmond körtér. Get off at the Petőfi utca stop in the XII district, cross the road and follow Pohár utca into a park, to find the *kastély*. Though rendered as "castle" in English, "*kastély*" generally signifies a manor house or chateau without fortifications, which Hungarian nobles began building after the Turks had been expelled – in this case by converting an older, ruined castle into a Baroque residence. Nowadays, its 29 rooms display furniture from the Gothic to the Biedermeyer epochs, owned by the Applied Arts Museum; the most outstanding exhibit is a walnut-veneered refectory from Trencsen Monastery. In July and August, **historical dances** and **concerts** are held in the grounds (☏207-5462 for information).

BUDAKESZI GAME PARK

Map 2, A5. Bus #22 from Moszkva tér (M2) to the MÁV Sanatorium stop. Daily 9am to dusk; ticket office closes 4pm on weekdays & 6pm at weekends & holidays; 300Ft, student 150Ft.

Better known to natives than it is to tourists, the **Budakeszi Game Park** (*Vadaspark*), right on the city limits, offers a chance to view fauna that is otherwise elusive in the Buda Hills, to breathe fresh air and to escape from the city – with the caveat that you should avoid coming at weekends or national holidays, and, in order to really get back to nature, get away from the zoological enclosures.

Since bus #22 stops fairly near to the Szépjuhászné halt on the Children's Railway, you can also visit the park as an extension of the "railway circuit" in the Buda Hills (p.65).

Oddly, the *Hotel Tanne* is better signposted than the *Vadaspark* itself, whose entrance is fifteen minutes' walk past the hotel. Turn off Budakeszi út, and follow the tarmac road past a quarry and a **restaurant** (daily noon–11pm), where shameless carnivores can consume the species in the park.

Away from the enclosures near the entrance (boars and deer to the left, fowl to the right) and the wooden **lookout tower** that affords a lovely view of the wooded hills and the village of Budakeszi with Budapest nowhere in sight, the woodland **paths** are pretty much deserted, and if it wasn't for the lack of signposting one could easily follow the *A túra* (5km) or *B túra* (3km) circuits posted at the entrance. As things are, however, you'd do better to simply follow the swathe cut for telephone pylons, where all kinds of wildflowers and butterflies flourish, and nobody ever goes.

WOLF'S MEADOW CEMETERY

Map 2, C6. Tram #59 from Moszkva tér to the entrance on Nemetvölgyi út. Mon–Fri 7am–9pm, Sat & Sun 9am–5pm; free.

Wolf's Meadow Cemetery (*Farkasréti temető*) in the hilly XI district of Buda contains the graves of many poets, writers and musicians, of whom the best known is **Béla Bartók**. His remains were ceremonially interred here in July 1988 following their return from America, where the composer died in exile in 1945. His will forbade reburial in Hungary so long as there were streets named after Hitler or Mussolini, but the return of his body was delayed for decades to prevent the Communists from capitalizing on the event. The Hungarian-born conductor **Sir Georg**

Solti was buried alongside Bartók in 1998. Ironically, the cemetery also contains the grave of **Mátyás Rákosi**, Hungary's Stalinist dictator, who died in exile in the USSR and was evidently deemed unworthy of inclusion in the Pantheon of the Working Class Movement at Kerepesi. Also look out for gravestones inscribed in the ancient runic Székely alphabet.

However, the real attraction is the amazing **mortuary chapel** by Imre Makovecz, whose wood-ribbed vault resembles the throat and belly of a beast. This awesome structure is one of Makovecz's finest designs, and can't help but make anyone who sees it curious to know more about his work, which can also be seen at Visegrád (see p.147), but, as it is in almost constant use by mourners, visitors should be as discreet as possible.

NEW PUBLIC CEMETERY

Map 2, I6. Tram #28 or #37 from Népszínház utca near Blaha Lujza tér (M2). Daily 8am–dusk; free.

The **New Public Cemetery** (*Új köztemető*) in the X district is the largest in Budapest, reflecting the city's growth in the latter half of the nineteenth century. Located beyond the breweries of Kőbánya, near the end of one of the longest tram rides in Budapest, its significance lies in the fact that it was here that Imre Nagy and 260 others, executed for their part in the Uprising, were secretly buried in unmarked graves in 1958. Any flowers left at **Plot 301** were removed by the police until 1989, when the deceased received a state funeral on Hősök tere. The plot is 2km from the main gates on Kozma utca; minibuses shuttle back and forth every twenty minutes. Near the graves, an ornate wooden gateway and headposts mark a mass grave now designated as a **National Pantheon** – as opposed to the

Communist pantheon in Kerepesi (see p.126).

In the adjacent **Jewish cemetery** (Sun–Fri 8am–2pm), where famous rabbis and Ernő Szép (author of *The Smell of Humans*) are buried, look out for the lovely blue Art Nouveau tomb of Sándor Schmidl, designed by Lechner and Lajta. The gates to the Jewish cemetery are 700m up the road; tram #37 runs past.

Excursions from Budapest

Although many provincial towns in Hungary are within three hours' journey of Budapest, the attractions covered in this chapter are all within an hour or so's travel. Foremost among them are the sites on the picturesque Danube Bend – the artists' colony and historic Serbian settlement of Szentendre; the cathedral town of Esztergom, where the Danube forms the border between Hungary and Slovakia; and the medieval ruins and Makovecz buildings at Visegrád – but you shouldn't overlook the former Imperial palace at Gödöllő, either.

SZENTENDRE

Map 8. 45min by HÉV train from Batthyány tér (M2). BKV passes valid to Budapest's limits.

Szentendre (St Andrew), 20km north of Budapest, is the most popular tourist destination in the vicinity of the capital and the easiest to reach. Despite its rash of souvenir shops, the centre remains a delightful maze of houses in autumnal colours, with secretive gardens and lanes winding up to hilltop churches. Szentendre's location on the lower slopes of the Pilis range is not only beautiful, but ensures that it enjoys more hours of sunlight than anywhere else in Hungary, making it a perfect spot for an artists' colony.

Before the artists moved in, its character had been forged by waves of refugees from Serbia. The first followed the catastrophic Serb defeat at Kosovo in 1389; the second, the Turkish recapture of Belgrade in 1690, causing 30,000 Serbs and Bosnians to flee. Six thousand settled in Szentendre, which became the seat of the Serbian Church in exile. Prospering through trade, they replaced their wooden churches with stone ones and built handsome town houses, but as Habsburg toleration waned and phylloxera (vine-blight) and floods ruined the local economy they trickled back to Serbia, so that by 1890 less than a quarter of the population was Serb. About seventy families of Serbian descent remain today.

Orientation

Szentendre's bus and train (HÉV) stations are next to each other, fifteen minutes' walk south of the centre. The jetty for ferries and hydrofoils between Budapest and Esztergom lies 500m to the north. For a free map of the town and any **information**, drop into Tourinform at Dumsta Jenő utca 22, a few minutes up the road leading into the centre, on the far side of the pedestrian underpass outside the HÉV station (March–Oct Mon–Fri 9.30am–4.30pm, Sat & Sun 10am–2pm; Nov–Feb Mon–Fri 10am–4pm; ☎26/317-965).

When you feel hungry, make a beeline for the *Aranysárkány* **restaurant** at Alkotmány utca 1A, just uphill from Fő tér, which serves delicious dishes such as honeyed goose with red cabbage, at reasonable prices (daily noon–11pm). For coffee, an ice-cream sundae or something stronger, try the *Café Cousin*, down an alley off Rákóczi utca.

Churches, museums and crafts

The **Pož arevačka Church** (Fri–Sun 11am–5pm) is the
first evidence of a Serbian presence. Typical of the churches
in Szentendre, it was built in the late eighteenth century to
replace an older wooden structure. Beyond the Bükkös
stream, Dumtsa Jenő utca continues past the **Marzipan
Museum and Pastry Shop** at no. 12, where the marzipan
creations include a model of the Hungarian Parliament,
while a left turn at Péter-Pál utca brings you to the **Peter-
Paul Church**, built in 1708, whose original furnishings
were taken back to Serbia after World War I. For details of
organ recitals there, ask at Tourinform.

Beyond the church, **Fő tér** swarms with tourists and
horse-drawn carriages, with diverging streets and alleys
leading to various galleries and museums. Don't miss the
Margit Kovács Museum on Vastagh György utca
(Tues–Sun 10am–6pm; 300Ft), whose wonderful collection
of ceramic hats never fails to delight. Her themes of leg-
ends, dreams, love and motherhood give her graceful sculptures and reliefs universal appeal; although her work isn't
particularly well known abroad, in Hungary, Kovács, who
died in 1977, is duly honoured as the nation's greatest
ceramicist.

The museum is down a sidestreet from the
Blagoveštenska Church on Fő tér, whose icons evoke all
the richness and tragedy of Serbian history. Look out for
the tomb of a Greek merchant of Macedonian origin to the
left of the entrance, and the Rococo windows and gate facing Görög utca. Next door, a portal carved with emblems
of science and learning provides the entrance to a former
Serbian school, now the **Ferenczy Museum** (mid-March–
Oct Tues–Sun 10am–6pm; Nov–mid-March Fri–Sun
10am–6pm; 300Ft) exhibiting paintings by the
Impressionist Károly Ferenczy, and of his eldest son Valér

SZENTENDRE

141

and younger twins Nóemi and Béni, who branched out into Expressionism, textiles and bronzeware.

From Fő tér you can ascend an alley of steps to gain a lovely view of Szentendre's rooftops and gardens from **Templom tér**, where **craft fairs** are frequently held to help finance the restoration of the Catholic **parish church**. Of medieval origin, with Romanesque and Gothic features, it was rebuilt in the Baroque style after falling derelict in Turkish times. The frescoes in its sanctuary were collectively painted by the artists' colony. North of Templom tér, the burgundy spire of the Orthodox episcopal cathedral or **Belgrade Church** rises above a walled garden; it is rarely open except for services (Sat 5pm, 6pm in summer; Sun 10am & 4pm), though you can view a **Serbian Ecclesiastical History Collection** (mid-March–Oct Wed–Sun 10am–4pm; Nov–mid-March Fri–Sun same hours; 200Ft) in the episcopal palace, whose icons, vestments and crosses come from churches in Hungary that fell empty after the Serbs returned to the Balkans and the last remaining parishioners died out.

From the church a lane leads down to Bogdányi utca, where the **Wine Museum** (daily 10am–10pm; 200Ft) does a fair job of describing Hungary's wine-making regions using maps, wine-bottle labels and other artefacts, but the optional wine-tasting costs a lot more than you'd pay to drink in a regular *borozó*.

Further on, an old millhouse is now a gallery for installation art, called the **Culture Mill** (Tues–Sun 10am–6pm; free), while the Kovács **Blue Dye Shop** showcases a traditional style of folk dyeing that was once popular with ethnic Germans and is now fashionable amongst Hungarians. You'll find more examples of local crafts up the hill at Angyal utca 5, where László Vincze operates his **Paper Mill** and gives demonstrations by appointment (Mon–Fri 7am–5pm, Sat 7am–2pm; ☎26/314-328; 200Ft).

In October, when the wine harvest is celebrated, there are **festivities** around the **Lázár Cross** honouring King Lázár of Serbia, whom the Turks beheaded after Kosovo (his body was brought here by the Serbs but later taken home), and the **Vinegrowers' Cross** beyond the **Preobrazhenska Church**.

The Village Museum

The fantastic **Szentendre Village Museum** (April–early Nov Tues–Sun 9am–5pm; 500Ft) is Hungary's largest open-air museum of rural architecture (termed a *skanzen*, after the first such museum, founded in a Stockholm suburb in 1891). Sited in rolling countryside 4km west of town, beside Sztaravodai út, it can be reached by buses from stand 7 of the bus terminal near the HÉV station, though they're quite infrequent after noon.

It takes at least two hours to tour the *skanzen*'s naturalistic ensembles from five ethnographic regions of Hungary. Downhill to the right, a village from the backward **Upper Tisza** region reveals that the homes of the poorest squires were barely superior to those of their tenants, yet rural carpenters produced highly skilled work, such as the circular "dry mill", the wooden belltower from Nemesborzova, and the Greek Catholic church from Mándok (on a hilltop).

Beyond a stream, rambling stone dwellings, a watermill and a washhouse cluster round an austere Catholic church from the wine-growing **Bakony-Balaton** uplands. Their split levels and free use of stone and timber contrasts with the flat, rectangular adobe or brick buildings of the Protestant market towns on the **Great Plain**, laid out along a wide road with a dyer's workshop, a tannery and a bakery at the end (where you can buy bread and milk-loaves). The house from Süsköd has a visitors' room or "clean room" laid out for Christmas celebrations with a nativity crib and a church-shaped box.

SZENTENDRE

Nearby is a more regimented section representing the ethnic German communities of the **Little Plain**, whose houses are filled with knick-knacks and embroidered samplers bearing homilies like "When the Hausfrau is capable, the clocks keep good time". The final ensemble is from **Western Transdanubia**, where heavy rainfall and dense forests gave rise to clusters of buildings linked by covered walkways, called *szer*. A school, mayor's house and a household in mourning are among them; on a nearby hilltop you'll find a wine press, cellars, and a tavern where you can taste local wines.

Demonstrations of **crafts** such as weaving, pottery and basket-making usually take place on the first and third Sunday of each month as well as on public holidays; other **folklore events** may occur from May to November – ask the museum (☎26/502-500, ⓦwww.sznm.hu) or Tourinform for precise dates.

VISEGRÁD

Bus (30min) or ferry (1hr 40min) from Szentendre; bus from the Árpád híd terminal (1hr 15min) or hydrofoil (50min) or ferry (3hr) from the Vigadó tér pier in Budapest.

Approaching **Visegrád** from the south, the hillsides start to plunge and the river twists shortly before you first catch sight of the citadel and ramparts of the ancient fortified site whose Slavic name means "High Castle". The view hasn't changed much since 1488, when János Thuroczy described its "upper walls stretching to the clouds floating in the sky, and the lower bastions reaching down as far as the river". At that time, courtly life in Visegrád was nearing its apogee and the palace of King Mátyás and Queen Beatrice was famed throughout Europe as a "paradiso terrestri". Today, Visegrád is a mere village that manages to conceal the remains of the palace off its main street, Fő utca, until the last moment, though the ramparts snaking down the hillside from the citadel and Solomon's Tower near the riverside are plainly visible from a distance.

The ruins

The **layout** of the ruins dates back to the thirteenth century, when Béla IV began fortifying the north against a recurrence of the Mongol invasion, while the construction of a royal palace below the hilltop citadel was a sign of greater security during the reign of the Angevins. However, its magnificence was effaced by the Turkish conquest, and later mud washing down from the hillside gradually buried the palace entirely. Later generations doubted its existence until the archeologist János Schulek unearthed one of the vaults in 1934, at Fő utca 23.

Now largely excavated and tastefully reconstructed, the **Royal Palace** (Tues–Sun: April–Oct 9am–5pm; Nov–March 8am–4pm; 300Ft) spreads over four levels or terraces. Founded in 1323 by the Angevin king Charles Robert, it was the setting for the Visegrád Congress of 1335, attended by the monarchs of Central Europe and the Grandmaster of the Teutonic Knights. Although nothing remains of this palace, the **Court of Honour** constructed for his successor Louis, which provided the basis for additions by kings Sigismund and Mátyás, is still to be seen on the second terrace. A pillastered **Renaissance loggia** surrounds a replica of the famous **Hercules Fountain**, which cools the tiled, gilded upper storey, overlooking the court. Other, cross-vaulted chambers have been reconstructed, and on the third terrace, where Mátyás and Beatrice resided, stands a copy of the **Lion Fountain**, bearing his raven crest and surrounded by dozens of sleepy-looking lions. In July the ruins provide a stage for **pageants** and **films** intended to recreate the splendour of Visegrád's Renaissance heyday.

VISEGRÁD

By walking north along Fő utca and turning right onto Solamon torony utca, you'll reach **Solomon's Tower**, secluded behind high walls. Its **Mátyás Museum** (May–Sept Tues–Sun 9am–5pm; 300Ft) exhibits finds from the palace, including a copy of the white Anjou Fountain of the Angevins and the red marble *Visegrád Madonna* carved by Tomaso Fiamberti, and fragments of the original Lion and Hercules fountains, which he probably also created.

Exiting at the rear of the tower, it's thirty minutes' walk up a steep path through the woods to the hilltop **Citadel** (May–Sept daily 9.30am–6pm; Oct–April Sat & Sun 10am–4pm; 400Ft), which can also be reached by a path signposted *Fellegvár* starting on Kálvaria utca, or by a bus (June–Aug only) from the Mátyás statue, which follows the scenic Panorama autóút into the hills. Though only partly restored, the citadel is mightily impressive, commanding a superb view of Nagymaros and the Börzsöny Mountains on the east bank of the Danube. Besides two **museums** devoted to medieval hunting, fishing, punishment and torture, there are outdoor displays of **archery** and **falconry** in the summer.

The Visegrád Hills

Thickly wooded and criss-crossed with paths, the **Visegrád Hills** are a popular rambling spot. From the car park near the citadel, you can follow the autóút and then a signposted path to the **Nagy-Villám observation tower**, or *Kilátó* (March–Oct daily 9am–7pm; Nov–Feb Sat & Sun 9am–6pm unless there's snow; 100Ft). Sited at the highest point on the Danube Bend, it offers a view that stretches as far as Slovakia. Nearby is a **summer bobsleigh course** (*Nyári Bobpálya*; April–Oct daily 9am–7pm, Nov–March Sat & Sun 9am–7pm; 280Ft, child 220Ft), where you can race down a one-kilometre metalled run (except on rainy days when the brakes are rendered ineffective).

One kilometre north of the tower lies Mogyoró-hegy (Hazelnut Hill) and a collection of wooden **buildings by Imre Makovecz**. As a promising architect in the Kádár years, Makovecz was branded a troublemaker for his out-spoken nationalism, banned from teaching and "exiled" to Visegrád's forestry department in 1977. Here he refined his ideas over the next decade, acquiring a following of stu-dents for whom he held summer schools. Employing cheap, low-technology methods, he taught them how to construct temporary buildings using raw materials such as branches and twigs. The Cultural House near *Jurta Camping* is an excellent example, with a turfed roof and a light, homely interior, while the oesophagus-like crypt of the Wolf's Meadow Cemetery in Budapest represents his apotheosis (see p.136).

ESZTERGOM

Map 9. By bus from the Árpád híd terminal (1hr 30min), train from Nyugati Station (1hr 30min), or hydrofoil (1hr 10min) from the Vigadó tér pier in Budapest.

Beautifully situated in a crook of the Danube facing Slovakia, **Esztergom** is dominated by its basilica, whose dome is visible for miles around – a richly symbolic sight, as it was here that Prince Géza and his son Vajk (the future king and saint Stephen) brought Hungary into the fold of Roman Catholic (not Orthodox) Christendom. Even after the court moved to Buda following the Mongol invasion, Esztergom remained the centre of Catholicism until the Turkish conquest, and resumed this role in the 1820s. Though the Church was persecuted during the Rákosi era, from the 1960s onwards the Communists settled for a modus vivendi; during the 1990s it regained much of its former influence. Esztergom itself makes an ideal day trip,

ESZTERGOM

147

combining historic monuments and small-town charm in just the right doses.

Orientation

If you arrive by bus from Visegrád, get off near the Basilica Hill rather than travelling on to the bus station where services from Budapest (via the inland route 10) terminate. Arriving at the train station, 1km further south, buses #1 and #5 run into the centre, while hydrofoils from Budapest tie up on the Danube embankment of Prímás-Sziget, fifteen minutes' walk away. For **information**, visit Gran Tours at Széchenyi tér 25, in the lower town between Prímás-Sziget and Bazilika-hegy (Oct–April Mon–Fri 8am–6pm; May–Sept Mon–Fri 8am–6pm, Sat 9am–noon; ☎33/313-756).

As in Szentendre, **restaurants** near the tourist sites are geared to coach parties and a fast turnover, but none is so bad or expensive that you feel compelled to look elsewhere. Indeed, it's hard to resist a meal in the cavernous cellars of the *Prímás Pince* (daily 10am–9.30pm), beneath Bazilika-hegy. On Prímás-Sziget, the *Hotel Esztergom*'s restaurant is excellent, or there's the rustic-style *Szálma Csárda* near the Budapest ferry-dock, serving fish and poultry; and should you stick around, the *Sörkert* has wild "tequila evenings".

The Basilica

Built upon the site of the first cathedral in Hungary, where Vajk was crowned as King Stephen by a papal envoy on Christmas Day 1000 AD, Esztergom's **Basilica** is the largest in the country, measuring 118m in length and 40m in width, capped by a dome 100m high. Liszt's *Gran Mass* (*Gran* being the German name for Esztergom) was composed for its completion in 1869. Admission (March–Sept

CARDINAL MINDSZENTY

When the much-travelled body of Cardinal József Mindszenty was finally laid to rest with state honours in May 1991, it was a vindication of his uncompromising heroism – and the Vatican realpolitik that Mindszenty despised.

As a conservative and monarchist, he had stubbornly opposed the postwar Communist takeover, warning that "cruel hands are reaching out to seize hold of our children, claws belonging to people who have nothing but evil to teach them". Arrested in 1948, tortured for 39 days and nights, and sentenced to life imprisonment for treason, Mindszenty was freed during the Uprising and took refuge in the US Embassy, where he remained for the next fifteen years – an exile in the heart of Budapest.

When the Vatican struck a deal with the Kádár regime in 1971, Mindszenty had to be pushed into resigning his position and going to Austria, where he died in 1975. Although his will stated that his body should not return home until "the red star of Moscow had fallen from Hungarian skies", his reburial occurred some weeks before the last Soviet soldier left, in preparation for the pope's visit in August of that year. Nowadays the Vatican proclaims his greatness, without any hint of apology for its past actions.

daily 7am–6pm; Oct–Feb Tues–Sun 7am–5pm) is free, but tickets are required for the spooky **crypt** (9am–4.45pm; 50Ft) where Cardinal Mindszenty (see box above) is buried; the **cupola** (May–Oct 9am–5pm; 100Ft), reached by three hundred steps and offering a superb view of Esztergom; and the collection of bejewelled croziers and kitsch papal souvenirs in the **treasury** (daily: May–Oct 9am–4.30pm; Feb–April, Nov & Dec 10am–4pm; 250Ft). The last is at the back of the nave, whose main altarpiece was painted by

ESZTERGOM

the Venetian Michelangelo Grigoletti, based on Titian's *Assumption* in the Frari Church in Venice. Don't miss the red and white marble **Bakócz Chapel** (below the relief of Christ on a donkey), whose Florentine altar was salvaged from the original basilica that was destroyed by the Mongols.

The Castle Museum

Near the basilica are the reconstructed remains of the palace founded by Prince Géza, now presented as the **Castle Museum** (Tues–Sun 10am–6pm; 400Ft). A royal seat for almost three hundred years, it was here that Béla III entertained Philip of France and Frederick Barbarossa on their way to the Third Crusade. The Renaissance prelate János Vitéz made it a centre of humanist culture, where Queen Beatrice spent her widowhood. Although it was sacked by the Turks and twice besieged before they were evicted in 1683, enough survived to be excavated in the 1930s. Traces of the frescoes that once covered every wall can be seen in the vaulted living hall from Béla III's reign, from which stairs ascend to the study of Archbishop Vitéz – known as the **Hall of Virtues** after its allegorical murals. Beyond lies the **royal chapel**, whose Gothic rose window and Romanesque arches were executed by craftsmen brought over by Béla's French wives, while the rooftop offers a panoramic view of Esztergom and the river.

During June and July, **plays** and **dances** are staged in the **Rondella** bastion on the hillside. Descending the hillside after your visit, notice the monumental **Dark Gate** – a tunnel built in the 1820s as a short cut between church buildings on either side of the hill – and the former primate's wine cellars, now the *Prímás Pince* restaurant.

The Víziváros and Prímás-Sziget

Below the castle ramparts lies the **Víziváros** district of Baroque churches and seminaries, where choirs can often be heard practising. Beyond the Italianate Baroque **Víziváros Parish Church**, the old Primate's Palace at Berényi utca 2 houses the **Christian Museum** (Tues–Sun 10am–6pm; 250Ft, audioguide 2500Ft), Hungary's richest hoard of religious art, featuring the largest collection of Italian prints outside Italy; Renaissance paintings and wood carvings by German, Austrian and Hungarian masters; a wheeled, gilded catafalque once used in Easter Week processions; and a tapestry entitled *St Stephen and his work*, woven by 34 artists for the millennium. In late July and early August, the international Monteverdi **choir festival** is held in the Parish Church and castle grounds (tickets from Cathedral Tours, Bajcsy-Zsilinszky út 26 ⊤33/515-620; Mon–Fri 9am–5pm, Sat 9am–noon).

From the church you can cross a bridge onto **Prímás-Sziget** (Primate's Island), a popular recreation spot whose banks are lined with weeping willows. On its far side, the new **Mária Valeria bridge** links Esztergom to the Slovak Štúrovo, across the Danube; only recently rebuilt for $17 million, it replaces the one blown up by the Germans on Christmas Day, 1944.

GÖDÖLLŐ

Map 2, N2. By HÉV from Örs vezér tere (M2) in Budapest to the Szabadság tér stop in Gödöllő (45min).

The small town of **Gödöllő** boasts a former Habsburg summer palace and a famous artists' colony, but being 30km northeast of Budapest rather than on the Danube Bend, it gets far fewer tourists than Szentendre, despite a reliable train service that enables visitors to enjoy an evening concert and return to the capital afterwards. Conveniently, the palace is just across the road from the HÉV stop, and the town museum two blocks away, near the market.

Gödöllő Palace

Gödöllő Palace (Tues–Sun: April–Oct 10am–6pm, Nov–March 10am–5pm, last tickets an hour before closing; 600Ft) was commissioned by a confidante of Empress Maria Theresa's, Count Antal Grassalkovich, and designed by András Mayerhoffer, who introduced the Baroque style of mansion to Hungary in the 1740s. In its heyday it rivalled the "Hungarian Versailles" at Esterháza for splendour; Emperor Franz Josef's wife Sissi stayed two thousand nights here, preferring it to Vienna. The palace suffered as a result of both world wars, being commandeered as a GHQ first by the Reds and then by the Whites in 1919–20, and pillaged by both the Nazis and the Red Army in 1944. One wing was later turned into an old people's home, while the rest was left to rot until the 1990s. Only the central block has been restored so far.

Reached by a grand staircase, the formal staterooms precede the apartments used by Franz Josef and Sissi – his decorated in grey and gold, hers draped in her favourite colour, violet. While Sissi's possessions are reverentially displayed right down to a nail from her horse's shoe, there's no sign to identify the secret staircase that she had installed for some privacy in a relentlessly public life.

Though it's possible to visit the unrestored bathhouse, riding hall and stables on a special tour (4000Ft; minimum 25 people) and there are **concerts** in the courtyard during August (details from ☎28/410-124), most visitors are content to stroll around the 28-hectare **park**, whose Palm House is now a garden centre.

Town Museum

While the **Gödöllő Town Museum** (Tues–Sun 10am–6pm; 300Ft) also has some of Sissi's stuff, it devotes more space to a prewar pharmacy, a 1950s' barber shop and other period interiors that speak volumes about social history, and a superb exhibition about the **Gödöllő Artists' Colony** that existed from 1901 to 1920. Inspired by the English Pre-Raphaelites and the Arts and Crafts movement of William Morris and John Ruskin, it took their communal, rural ethos even further, seeking pure wellsprings of Magyar culture in remote Transylvanian villages and ancient Hungarian myths. Their tapestries, paintings and prints are exquisite, but their romanticism was tinged with the hatred of modernity that characterized Hungarian Fascism. A vitriolic etching entitled *Feminism* shows a father having his brain sucked out by a bawling infant while its mother lounges in the background, smoking. If you'd like to know more about the artists, the museum's curator runs occasional **walking tours** of their former haunts (ⓔgodolloimuzeum@mail.digitel2002.hu).

LISTINGS

Accommodation

The availability of accommodation in Budapest has improved markedly in recent years, although many of the new hotels are at the luxury end of the market. Predictably, demand is heaviest and prices highest in the summer, when the city feels like it's bursting at the seams. Christmas, New Year, the Spring Festival in March/April and the Grand Prix in August are also busy periods, with most hotels charging higher rates. Even so, it should always be possible to find somewhere that's reasonably priced, if not well sited.

Slightly cheaper than hotels are **pensions**, often offering the same facilities as small hotels, with en-suite bathrooms

ACCOMMODATION PRICE CODES

All accommodation in this guide is graded according to the price bands given below. Note that prices refer to the cheapest available double room in high season or, in the case of campsites, the price of two people sharing a tent. 100Ft is roughly equivalent to $0.45 or DM1.

❶ Under 2000Ft	❹ 6000–8500Ft	❼ 20,000–27,000Ft
❷ 2000–4000Ft	❺ 8500–13,000Ft	❽ 27,000–40,000Ft
❸ 4000–6000Ft	❻ 13,000–20,000Ft	❾ Over 40,000Ft

ACCOMMODATION BOOKING AGENCIES

American Express V, Deák Ferenc utca 10 (Mon–Fri 9am–5.30pm, Sat 9am–2pm; ☎235-4330). Note that there is a $20 service fee for non-cardholders.

Budapest Tourist ⓦwww.budapesttourist.hu. Nyugati Station, downstairs in the underpass in front of the station (Mon–Fri 9am–5pm, Sat 9am–noon; ☎332-6565). XII, Déli Station, in the mall by the metro entrance (Mon–Thurs 9am–5pm, Fri 9am–4pm; ☎225-7489). VII, Erzsébet körút 41 (Mon–Thurs 10am–6pm, Fri 10am–5pm, Sat 9am–1pm; ☎342-6521).

Cooptourist ⓦwww.cooptourist.hu. Skála Métro department store, opposite Nyugati Station (Mon–Fri 9am–4.30pm; ☎312-4867). V, Bajcsy-Zsilinszky út 17 (Mon–Fri 9am–5pm; ☎311-7034). V, Kossuth tér 13 (Mon, Tues, Thurs & Fri 8am–4pm, Wed 8am–5pm; ☎332-6387).

Express ⓦwww.express-travel.hu. V, Semmelweis utca 4 (Mon–Thurs 8.30am–4.30pm, Fri 8.30am–3pm; ☎317-8045).

HungarHotels ⓦwww.danubiusgroup.com. V, Petőfi Sándor utca 16 (Mon–Fri 9am–5pm; July & Aug also Sat 9am–noon; ☎318-3393, ☞318-0894).

Ibusz ⓦwww.ibusz.hu. V, Ferenciek tere 10, on the corner of Petőfi Sándor utca (Mon–Fri 8.15am–5pm; ☎485-2716). V, Vörösmarty tér 6, facing the British Embassy (Mon–Fri 8.15am–5pm; ☎317-0532). VII, Dob utca 1 (Mon–Fri 8am–4pm; ☎322-7214).

Tribus V, Apáczai Csere János utca 1 (open 24hr; ☎1/266-8042).

Vista Visitor Center ⓦwww.vista.hu. VI, Paulay Ede utca 7 (Mon–Fri 9am–8pm, Sat 9am–6pm; ☎267-8603).

and other mod cons. For both hotels and pensions, it's essential to phone ahead and book.

If you're on a tight budget, your best bet is a hostel or a

room or apartment in a private house. As well as the usual dormitory accommodation, most **hostels** can also offer double rooms. **Private rooms** and apartments can be arranged through a tourist agency, and while the location might not be perfect, you should have no problem finding one at any time of year. Budapest also has several **campsites**, where tent space can usually be found, even if all the **bungalows** are taken.

The following recommendations are divided according to type of accommodation, and subdivided by area. Of the **booking agencies** listed in the box opposite, only American Express and HungarHotels deal exclusively with hotel accommodation. The rest can make reservations in hotels and book private rooms and hostel and student-type accommodation – Tribus and the less helpful Cooptourist are the most expensive.

HOTELS AND PENSIONS

Both hotels and pensions are in high demand, so it's sensible to **book** before leaving home or, failing that, through an agency (see opposite) or any airport tourist office on arrival. Star ratings give you a fair idea of standards, though facilities at some of the older three-star places don't compare with their Western equivalents, even if room prices are similar. Almost all hotels reduce their rates out of season.

The greatest choice of hotels can be found in **Pest**, where there's more in the way of restaurants and nightlife – and more traffic noise, too. The prime spots are along the river bank, with views across to Várhegy; having said that, all the really grand hotels were destroyed during the war, and their replacements don't have quite the same elegance. Staying out of the centre is a viable option, since most places are within reach of a metro station.

VÁRHEGY, VÍZIVÁROS, TABÁN AND GELLÉRT-HEGY

Ábel Panzió

Map 2, D6. XI, Ábel Jenő utca 9 ⊤381-0553, ⨍372-0299, Ⰵwww.hotels.hu/abelpanzio. Tram 61 from Móricz Zsigmond körtér.

The most appealing pension in Budapest, a 1913 villa with beautiful Art Nouveau fittings in a quiet street twenty minutes from the *Belváros*. Just ten rooms, so essential to book in advance. ❻

Art'otel

Map 5, G4. I, Bem rakpart 16–19 ⊤487-9487, Ⰵwww.parkplazaww.com. Batthyány tér (M2).

The first boutique hotel in the city is an award-winning venture (part of a chain) that combines eighteenth-century buildings – comprising beautiful large rooms with original doors and high ceilings – with a modern wing affording marvellous views over the river. Well-equipped rooms come with all mod cons and bright-red dressing gowns. The furnishings, wall decorations and crockery were all designed by one American artist – they couldn't find a Hungarian artist who could mass-produce their art quickly enough. ❽

Astra Hotel

Map 5, F3. I, Vám utca 6 ⊤214-1906. ⰅWww.virtualhungary .com/astra. Batthyány tér (M2).

Small hotel in a converted 300-year-old building at the foot of the castle near Batthyány tér. Nine well-furnished a/c rooms with minibar. ❼

Budapest Hilton

Map 5, D3. I, Hess András tér 1–3 ⊤488-6600 ⰅWww.danubiusgroup.com/ hilton. Várbusz from Moszkva tér (M2).

By the Mátyás Church on Castle Hill, with superb views across the river, this five-star hotel incorporates the remains of a medieval monastery and hosts summertime concerts in the former church. Luxurious to a fault. There is a new *Hilton* attached to the WestEnd City Center mall by Nyugati Station in Pest, well-positioned for the business market. ❾

Burg

Map 5, D3. I, Szentháromság tér 7 ☏212-0269, ✉hotel.burg@mail.datanet.hu. Várbusz from Moszkva tér (M2). Small hotel right opposite the Mátyás Church. All rooms have en-suite bathrooms, minibar and TV. ❼

Carlton Hotel

Map 5, E6. I, Apor Péter utca 3 ☏224-0999, ⓦwww.hotels.hu/carlton. Bus #86 from Batthyány tér (M2). Four-star hotel well situated by the Lánchíd, below Castle Hill. Modern, comfy interior, but slightly lacking in atmosphere. Rooms have minibar and TV and there's also parking space. The Habsburg family stayed here for a wedding in the city in 1998. ❽

Charles Apartments

Map 3, D12. XI, Hegyalja út 23 ☏212-9169, ⒻFax202-2984, ⓦwww.charleshotel.hu. Bus #8 from Március 15. tér, near Ferenciek tere (M3).
Friendly place situated on the hill up from the Erzsébet bridge on the main road to Vienna, a short bus ride from the centre of Pest. Rooms facing the inner yard are quieter; all come with cooking facilities, minibar and TV, and there's also a business room with Internet access, plus bikes for rent. Parking costs 1300Ft extra. ❺

Gellért Hotel

Map 3, H14. XI, Szent Gellért tér 1 ☏385-2200, ⓦwww.danubiusgroup.com/gellert. Tram #47 or #49 from Deák tér.
One of Budapest's most famous old hotels, whose character will hopefully survive its gradual refurbishment. The facade, floodlit at night, is magnificent, as is the thermal pool (free for guests). The hotel has an excellent café. ❾

HOTELS AND PENSIONS

Kulturinnov Hotel

Map 5, D3. I, Szentháromság tér 6 ☎355-0122, ℻375-1886, ⓔmka3@matavnet.hu. Várbusz from Moszkva tér (M2).
Well positioned for sightseeing, in a large neo-Gothic building right by Mátyás Church. The hotel is badly signed in the main entrance on the first floor. Spacious, quiet rooms with minibar, but no TV; breakfast included. The hotel also hosts Hungarian cultural events, concerts and exhibitions. ❼

Orion

Map 3, G10. I, Döbrentei utca 13 ☎356-8583, ⓦwww.hotels.hu/orion.
Small, modern place in the Tabán district, just south of Várhegy. Rooms have TV and minibar – those at the front can be noisy – and there's a sauna available for guests. ❼

Victoria Hotel

Map 5, F5. I, Bem rakpart 11 ☎457-8080, ⓦwww.victoria.hu. Bus #86 from Batthyány tér (M2).

Located on the embankment directly below the Mátyás Church, with excellent views of the Lánchíd and the river, this very friendly, small hotel is run by helpful staff and has a/c rooms with minibar and TV. There's also a sauna and parking facilities. ❼

ÓBUDA, BUDA HILLS AND BEYOND

Beatrix Panzió

Map 2, B4. II, Szehér út 3 ☎275-0550, ℻394-3730, ⓦwww.beatrixhotel.hu. Bus #56 from Moszkva tér (M2).
Friendly eighteen-room pension in the villa district northwest of Moszkva tér. There's a bar on the ground floor, plus a sauna. ❻

Budapest Hotel

Map 2, B5. II, Szilágyi Erzsébet fasor 47 ☎488-9800, ⓦwww.danubiusgroup.com/hungarhotels/budapest.html. Bus #56 or tram #56 from Moszkva tér (M2).
Cylindrical tower facing the Buda Hills, opposite the

lower terminal of the Cogwheel Railway, 500m from Moszkva tér. 1970s decor in the lobby but good views over the city from the upper floors. Air-conditioned rooms come with TV and minibar, and there's a sauna, fitness room and business centre, too. ❽

Buda Villa Panzió
Map 2, C5. XII, Kiss Áron utca 6 ☎275-0091, ☏275-1687, ⓦwww.budapansio.hu. Bus #156 from Moszkva tér (M2). Comfortable small pension in the hills just above Moszkva tér. There's a bar in the lounge on the first floor, and the small garden is perfect for relaxing in after a day's sightseeing. Breakfast is included. ❺

Csillaghegy Strand Hotel
Map 2, C5. III, Pusztakúti utca 3 ☎368-4012. HÉV train to Csillaghegy from Batthyány tér (M2).
Situated in the northern suburbs, but only ten minutes by HÉV from Batthyány tér. Free entry to the hotel's

outdoor thermal pool; breakfast included. ❸

Jäger–Trió Panzió
Map 2, B7. XI, Ördögorom út 20D ☎246-4558, ⓔjagertrio@ax.hu. Bus #8 from Március 15 tér to the end of the line, then it's a ten-minute walk. Friendly, family-run place in the Sasad district in the hills. Open March 15–Nov 15. ❺

Pál Panzió
Map 7, A4. III, Pálvölgyi köz 15 ☎388-7099. Bus #65 from Kolosy tér.
Small, welcoming pension with eight double rooms, situated in the hills near the Pálvölgy Stalactite Cave. ❺

Panda Hotel
Map 2, C4. II, Pasaréti út 133 ☎394-1932, ☏394-1002, ⓦwww.budapesthotels.com/ hotels/Panda.asp. Bus #5 from Moszkva tér (M2).
Pleasant, modern hotel only a ten-minute bus ride from Moszkva tér. All rooms have TV and minibar, most have showers, and three have baths. Sauna available. ❻

HOTELS AND PENSIONS

San Marcó Panzió

Map 7, E4. III, San Marcó utca 6 ⊤388-9997. Bus #60 from Batthyány tér (M2). Friendly Óbuda pension with shared bathrooms. **⑤**

Touring Hotel

Map 2, E1. III, Pünkösdfürdő utca 38 ⊤250-3184. HÉV train to Békásmegyer from Batthyány tér (M2).

On the northern edge of the city, about 11km from the centre, but only 15min by HÉV. Basic one-star hotel with tennis court, pool tables and restaurant. All rooms have TV and minibar and there's a swimming pool at the *strand* down the road. **④**

Tusculanum Hotel

Map 2, E3. III, Záhony utca 10 ⊤387-1440, ⓦwww.tusculanum.hu. HÉV train to Aquincum from Batthyány tér (M2). Comfortable, if characterless, new establishment, near the ruins of Aquincum. All rooms come with bathroom and TV. Breakfast is included, and guests can use the tennis court next door. **⑤**

MARGIT SZIGET

Danubius Grand Hotel

Map 2, E4. XIII, Margit sziget ⊤452-6200, ⓦwww.danubiusgroup.com. Bus #26 from Nyugati pu (M3). The island's original *fin-de-siècle* hotel, totally refurbished for wealthy tourists, here to enjoy the island's seclusion and fresh air. Its uglier modern sister hotel (with the same telephone number) next door, the *Thermal*, is now home to the sauna, gym and the thermal springs that made this a fashionable spa resort around the turn of the last century. **⑨**

BELVÁROS

Hotel Anna

Map 4, F10. VIII, Gyulai Pál utca 14 ⊤338-4644, ⓔannahotel@matavnet.hu. Located in a quiet street in central Pest, this hotel offers small, basic rooms – twin beds only – with TV and showers. Off-street parking. **⑦**

HOTELS AND PENSIONS

Hotel Art (Best Western)

Map 6, D8. V, Királyi Pál utca 12 ☎266-2166, ℻266-2170, ⓦwww.bestwestern.com. Kálvin tér (M3).

Not to be confused with the newer *Art'otel* in Buda, this small hotel is situated in a quiet backstreet of Pest. Rooms are quite cramped, but have air conditioning, minibar, phone and TV, though only Hungarian and German channels. Sauna, fitness room and laundry service. ❼

Astoria Hotel

Map 6, F6. V, Kossuth utca 19 ☎484-3200, ⓦwww.danubiusgroup.com/ hungarhotels/astoria.html. Astoria (M2).

A refurbished, vintage hotel on the major junction in central Pest to which it gave its name. Good-sized rooms have a sofa, safe, minibar, phone and TV. As well as the wonderful coffee house, there's a restaurant complete with Hungarian gypsy band. ❼

Carmen Mini Hotel

Map 6, F5. V, Károly körút 5/b ☎352-0798, ℻318-3865, ⓔcarmen8@matavnet.hu. Deák tér (M1/2/3) or Astoria (M2).

Small hotel in a couple of converted flats in the centre of town, a minute's walk from the main synagogue. Rooms have TV, bath and shower. Breakfast included. ❻

City Panzió Mátyás

Map 6, B6. V, Március 15 tér 8 ☎338-4711, ℻317-9086, ⓦwww.taverna.hu. Ferenciek tere (M3).

Centrally located place offering simple rooms with TV and minibar. A buffet breakfast is served downstairs in the *Mátyás Pince* restaurant, painted inside like the Mátyás Church. The hotel overlooks the main road leading onto the Erzsébet híd, so it's best to ask for a courtyard room if you want some quiet, though corner rooms compensate with a great view of the river. Secure parking. ❼

ELTE Peregrinus Vendégház

Map 6, C8. V, Szerb utca 3 ☎266-4911, ℻266-4913. Kálvin tér (M3).

HOTELS AND PENSIONS

165

Elegant but friendly place in a quiet street in central Pest. Double rooms are spacious with high ceilings, but cramped bathrooms. It belongs to the university, so all rooms have writing tables to meet the needs of academic visitors. Buffet breakfast included. ❼

Kempinski Corvinus
Map 6, D3. V, Erzsébet tér 7–8 ⓣ 429-3777, ⓕ 429-4777, ⓦ www.kempinski-budapest.com. Deák tér (M1/2/3).
A flashy, smug five-star establishment on the edge of the Belváros, which counts Madonna and Michael Jackson amongst past guests. Tastefully furnished rooms offer every luxury, right down to a phone extension in the bathroom. Swimming pool, sauna, solarium, fitness room and underground garage. ❾

K&K Opera
Map 4, C7. VI, Révay utca 24 ⓣ 269-0222, ⓕ 269-0230, ⓦ www.kkhotels.com. Opera (M1).

Bright, modern and fully a/c four-star hotel right by the Opera House, with underground parking. Rooms – all with minibar, TV, safe and phone – are pleasantly furnished. Buffet breakfast included. ❽

Le Meridien
Map 6, D3. V, Erzsébet tér 9–10 ⓣ 429-5500, ⓕ 429-5555, ⓦ www.lemeridien-budapest.com. Deák tér (M1/2/3).
Originally built for the Adria insurance company at the turn of the twentieth century, this building housed the police headquarters in the Communist years until it was totally gutted and reopened as a luxury hotel in 2000 – a welcome rival for the *Kempinski* next door. The hotel is magnificently furnished throughout, and its well-equipped rooms are perhaps the most tasteful in the city. Parking and swimming pool. ❾

Marriott Budapest
Map 6, B3. V, Apáczai Csere János utca 4 ⓣ 266-7000,

HOTELS AND PENSIONS

Ⓟ 266-5000,
Ⓦ www.marriott.com.
Vörösmarty tér (M1) or
Ferenciek tere (M3).
There's a view of the Danube
from every room in this
older, five-star hotel.
Excellent buffet grill and
afternoon chamber music in
the lounge area. Facilities
include a sauna, squash court,
parking and babysitting
service. ❾

Medosz Hotel
Map 4, D5. VI, Jókai tér 9
Ⓟ 374-3000. Oktogon (M1).
Ugly but comfortable hotel
in a former trade union
hostel overlooking a square
near Oktogon. Small, bright
rooms with bath and TV
make this good value for the
location. ❺

Mercure Museum
Map 6, G7. VIII, Trefort utca 2
Ⓟ 485-1080,
Ⓦ www.pannoniahotels.hu/
muzeum. Astoria (M2).
In a quiet street close to
Astoria, this new hotel is
housed in an imaginatively
transformed Pest apartment
block, with the restaurant in

the glass-roofed courtyard.
Small but well-equipped air-
conditioned rooms come
with en-suite bathrooms,
hairdryers, satellite TV and
minibar. Breakfast not
included. Off-street parking
available. ❼

Nemzeti Hotel
Map 4, G9. VIII, József körút 4
Ⓟ 269-9310, Ⓟ 314-0019,
Ⓦ www.mercure-nemzeti.hu.
Blaha Lujza tér (M2).
Small but elegant rooms in an
Art Nouveau-style building
overlooking Blaha Lujza tér.
Rooms facing on to the
square have double glazing
but the courtyard ones are
quieter. The glass-roofed
restaurant and the staircase are
both magnificent. Breakfast
included. ❼

BEYOND THE
NAGYKÖRÚT

Benczúr Hotel
Map 4, H3. VI, Benczúr utca
35 Ⓟ 479-5650, Ⓟ 342-1558,
Ⓦ www.hotelbanczur.hu. Hősök
tere (M1).
Modern, functional hotel on a

leafy street off Andrássy út, with a nice garden at the back and parking in the yard (850Ft extra). Pleasant rooms all have bath, TV and phone. In the other wing of the building is the *Hotel Pedagógus*, a sister establishment offering fewer frills and a slightly cheaper rate. **❼**

Radio Inn
Map 4, H3. VI, Benczúr utca 19 ⓣ342-8347, ⓕ322-8284. Bajza utca (M1).
Spacious, if slightly gloomy rooms, complete with kitchen, extra living room and TV. Situated in a leafy street, by the Chinese and Vietnamese embassies. Pleasant garden. **❻**

Thermal Hotel Helia
Map 2, E4. XIII, Kárpát utca 62–64 ⓣ270-3277. Trolley bus #79 from Margit híd or Dózsa György út (M3).
Finnish-owned modern four-star hotel with thermal baths, well situated near the river in northern Pest. **❾**

HOSTELS

Budapest has a good choice of **hostels**. As well as the usual dormitory accommodation, many hostels also have double rooms. A double costs around 5000Ft or more – much the same as a room in a private house. This does include 24-hour information from the English-speaking staff at the reception desk, but the rooms often have very basic student furniture. Unless stated otherwise, the hostels listed below are open year round – student dormitories are open during July and August only, many of them located in the university area south of Gellért-hegy.

You should have no trouble finding a bed at any time of year, though in summer it's best to **book** ahead (see box on p.158 for details) if you want to be sure of getting the hostel of your choice. Many hostels tout for business on incoming international trains and some of the larger ones offer transport to the hostel, which can make arrival less daunting.

The Tourist Information Centre office in Keleti Station (in the big side hall down by platform 6, on the left of the station as you face the trains) can give you information about more of the summer-only hostels and make bookings (daily: June–Aug 7am–11pm; Sept–May 7am–9pm; ℗ 343-0748). The main office of the Hungarian Youth Hostel Association is at Baross tér 15/III/6 across the road from Keleti station (Mon–Fri 8am–4pm, ℗ 413-2065, ⓦ www.backpackers.hu).

Back Pack

Map 2, D7. XI, Takács Menyhért utca 33 ℗ 385-8946, ⓔ backpackguest@hotmail.com. Tram #49 or bus #7 from Astoria (M2) to Tétényi út stop in Buda. Charming, clean, fifty-bed hostel with a shaded garden, just twenty minutes from the centre. Lots of information on the city, sport and fitness, and they also organize cave trips. Dorm bed 1800Ft, doubles ❸

Best Hostel

Map 4, D4. VI, Podmaniczky utca 27, 1st floor ℗ 332-4934, ⓦ www.besthostel.hu. Rambling friendly hotel in a typical tall Pest apartment, close to Nyugati train station. Cooking facilities. Dorm bed 2500Ft, doubles ❷

Caterina Youth Hostel

Map 4, E6. V, Andrássy út 47 ℗ 291-9538 or 342-0804, ⓦ www.extra.hu/caterin. Oktogon (M1). Thirty-two beds crammed into every corner of this flat on the third floor of a grand Pest apartment block near Oktogon (note the fantastic entrance way). Laundry facilities. Dorm bed 2500Ft.

Citadella

Map 3, G13. I, Citadella sétány ℗ 466-5794, ⓦ www.hotels.hu/hotelcitadella. Bus #27 from Móricz Zsigmond körtér, then a ten-minute walk to the top of the hill. Breathtaking views of the city in this well-sited hostel, but note that the weekend disco in the neighbouring nightclub sets the whole place shaking. Arrive early to get a bunk. Ten- and fourteen-bed dorms 1850Ft, doubles ❺

HOSTELS

Diáksport Hotel

Map 2, F5. XIII, Dózsa György
út 152 ⊤340-8585,
Ⓦwww.travellers-hostels.com.
Dózsa György út (M3).
Clean, lively but run-down
hostel near the centre, with
internet access – but at 550Ft
for 30min you're better off
going to an internet café.
Entrance is at the side in
Angyalföldi út. Cave trips
organized. Dorm bed 3000Ft,
doubles ❸

Landler

Map 2, E6. XI, Bartók Béla út
17 ⊤463-3621. Tram #47 or
#49 from Deák tér (M1/2/3).
Open July & Aug only.
One of the older hostels,
housed in the Baross Gábor
Kollégium, near the Gellért
Baths. Two- and three-bed
rooms, with high ceilings.
Dorm bed 3700Ft.

Museum Guest House

Map 4, F12. VIII, Mikszáth
Kálmán tér 4, 1st floor ⊤318-
9508, ⒺIotus@freemail.c3.hu.
In the streets behind the
National Museum, handy for
the bars and cafés in the
centre. Three clean, spacious
dorms, each sleeping seven or
eight on mattresses on the
floor. Cave trips organized.
Free internet access in the
evening. Dorm bed 2200Ft.

Ráday Youth Hostel

Map 4, E14. IX, Ráday utca
43–45 ⊤218-4766. Kálvin tér
(M3). Open July & Aug only.
Near Kálvin tér, with basic
student hostel furniture, tall
rooms of two to six beds or
dormitories. Dorm bed
2000Ft.

Yellow Submarine

Map 4, D4. VI, Teréz körút 56,
⊤ & Ⓕ331-9896,
Ⓔyellowsubmarine@mail.interw
are.hu. Nyugati Station (M3).
Pleasant hostel in a typical old
Pest apartment on the
Nagykörút, with 65 bunk
beds in large rooms with high
ceilings. It's on the third floor
(no lift). Also organizes
canoeing, cycling and cave
tours. Dorm bed 2500Ft,
doubles ❹

HOSTELS

PRIVATE ROOMS AND APARTMENTS

There are **private rooms** throughout the city, many in locations where a hotel would be unaffordable. Depending on district and amenities, **prices** for a double room range from 2500 to 6000Ft a night. Note, however, that rates are thirty percent higher if you stay for fewer than four nights, making pensions or hostels more economical for short-staying visitors. Single rooms are virtually non-existent, so solo travellers will almost certainly have to pay for a double. **Apartments**, from 8000Ft a night, are not as common as rooms, but you should be able to find an agency with one on its books.

It's easy enough to get a room from one of the **touts** at the train stations, but it's safer to go through a tourist agency, where you book and pay at the counter signposted *fizetővendég*. The three main **agencies** – Budapest Tourist, Cooptourist and Ibusz (see box on p.158) – all handle private rooms, as does the To-Ma Travel Agency at V, Október 6 utca 22 (☏ 353-0819, ⓦ www.tomatour.tsx.org).

Since rooms are rented unseen, it pays to take some trouble over your choice. Your host and the premises should give no cause for complaint (both are checked out), but the **location** or ambience might. For atmosphere and comfort you can't beat the nineteenth-century blocks where spacious, high-ceilinged apartments surround a courtyard with wrought-iron balconies – most common in Pest's V, VI and VII districts, and the parts of Buda nearest the Vár. It's best to avoid the rundown VIII and IX districts unless you can get a place inside the *körút* (boulevard). Elsewhere – particularly in Újpest (IV district), Csepel (XXI) or Óbuda (III) – you're likely to end up in a box on the twelfth floor of a *lakótelep* (housing estate). The *Budapest Atlasz* (see p.9) is invaluable for checking the location of sites and access by public transport.

Because many proprietors go out to work, you might not be able to take possession of the room until 5pm. Some knowledge of Hungarian facilitates **settling in**; guests normally receive an explanation of the boiler system and multiple door keys (*kulcs*), and may have use of the washing machine (*mosógép*).

CAMPING

Budapest's **campsites** are generally well equipped and pleasant, with trees, grass and sometimes even a pool. They can get crowded between June and September, when smaller places might run out of space. It is, however, illegal to camp anywhere else, and the parks are patrolled to enforce this. The campsites listed here are all in Buda, since the Pest ones are far out and not very inviting. Tourinform (see p.8) can point you in their direction if you need them.

Csillebérci Camping
Map 2, B6. XII, Konkoly Thege M. út 21 ☎395-6537, ⓦwww.datanet.hu/csill. Bus #21 from Moszkva tér (M2), then a short walk. Open all year.
Large, well-equipped site with space for 1000 campers. A range of bungalows is also available.

Római Camping
Map 2, E2. III, Szentendrei út 189 ☎368-6260. ⓔromai@matavnet.hu. HÉV from Batthyány tér (M2). Open all year.
Huge site with space for 2500 campers beside the road to Szentendre in Római Fürdő (25min by HÉV). Higher than average rates include use of the nearby swimming pool.

Zugligeti Niche Camping
Map 2, B5. XII, Zugligeti út 101 ☎200-8346, ⓔcamping.niche@matavnet.hu. Bus #158 from Moszkva tér (M2). Open April–Oct.

At the end of the #158 bus route, opposite the chairlift up to János-hegy, this is a small, terraced ravine site in the woods with space for 260 campers and good facilities, including a pleasant little restaurant occupying the former tram station at the far end.

Restaurants

It's remarkably easy to spend your time in Budapest going from restaurant to coffee house and back, filling in the time between with a little sightseeing. The city is well stocked with affordable eating places offering hearty traditional fare. In the last few years there's also been a marked increase in the number of restaurants serving more sophisticated cuisine, not to mention the best in Hungarian wine. Places like *Arcade*, *Krizia*, *Chapter One*, *Chez Daniel* and *Lou Lou*, though expensive even by Western standards, have become extremely popular. There has also been a welcome diversification recently, with many new places offering Chinese and Japanese food. A development popular with foreign residents in the city are Sunday brunches, giving you as much as you can eat for a fixed price: *Gundel* by the Városliget is the best location, but many of the top hotels, including the *Marriott Hotel* and the *Hilton Hotel* in the castle, also offer an excellent spread. Restaurants with Hungarian gypsy bands tend to be touristy, but do have a certain distinctive charm.

The places listed below range from rough-and-ready backstreet diners to glittering citadels of *haute cuisine* – it's worth checking out both ends of the spectrum. You can generally reckon that the places further from the Belváros or Várhegy will be cheaper.

If a restaurant doesn't have a menu (*étlap*) in German (which most waiters understand) or English, the food and drink vocabulary on pp.176–177 should help when **ordering meals**. Simply pointing to dishes on the menu or neighbouring tables is a bit risky.

Smoking is still the general rule in Budapest's restaurants – and Hungarians smoke a lot. Only the more upmarket places like *Lou Lou* and the more expensive hotel restaurants have a non-smoking section.

As forint prices rise continuously, we have classified restaurants in comparative terms. Expect to pay under £10/$14 per head for a full meal with drinks in an **inexpensive** place; £10–20/$14–28 in a **moderate** restaurant; and £30/$42 upwards in an **expensive** one.

Snacks are covered at the end of this chapter. Note also that bars and coffee houses sometimes serve food; see chapters 15 and 16 for listings.

It's wise to **reserve** a table if you're determined to eat in a particular restaurant; if you haven't, and it's full, you can usually find an alternative within a couple of blocks. We've included phone numbers where booking is advisable. Booking is a must on August 20, St Stephen's Day, when crowds flock to the restaurants after the firework displays have ended.

The standard policy for **tipping** is to give an extra ten to fifteen percent of the total when you pay your bill. Some restaurants include this in their menu prices, but they will not always draw your attention to the fact. Waiters in Budapest do very easily make "mistakes" with the bill, and foreign visitors are especially easy targets for **overcharging**. There have been reports of single male visitors being lured into restaurants by women who have befriended them and at the end of the meal being landed

RESTAURANTS

A FOOD GLOSSARY

What follows is by no means a comprehensive list of Hungarian
dishes, though by combining names and terms it should be possible to decipher most things that you're likely to see on a menu,
or to ask for basic items.

Soups (levesek)

erőleves	meat consommé with noodles (*tésztával* or *metélttel*), liver dumplings (*májgom bóccal*) or a raw egg on top (*tojással*)
gombaleves	mushroom soup
gulyásleves	goulash in its original Hungarian form as a soup
halászlé	a rich paprika fish soup
jókai bableves	bean soup flavoured with smoked meat
tarkonyos borjúraguleves	lamb soup flavoured with tarragon

Appetizers (előételek)

hortobágyi palacsinta	pancake stuffed with minced meat and served with creamy paprika sauce
körözött	a paprika-flavoured spread made with sheep's cheese and served with toast
rántott gomba	mushrooms fried in breadcrumbs, sometimes stuffed with sheep's cheese (*juhtúróval töltött*)

Fish dishes (halételek)

fogas	a local fish of the pike-perch family
harcsa	catfish
pisztráng	trout
ponty	carp

RESTAURANTS

Meat dishes (húsételek)

bélszin	sirloin
csirke	chicken
kacsa	duck
kolbász	spicy sausage
liba	goose
máj	liver
marha	beef
őz	venison
sertés	pork
vaddisznó	wild boar
bécsi szelet	Wiener schnitzel
cigányrostélyos	"gypsy-style" steak with brown sauce
hagymás rostélyos	braised steak piled high with fried onions
paprikás csirke	chicken in paprika sauce

Accompaniments (köretek)

galuska	noodles
hasábburgonya	chips
krokett	potato croquettes
rizs	rice

Vegetables (zöldségek)

bab	beans
burgonya/krumpli	potatoes
gomba	mushrooms
hagyma	onions
lecsó	tomato and green pepper stew
káposzta	cabbage
paprika – édes or *erős*	peppers – sweet or hot

with an astronomical bill – which the unfortunate diner is forced to pay by beefy bouncers. Other more common tactics include issuing menus without prices, offering expensive "specials of the day", hiking up the bill or charging exorbitant amounts for the wine. Insist on a proper menu (including prices for drinks) and don't be shy about querying the total. The US embassy regularly updates its list of restaurants to avoid on its website Ⓦ www.usis.hu/tourist.htm (see p.74).

In addition to salt and pepper, a typical Hungarian restaurant is likely to set paprika on the table too. This is the mild rather than the hot variety, which is brought in separately with dishes such as fish soup. Confusingly, the pepper holder usually has just one hole in the top while the salt pot has lots of holes – the opposite of what you commonly find on a British table.

RESTAURANTS

CENTRAL BUDA

Arcade
Map 3, A10. XII, Kiss János alt. utca 38 ☏ 225-1969. Ten-minute walk from Déli pu (M2). Tues–Sun 11am–11pm.
Expensive.
A new, upmarket restaurant set up by the owners of *Café Kör* in Pest, serving excellent international cuisine, including delicious duck steak in maple syrup. The good range of top Hungarian wines includes *Gere Kopár*, a deep-flavoured red, which, at over 3000Ft a small glass, should be savoured slowly.

Gusto's
Map 3, E2. II, Frankel Leo utca 12 ☏ 316-3970. Tram #4 or #6 from Moszkva tér or the Nagykörút.

Mon–Sat 10am–10pm.
Inexpensive.
A cosy little bar with a small summertime terrace, near the Buda side of Margit híd. Its small menu includes good salads and wines, as well as the best *tiramisu* in town. Booking essential.

Horváth
Map 5, A5. I, Krisztina tér 3. Tram #18 from Déli pu (M2).
Daily noon–11pm. Inexpensive.
Small, popular restaurant just down from Déli Station, near the tunnel beneath Várhegy. Despite its name, which means "Croat" in Hungarian, it serves traditional Hungarian dishes; the speciality of bone marrow served with toast and garlic is recommended.

Marcello
Map 2, E6. XI, Bartók Béla út 40 ☎ 466-6231. Tram #47 or #49 from Deák tér (M1/2/3).
Mon–Sat noon–10pm.
Inexpensive.
An inconspicuous basement place near Móricz Zsigmond körtér serving good pizzas.

Márkus Vendéglő
Map 3, B3. II, Lövőház utca 17 ☎ 212-3153. Moszkva tér (M2).
Daily 9am–1am. Inexpensive.
Friendly Hungarian restaurant near Moszkva tér, right by the Millenarium Park. Large portions of reliable Hungarian dishes, such as *Jókai bableves* and variously stuffed turkey dishes, all recommended. Menus in English available.

Marxim
Map 3, C3. II, Kis Rókus utca 23. Tram #4 or #6 or a five-minute walk from Moszkva tér (M2).
Mon–Fri noon–1am, Sat noon–2am, Sun 6pm–1am.
Inexpensive.
Popular pizza restaurant located just off Margit körút, whose decor makes humorous digs at Stalin and Communism.

Rivalda
Map 5, D6. I, Szinhaz utca 5–9 ☎ 489-0236. Várbusz from Moszkva tér (M2).
Daily 11.30am–11.30pm.
Expensive.

A smart, new restaurant close to the Royal Palace attracting a loyal, local clientele, not just tourists – unlike so many other places on Castle Hill. High-standard cooking (the chicken with mustard maple syrup and the chocolate gateau are especially recommended) and wacky, theatrically inspired decor.

Tabáni Kakas
Map 5, C9. I, Attila út 27 ☎375-7165. Tram #18 from Déli pu (M2).
Daily noon–midnight.
Inexpensive.
Popular old place specializing in poultry – it does an excellent goose leg with mashed potatoes and cabbage (*sült libacomb*) – but also has good fish dishes, such as catfish paprika (*paprikás harcsa*).

ÓBUDA AND THE BUDA HILLS

Búfelejtő
Map 2, C6. XI, Nématvölgyi út 136. Tram #59 from Moszkva tér (M2).

Daily 11am–midnight.
Inexpensive.
The "Comforter" – opposite the Wolf's Meadow cemetery – offers the consolation of fine Hungarian food and a pleasant terrace.

Fenyőgyöngye
Map 2, C4. II, Szépvölgyi út 155 ☎325-9783. Bus #65 from Kolosy tér.
Daily noon–midnight.
Inexpensive.
A pleasant restaurant out in the woods on the northwest edge of the city, serving standard Hungarian fare. Recommended are the Transylvanian stuffed cabbage and the *Füredi Fimom Falatok* – spicy sausage wrapped in pork and served in a paprika sauce.

Kerék
Map 7, F5. III, Bécsi út 103 ☎250-4261. Bus #60 from Batthyány tér (M2).
Daily noon–11.30pm.
Inexpensive.
A small place serving traditional Hungarian food with *srámli* (accordion) music

provided by a couple of old musicians. Outside seating in summer.

Kisbuda Gyöngye
Map 7, E3. III, Kenyeres utca 34 ⊤368-6402. Bus #60 from Batthyány tér (M2).
Daily noon–midnight.
Expensive.
Good food in finely decorated *fin-de-siècle*-style surroundings out in Óbuda. Pleasant courtyard and violin music. Booking essential.

Náncsi Néni
Map 2, B4. II, Ördögárok út 80 ⊤397-2742. Bus #56 from Moszkva tér (M2).
Daily noon–11pm. Moderate.
Popular family restaurant with a large terrace in the leafy suburb of Hűvösvölgy, ten minutes' walk from the terminus of bus #56. Excellent, well-cooked Hungarian food – very tasty starters and the best *túrós gombóc* (sweet curd dumpling) in the city – and live music too. Booking essential.

CENTRAL PEST

Al-Amir
Map 4, D8. VII, Király utca 17 ⊤352-1422. Deák tér (M1/2/3).
Daily 11am–11pm. Inexpensive.
Syrian restaurant serving excellent salads and hummus, making it a haven for vegetarians in this city of carnivores. If that isn't enough, the array of Arabic sweets is most enticing. No alcohol served.

Belcanto
Map 4, D7. VI, Dalszínház utca 8 ⊤269-2786. Opera (M1).
Daily noon–3pm & 5.30–midnight. Expensive.
Good international fare in a smart establishment right by the Opera House. The waiters often burst into song, making for a lively atmosphere.

Berlini Sörkatakomba ("Beer Catacombs")
Map 4, D12. IX, Ráday utca 9 Kálvin tér (M3).
Daily 11am–3am. Inexpensive.
Smoky cellar restaurant with

a genial atmosphere; popular with the younger generation. Serves up lots of that old Hungarian staple – different meats deep-fried in breadcrumbs.

Café Kör

Map 6, E1. V, Sas utca 17 ☎311-0053. Arany János utca (M3).

Mon–Sat 10am–10pm. Moderate.

Buzzy, friendly place near the Basilica with a very relaxed feel. Good grilled meats, salads and wines. The specials of the day written up on the wall are recommended – the staff speak English and can advise on your choice. Booking essential.

Chapter One

Map 4, A5. V, Nador utca 29 ☎354-0113. Kossuth tér (M2).

Daily 9am–midnight or until the last guest leaves. Expensive. Flashy new place near the Parliament set up by an English/Dutch/Hungarian trio with a bright, stylish interior, comfy chairs and loud music attracting a smart clientele. Its unusual

international cuisine, such as chicken in a lime sauce, marks it out from all its rivals.

Fausto's

Map 6, G6. VII, Dohány utca 3 ☎269-6806. Astoria (M2).

Daily noon–3pm & 7pm–midnight. Expensive. Fresh daily specials and homemade pasta in perhaps the best Italian restaurant in town, located near the main synagogue. Specializes in food from northern Italy, and has a good selection of Italian wines and spirits.

Fészek Klub

Map 4, E7. VII, Kertész utca 36 ☎322-6043. Tram #4 or #6 from Nyugati tér (M3) or Blaha Lujza tér (M2).

Daily noon–2am. Inexpensive. A long-established artists' club that draws many of its diners from that world. Delightful leafy courtyard in summer, with cool arcades and a grand dining room in winter, though the food and service can be a let-down. Entry 50Ft unless you book in advance.

Gandhi
Map 4, A7. V, Vigyázó Ferenc utca 4 ⊕269-4944. Tram #2 to Roosevelt tér.
Daily noon–11pm. Inexpensive.
Despite its name, this vegetarian cellar restaurant near Roosevelt tér is not limited to Indian cuisine, offering two set menus, a wide selection of salads, and forty types of tea. It's all very meditative and calming, with prayer wheels for the Hindu, Buddhist, Muslim, Jewish and Christian faiths – Gandhi apparently named all five when asked which religion he belonged to.

Govinda
Map 6, A7. V, Belgrád rakpart 18. Ferenciek tere (M3).
Tues–Sun noon–9pm.
Inexpensive.
Hare Krishna vegetarian restaurant overlooking the river. Serves good set meals, accompanied by the whiff of soporific incense. No alcohol served. No credit cards.

Greens
Map 6, F5. VII, Dob utca 3 ⊕352-8515. Deák tér (M1/2/3).
Daily 11am–2am. Inexpensive.
Cellar restaurant offering the Hungarian speciality *főzelék* (vegetable stews): the garlicky creamed spinach, creamed pumpkin and lentil stews are served with meat, a fried egg, or just by themselves.

King's Hotel
Map 4, E8. VII, Nagydiófa utca 25–27 ⊕352-7675. Tram #4 or #6 from Nyugati tér (M3) or Blaha Lujza tér (M2).
Daily noon–9.30pm. Moderate.
Mehadrin kosher food, which is rare in this town, and it's reasonably good too. The best place in town to meet Hasidic pilgrims heading east. You have to pay in advance for Sabbath meals.

Kiskacsa
Map 4, D8. VII, Dob utca 26, Deák tér (M1/2/3).
Mon–Sat noon–11pm. Inexpensive.
Small friendly joint ten minutes up from the big synagogue, serving traditional Hungarian fare. You get three dice with your bill and if you roll three sixes your meal is on the house.

Krizia

Map 4. D6. V, Mozsár utca 12
⊤331-8711. Opera (M1).
Mon–Sat noon–3pm &
6.30pm–midnight. **Expensive.**
Top-class Italian restaurant,
one of the best in town,
conveniently located near the
Opera. Recommended are
the mouth-watering warm
salmon *carpaccio* and the
delicious *tiramisu*.

Lou Lou

Map 4, A7. V, Vigyázó Ferenc
utca 4 ⊤312-4505. Tram #2 to
Roosevelt tér.
Mon–Fri noon–3pm &
7pm–midnight, Sat
7pm–midnight.
The menu has French
influences but goes far wider
than that, with interesting
dishes such as a delicious
lamb steak in an orange and
coffee bean sauce. Top
Hungarian wines too. No-
smoking section.

Marquis de Salade

Map 4, C5. VI, Hajós utca 43
⊤302-4086. Arany János utca
(M3).
Daily 11am–midnight.
Moderate.

Trendy place that has
expanded into a vast
downstairs section, offering
Japanese, Greek, Azerbaijani
and other cuisines. Zesty
salads make this a favourite
destination for vegetarians.
Special business lunch offer
from 11am to 6pm. No credit
cards.

Múzeum Kávéház

Map 6, E8. VIII, Múzeum körút
12 ⊤267-0375. Astoria (M2).
Mon–Sat 10am–1am.
Expensive.
Excellent traditional
Hungarian food in a grand
nineteenth-century restaurant
– note the Zsolnay tiles and
the frescoes on the ceiling.
Rather old-school, with a
pianist singing kitschy songs
in the background. Near
Astoria metro. Booking
essential.

Okay Italia

Map 4, C3. XIII, Szent István
körút 20. Nyugati pu (M3).
Daily noon–midnight.
Inexpensive.
One of the most popular
Italian restaurants in
Budapest. Bright interior,

speedy service, and delicious pasta and pizza.

Papageno

Map 6, E5. V, Semmelweis utca 19 ☎485-0161. Deák tér (M1/2/3).
Mon–Fri 11.30am–midnight, Sat 12.30pm–midnight. Moderate.
A small bistro in a quiet street near the Astoria. The experienced chef specializes in pasta dishes. A very good lunchtime place, though you'll need to book.

Shiraz

Map 4, E13. IX, Ráday utca 21. Kálvin tér (M3).
Daily noon–midnight.
Inexpensive.
Friendly Persian establishment serving tasty regional dishes – good salads make it attractive to vegetarians.

Via Luna

Map 4, C6. V, Nagysándor József utca 1 ☎312-8058. Arany János utca (M3).
Daily noon–11.30pm.
Inexpensive.
Popular Italian restaurant a few minutes' walk from Szabadság tér. Widely spaced

tables, with bunches of dried herbs decorating the interior, giving a rustic trattoria feel. Good fresh salads, soups, and Parma ham, but the canned vegetables and olives would cause a scandal if the restaurant was in Italy.

Vörös és Fehér ("Red and White")

Map 4, D6. VI, Andrássy út 41 ☎413-1545. Oktogon (M1)
Daily 11am–midnight.
Moderate.
This new wine bar sets a high standard, serving excellent tapas-style food, salads and snacks accompanied by top Hungarian vintages – you can drink most wines by the glass and the friendly staff can advise what goes well with what. Worth booking.

BEYOND THE NAGYKÖRÚT

Bagolyvár

Map 4, H1. XIV, Állatkerti körút 20 ☎321-3550. Hősök tere (M1).
Daily noon–11pm. Moderate.
Sister to the illustrious *Gundel*

restaurant next door (see below), so standards are high, but prices much lower. Prides itself on creating the atmosphere of a prewar middle-class home and serves up home-style cooking to match. Pleasant terrace backing onto the zoo.

Chez Daniel
Map 4, E4. VI, Szív utca 32 ☎302-4039. Kodály körönd (M1).
Daily noon–10.30pm. **Expensive.**
An excellent French restaurant in a cellar, run by idiosyncratic master chef, Daniel, that's arguably the best in town. The new courtyard dining area has just the right atmosphere. Booking recommended.

Erzsébet királyné
Map 2, G7. XIV, Stefánia út 34–36 ☎363-3300. Fifteen-minute walk from Hősök tere (M1), or trolley bus #74 from Dohány utca.
Daily noon–9pm. **Inexpensive.**
If you can't afford *Gundel*, treat yourself to a long al fresco meal in the garden of a

villa built for "Sissi", the wife of Emperor Franz Josef, and complete with a sweeping staircase and wedding banquets at weekends. Hearty, richly-sauced Hungarian dishes.

Firkász
Map 4, B1. XIII, Tátra utca 18 ☎450-1118. Nyugati pu. (M3).
Mon–Thurs & Sun noon–midnight, Fri & Sat noon–2am. **Inexpensive.**
New place done up like a turn-of-the-twentieth-century journalists' haunt, serving good Hungarian food.

Gundel
Map 4, H1. Állatkerti körút 2 ☎321-3550. Hősök tere (M1).
Daily noon–4pm & 7pm–midnight. **Expensive.**
Budapest's most famous restaurant since 1894, it's now run by the Hungarian-American restaurateur, George Lang. Zsolnay porcelain and silver service, a ballroom, garden and terrace and a gypsy band maintain the atmosphere of elegance from before the war, when

RESTAURANTS

Gundel was the haunt of Budapest's social elite. Its menu is fantastically expensive, though the all-you-can-eat Sunday brunch (11am–3pm; 3400Ft) offers a cheaper way to sample its delights. Booking and smart dress required.

FAST FOOD, SNACKS AND LUNCH

Budapest has taken to **fast food** in a big way, with over forty branches of *McDonald's* and plenty of *Pizza Huts* and *Burger Kings* too. On a more positive note, you'll find excellent Chinese stand-up joints – *gyors büfé* – all over town, many of them serving very good and cheap fare. A Hungarian peculiarity are the *étkezde* – small, lunchtime diners where customers sit at shared tables to eat hearty home-cooked food. Few of the places listed below take credit cards.

Café Karinthy
Map 2, E6. XI, Karinthy Frigyes út 22. Tram 6, 18, 19, 47 or 49 to Móricz Zsigmond körtér.
Daily 8am–10pm.
Relaxed large café serving great breakfasts and omelettes, sandwiches, salads and light snacks.

Duran Sandwich Bar
Map 4, B7. V, Október 6 utca 15. Arany János utca (M3) and **Map 4, B7.** II, Retek utca 18. Moszkva tér (M3)
Mon–Fri 8am–6pm, Sat 9am–1pm.
A sandwich and coffee bar – still a rare combination in Budapest, oddly enough.

Falafel
Map 4, D6. VI, Paulay Ede utca 53. Opera (M1).
Mon–Fri 10am–8pm, Sat 10am–6pm.
Small self-service falafel joint five minutes' walk from the Opera House. You can eat as much as you can cram into the pitta bread. Some seating in the upstairs gallery.

Három Testvér ("Three Brothers")

Map 4, C3. VI, Teréz körút 62.
Daily 9am–3am.
Chain of Turkish kebab bars offering quick, cheap and good food. Good range of salady bits too.

Kádár Étkezde

Map 4, E8. VII, Klauzál tér 10.
Tram #4 or #6 from Nyugati tér (M3) or Blaha Lujza tér (M2).
Mon–Sat 11.30am–3.30pm; closed mid-July–mid-Aug.
Cheap lunch place in the heart of the Jewish quarter. The food, such as *sólet*, the bean stew speciality served on Fridays and Saturdays, is that of the non-kosher assimilated Budapest Jewry. Friendly atmosphere, with diners sharing tables equipped with soda siphons, and photos and caricatures of Hungarian and visiting celebrities on the walls.

Lánchíd

Map 5, E6. I, Fő utca 4.
Daily 9am–11pm.
Atmospheric small bar serving hot and cold sandwiches, handily placed at the Buda end of the Chain Bridge.

Marie Kristensen Sandwich Bar

Map 4, E12. IX, Ráday utca 7. Kálvin tér (M3).
Mon–Fri 8am–10pm.
In theory this place behind Kálvin tér has a Danish flavour, but in practice it is basically a decent regular sandwich bar.

Mini Étkezde

Map 4, E7. VII, Dob utca 45.
Tram #4 or #6 from Nyugati tér (M3) or Blaha Lujza tér (M2).
Mon–Fri 11.30am–3pm; closed mid-July–mid-Aug.
A cheap lunchtime diner just off Klauzál tér. Less crowded than the *Kádár* round the corner, but just as good. Menus are in Hungarian only. Don't miss the tasty elderflower cordial (*bodza szörp*).

Mirákulum

Map 4, B6. V, Hercegprimás utca 19.
Open daily 9am–1am.

Handy breakfast joint near Arany János utca station (blue metro), with smoking and non-smoking sections.

Museum of Contemporary Art

Map 5, D7. I, Wing A, Buda Royal Palace. Várbusz from Moszkva tér (M2).

Tues–Sun 10am–4pm.

Excellent café on the museum's upper floor, with fast service and very tasty Hungarian food. The best-value place on Castle Hill – though you'll have to pay the admission to the museum as well.

Self-service Canteen

Map 6, B2. V, Szende Pál utca 3. Vörösmarty tér (M1).

Mon–Fri noon–3pm.

Standard Hungarian food at this super-cheap lunch spot just round the corner from Vörösmarty tér.

Szahara

Map 4, F13. VIII, József körút 84–86. Ferenc körút (M3)

Open 24 hours a day (closes around 9/10am for an hour's cleaning).

Clean, bright joint that has a wide range of tasty Middle Eastern food, eaten at shared tables. No smoking inside, though there are some tables outside in summer. It's easy to order: just point to the pictures of the food on the menu.

Thai Szendvics

Map 4, D4. VI, Teréz körút 46.

Daily 10am–midnight.

Fast food like they serve it back in Thailand: filling plates of noodles, meat and vegetables, cooked in the wok in front of your eyes and served up in seconds. Pay the cashier, who barks out your order to the cooks.

Tower Restaurant

Map 4, B7. 10th floor of the Central European University, V, Nádor utca 9.

Mon–Fri 10am–8pm (from noon to 2pm university members get priority).

Excellent inexpensive university café open to all, run by the same people as the café in the Museum of Contemporary Art.

FAST FOOD, SNACKS AND LUNCH

Zöldfaló Salad Bar

Map 3, B5. XII, Csaba utca 8
(entrance on Hajnóczy utca).
Moszkva tér (M2).
Mon–Fri 10am–6pm.

Five minutes' walk from
Moszkva tér, this place serves
falafels and as much salad as
you can eat.

Coffee houses and patisseries

offee houses (*kávéház*) are one of the city's big treats. At the end of the nineteenth century Budapest had hundreds of them, providing meeting places for the city's bohemian intelligentsia – artists, writers, journalists and lawyers. Living conditions in the rapidly growing city were often poor, and the coffee houses offered warmth and a place to work, with sympathy drinks or credit for those down on their luck. Stories abound of the quirks of some of the regulars, such as the writer who would always come to his table at three o'clock in the morning and work all night by candlelight.

Today's coffee houses and **patisseries** (*cukrászda*) are less romantic but still full of character, whether fabulously opulent, with silver service, or homely and idiosyncratic. They are still very much in use, with daily life in Budapest punctuated by the consumption of black coffee drunk from little glasses or cups (*eszpresszó*), though cappuccinos are now standard fare too.

BUDA

Ági Rétes
Map 3, B4. II, Retek utca 19.
Moszkva tér (M2). Mon–Fri
10am–6pm.
Patisserie with the best *rétes*
(strudel) in town just near
Moszkva tér, all baked on the
premises.

Angelika
Map 3, F5. I, Batthyány tér 7.
Batthyány tér (M2).
Daily 10am–midnight.
Quiet but smoky atmosphere
in beautiful vaulted rooms
next to St Anne's Church in
the Víziváros, with a lively
terrace.

Daubner
Map 7, E7. II, Szépvölgyi út
20. Bus #60 from Batthyány tér.
Daily 10am–7pm.
Excellent cakes and pastries
in this patisserie (no seating),
ten minutes' walk up from
Kolosy tér, towards the
Pálvölgyi Caves.
Recommended are the *szilvás
papucs* (plum slippers) – plums
folded in a Danish pastry.
The long queues at weekends
testify to the place's
popularity.

Miró
Map 5, C3. I, Úri utca 30.
Várbusz from Moszkva tér (M2).
Daily 9am–midnight.
Groovy place with a young,
relaxed atmosphere, down the
road from the Mátyás Church
on Várhegy. Furnished in a
Miróesque style, with
curious, not very
comfortable, chairs. Snacks
and sandwiches.

Ruszwurm
Map 5, D3. I, Szentháromság
tér 7. Várbusz from Moszkva tér
(M2).
Daily 10am–8pm.
Diminutive Baroque coffee
house and the oldest in
Budapest, operating since
1827. Almost impossible to
get a seat in summer.
Delicious cakes and ices.

PEST

Astoria Kávéház
Map 6, F6. V, Kossuth utca 19.
Astoria (M2).
Daily 7am–11pm.

A grand, turn-of-the-twentieth-century coffee house-cum-bar on the ground floor of the *Astoria Hotel*, whose central location makes it a convenient meeting place. The comfy armchairs have sadly disappeared, but it's still a good place to watch the locals discuss their business.

Café Picard

Map 4, A4. V, Falk Miksa utca 10. Kossuth tér (M2).

Mon–Fri 7am–10pm, Sat 9am–10pm.

Elegant small French café near Parliament, serving good breakfasts – fresh croissants and excellent coffee – and lunches.

Central Kávéház

Map 0, D7. V, Károlyi Mihály utca 9. Ferenciek tere (M3)

Daily 8am–midnight/1am.

Large old coffee house recently restored to its former grandeur. Also serves a wide range of food throughout the day, from cheap favourites like creamed spinach to more expensive dishes.

Eckermann

Map 4, D6. VI, Andrássy út 24. Opera (M1).

Mon–Sat 8am–10pm.

One of the best cafés around, attached to the Goethe Institute right by the Opera House. Popular with young artists and writers – and also with bag thieves, take note. Excellent large coffees, tasty Balkan *burek* pastry and other snacks, and free Internet access (from 2pm).

Frőhlich

Map 4, D8. VII, Dob utca 22. Deák tér (M1/2/3) or Astoria (M2).

Mon–Thurs 9am–6pm, Fri 7.30am–3pm, Sun 10am–4pm; closed Sat & Jewish holidays.

Kosher café and a fantastic hub of Jewish community life five minutes' walk from the Dohány utca synagogue, presided over by the Frőhlich family. Specialities such as *flodni* (apple, walnut and poppy-seed cake) are worth tasting.

Gerbeaud

Map 6, C2. V, Vörösmarty tér 7. Vörösmarty tér (M1).

Daily 9am–9pm.
A Budapest institution with a gilded salon and terrace. Popular with tourists but the service is good – and they don't rip you off as often happens in the loud *Café Art* across the square. The cakes are great and the creamy and chocolatey Mexican coffee superb – though it's quite pricey.

Ibolya
Map 6, C6. V, Ferenciek tere 5. Ferenciek tere (M3).
Mon–Sat 8am–11pm, Sun noon–10pm.
Iced coffee outside in the summer, or sticky cakes, *Szalon sör* (a beer from the southern Hungarian town of Pécs), and a smoky atmosphere indoors all year round in this popular student meeting place.

István Cukrászda
Map 4, B7. V, Október 6 utca 17. Arany János utca (M3).
Daily 10am–6pm.
Small friendly café near the Basilica. You pay for your cakes and coffee on the

ground floor, then head upstairs to find a table. Your order arrives on the mini-lift.

Király
Map 4, D8. V, Király utca 19. Deák tér (M1/2/3).
Daily 10am–midnight.
Cosy café above a patisserie serving delicious cakes and ice cream, all made on the premises.

Lukács
Map 4, F4. VI, Andrássy út 70. Kodály körönd (M1).
Mon–Fri 8am–8pm, Sat & Sun 10am–8pm.
One of the older coffee houses, recently restored to its full grandeur. In the 1950s this was apparently the local café for the Communist secret police, who had their headquarters down the road at no. 60.

Múzeum Cukrászda
Map 6, F7. VIII, Múzeum körút 10. Astoria (M2).
Daily 24 hours.
Friendly student hangout next to the National Museum, with *pogácsa* (cheese scones)

on the table. Fresh pastries arrive early in the morning.

Művész
Map 4, D6. VI, Andrássy út 29. Opera (M1).
Daily 8am–midnight.
Stunning old coffee house that's now getting a bit shabby. Valued for its location, just across from the Opera House, its decor and its clientele – including some wonderful fur-hatted old ladies. The cakes and service are average.

Sport
Map 4 C6. V, Bank utca 5. Arany János utca (M3)
Mon–Fri 7am–6pm.
1970s furniture and service and good cakes in this fine example of an ancien-regime café.

Szalay
Map 4, A5. V, Balassi Bálint utca 5. Kossuth tér (M2).
Daily except Tues 9am–7pm, Nov–March closed Mon too.
Just near the Parliament, this café is one of the few remaining old-style cake shops in Budapest, run by a dynasty of bakers. Excellent cakes and ice creams.

Zsolnay
Map 4, D4. VI, Teréz körút 43. Nyugati pu. (M3).
Daily 10am–10pm.
In spite of its unlikely location on the first floor of the *Béke Radisson Hotel* and its modern interior, the *Zsolnay* is a popular meeting place. Its cakes, served on Zsolnay porcelain, are close contenders for the best in town.

COFFEE HOUSES AND PATISSERIES

Bars and clubs

Budapest's nightlife scene is small – spend a few evenings drinking and clubbing and you'll be spotting familiar faces. It is centred on three main areas: Liszt Ferenc tér – the place to see and be seen – running between Andrássy út and the Music Academy; semi-pedestrianized Ráday utca, which, with its innumerable cafés and terraces, styles itself the Budapest Soho; and Krudy Gyula utca, behind the National Museum. Another growth area has been summer outdoor bars, such as the *Romkert* and *West Balkan*, but since most of these also have dance floors, they are covered under "Dance spots" on p.200. The majority of *borozó* or wine bars are nothing like their counterparts in the West, being mainly working men's watering holes, offering such humble snacks as *zsíros kenyér* (bread and pork dripping with onion and paprika). Conversely, beer halls (*söröző*) are often quite upmarket, striving to resemble an English pub or a German bierkeller, and serving full meals. The addition of *pince* to the name of an outlet signifies that it is in a cellar; many of the new places stink of mould until the crowds arrive.

Most places open around lunchtime and stay open until after midnight, unless otherwise stated, though bars in residential areas have to close their terraces at 10pm. See p.74 for warnings about **rip-offs** in restaurants, which apply equally to bars. There have been reports of foreign male travellers being lured into bars by local women and then being made to pay hefty bills for drinks by bouncers. **Váci utca** is particularly notorious for this.

Some **clubs** and **discos** in the city are still run by the universities, though there's an increasing number of private ventures, some of which have a fairly strict entrance policy. Various mafias operate in town – Hungarian, Russian, Ukrainian and others – and there is a big demand for bouncers, whose presence is felt at many of the bars and clubs in town. The best advice is not to mess with them.

BARS

BUDA

Bambi
Map 3, F2. I, Frankl Leó utca 2–4.
Mon–Fri 7am–9pm, Sat & Sun 9am–8pm.
One of the few surviving Socialist-Realist bars, with red plastic-covered seats and stern waitresses serving drinks, plus breakfast, lunch, snacks and cakes all day long.

Kecskeméti Borozó
Map 3, C4. II, Széna tér.
Mon–Sat 9am–11pm.
Smoky, sweaty and crowded stand-up wine bar by Moszkva tér, on the corner of Retek utca. They serve up that staple of Hungarian bar fare, *zsíros kenyér*, bread with lard, paprika and onions. A notice on the wall saying "We do not serve drunks" seems to be paid scant regard in practice.

Libella
Map 3, I14. XI, Budafoki út 7.
Mon–Sat 8am–11pm, Sun 10am–11pm.
Friendly, unmarked bar near the *Gellért Hotel*. A young, alternative crowd comes here for bar snacks, chess and draughts.

Móri Borozó

Map 3, C4. I, Fiáth János utca 16.

June–Aug daily 4–11pm;
Sept–May Mon–Sat 2–11pm,
Sun 2–9pm.

Cheap and cheerful neighbourhood wine bar attracting a young crowd. Darts and bar billiards in the room at the far end.

Ponyvaregény

Map 2, E6. XI, Bercsényi utca 5.

Daily 10am–2am.

The books around the walls (the name means "pulp fiction") and the sofas give this spacious cellar bar a very friendly feel.

Tabáni Teázó

Map 3, F10. I, Attila út 27.

Daily 11am–1am.

Quiet place near Dózsa György tér, west of Várhegy, that specializes in tea, but sells alcohol too.

PEST

Café Mediterrán

Map 4, E6. VI, Liszt Ferenc tér 11.

Daily 11am–2am.

The least posey place on this posiest of squares. Red walls, cane furniture, a big terrace in summer and a relaxed atmosphere.

Castro

Map 4, E14. IX, Ráday utca 35.

Daily 10am–midnight/1am.

A popular place attracting a mix of locals and expats. The Serb chef rustles up excellent food, such as spinach pies. Internet access too.

Crazy Jungle Café

Map 4, D4. VI, Jókai utca 30.

Open daily noon–1am.

Lively and very long cellar bar with a huge variety of beer and a karaoke machine.

Darshan Udvar

Map 4, F12. VIII, Krúdy Gyula utca 7.

Mon–Wed 11am–1am,
Thurs–Sat 11am–2am & Sun 6pm–midnight.

This is the largest bar in a growing complex of bars, cafés and shops. Set at the back of a courtyard, with hippy Gaudiesque decorations, good food and

world music. Service is
leisurely.

Fortuca Bistro
Map 4, E6 VI, Liszt Ferenc tér
10.
Daily 11am–1am.
Another new place with a
terrace in this popular square,
with high ceilings and a Tex-
Mex interior. Good, cheap
food of a mixed Mediterranean
-cum-Mexican kind.

Martinez
Map 6, F5. VII, Dohány utca 1.
Daily 11am–2am.
This was one of the first bars
in the city devoted purely to
cocktails, and its staff know
how to wield a shaker. Right
opposite the Dohány utca
synagogue, making it a useful
meeting place.

Old Man's Music Pub
Map 4, F8. VII, Akácfa utca 13.
Daily 3pm–dawn.
Large, popular joint near
Blaha Lujza tér. Live local
acts, and good food.

Paris-Texas
Map 4, E13. IX, Ráday utca 22.
Daily 9am–dawn.
Stylish bar near Kálvin tér
with a very French
atmosphere. Good bar
snacks.

Portside
Map 6, G6. VII, Dohány utca 7.
Sun–Thurs noon–2am, Fri & Sat
noon–4am.
Large cellar bar offering beer
and delicious food – the
grilled cheese with vegetables
is a vegetarian's delight. Pool
tables to the left of the
entrance.

Tokaji Borozó
Map 4, B3. V, Folk Miksa utca
32.
Mon–Fri noon–10pm, Sat
4–10pm.
Crowded, smoky old-style
wine bar serving wines from
the Tokaj region, as well as
snacks such as *lapsánka*
(potato pancakes) and *zsíros
kenyér*.

DANCE SPOTS

With posters all around town advertising raves and discos, it won't take long to find your way around Budapest's small clubbing scene. Another good place to look is in *Pesti Est*, the free listings magazine found in cinemas and bars all around town; look up the "*Könnyű*" section at the back. All the venues listed below are in town, but there are regular all-night raves further out in places like Törökbálint and Etyek – buses (*parti buszok*) are usually laid on for these, leaving from Moszkva tér and Móricz Zsigmond körtér – it will say on posters where buses go from.

Entry to **clubs** and **discos** usually ranges from 200 to 1000Ft. Dancing often starts late, sometimes after midnight. You'll also find dancing in some of the bars listed on pp.197–199, including the *Old Man's Music Pub*, as well as in the three big arts centres, the Petőfi Csarnok (see p.110), Almássy téri Szabadidő Központ (see p.215), and the Trafó (see p.215). The gay and lesbian scene is covered separately on p.204.

For a different experience, look out for the monthly *Cinetrip* dance parties (ⓦ www.cinetrip.hu) held in the old Turkish Rudas baths and at other venues, with films and weird lighting added to the mix.

TURNTABLE WIZARDS

Budapest may not rate as the rave capital of the world, but it has thrown up a few local stars. Names to look out for include Yonderboi, Keyser and Shuriken (easy listening), Palotai, Titus and Mango (drum'n'bass) Norman (house) and Superbeat (nujazz). If you're into goa, the slightly gentler version of your run-of-the-mill techno, look out for DJs Virág and Oleg, while Tommy Boy is a mainstream DJ playing mainly acid jazz.

Cha Cha Cha

Map 6, E9. IX, Kálvin tér subway.
Mon–Fri 7am–2am, Sat
10am–2am.

Glam 1970s bar with fake
zebra furnishings and a
louche feel. Despite its
strange location, it attracts a
big crowd, which spills out
into the concourse, and there
are DJs Thursday to Saturday
nights.

E-Klub

Map 2, G6. X, Népliget (at the
Planetarium).
Fri & Sat 8pm–5am.

Formerly in block E of the
Technical University across
the river, this once-wild
cattle market for engineering
students has been exiled to
outer Pest. Today a more
mixed crowd packs the two
discos on different floors, and
there's beer galore. Live rock
music on Fridays.

Franklin Trocadero

Map 4, B3. V, Szent István
körút 15.
Tues–Sat 9pm–4am.

The best place in town for
Latin music, and the best

dancers too. Hot and steamy
once it gets going.

Kashmir Underground

Map 4, F13. IX, Üllői út 151.
Wed–Sat 10pm–6am.

New, hip place near Ferenc
körút metro station (M3).

Közgáz DC

Map 4, D13. IX, Fővám tér 8.
Fri 8.30pm–3am.

Massive, sweaty party scene
at the southern end of the
Economics University, with
a live rock band and non-
stop disco, two films and a
karaoke show, plus a "tea
house", ice-cream bar and
lots of beer.

Nincs Pardon

Map 4, G7. VIII, Almássy tér 11.
Daily noon–4am.

Bar/nightclub with a small
dance floor, variable music,
and open sandwiches at the
bar. Packed on Saturdays.

Old Man's Music Pub

Map 4, F8. VII, Akácfa utca 13.
Daily 3pm–dawn.

Very popular place in the
centre of town, though

DANCE SPOTS

expensive by Hungarian standards. Good for dancing and Hungarian food.

Petőfi Csarnok

Map 2, F5. XIV, Zichy Mihály út 14.

The raves organized by Tilós Rádió and other DJs are the best dance events at this large youth centre near the back of the Városliget. Otherwise it offers everything from Greek folk dancing (Sun in summer) down to the Kelly Family club. Turn up on the wrong night and you'll stumble into the Star Trek club.

Piaf

Map 4, D6. VI, Nagymező utca 20.

Daily 10pm–well after dawn.

This fashionable bar on "Broadway" charges 500Ft to enter, unless you know a regular and can give their name at the door (you have to ring the bell). Basically it's a room and a cellar graced by the odd film star and lots of wannabes, with occasional jazz or rock sets.

Romkert

Map 3, G12. I, Döbrentei tér 9 ☎344-3155.

March–Oct Mon–Fri noon–2/3am, Sat 6pm–4/5am, Sun 6pm–2/3am.

This popular outdoor nightspot beside the Rudas Baths draws yuppies and bimbos on the prowl, and offers cocktails, tasty bar food (reserve a table if you're going to eat) and a small dance floor.

Süss fel nap

Map 4, B3. V, corner of Honvéd utca and Szent István körút.

Daily 8pm–4am.

Big club with a young crowd. Mixed music and occasional live acts.

West Balkan

Map 2, E7. XI, Kopaszi-gát.

May–Sept daily 5pm–dawn.

Lively dance spot which attracts top DJs and big crowds, despite its being out of the city. It's ten minutes' walk south along the river bank from the Buda end of Petőfi Bridge – or there are

DANCE SPOTS

bicycle rickshaws from the
bridge or *Zöld Pardon*.

Zöld Pardon
Map 2, E7. XI, Goldmann
György tér.
Daily 9am–6am (kitchen
noon–6am).

Large, heaving outdoor bar
near the Petőfi bridgehead,
where hundreds of teenagers
dance to drum 'n' bass, deep
house and jungle. Visit their
website for a preview:
Ⓦ www.zp.hu. Punch-ups and
knifings despite heavy security.

DANCE SPOTS

●

Gay Budapest

Budapest's gay scene has taken wing in recent years, with new, overtly gay clubs replacing the old, covert meeting places, and the appearance of a trilingual monthly listings magazine, *Mások* ("Outsiders"). However, gays must still tread warily and lesbians even more so. The Hungarian word for gay is *meleg* – *warm*, while the pejorative term is *buzi* (from the word *buzeráns*, which has the same roots as *bugger*).

Aside from the bars and clubs listed below, the **Turkish baths** are a popular meeting place – Király Baths for the younger crowd, where you'll find a lot of Romanian prostitutes; the Rácz for the more middle-aged gays; and the Rudas Baths, where a more mixed crowd is found mainly after 6pm – but, as tends to be the case in Budapest, these are gay hangouts for men only. The same is true of the first private gay bath, Magnum Sauna & Gym at VIII, Csepreghy utca 2 (Mon–Thurs & Sun 1pm–1am, Fri & Sat 1pm–6am; 1600Ft; ☎267-2532, ⓦgayguide.net/Budapest/Magnum; Ferenc körut metro). The best spot for lesbians is the *Eklektika* bar (see p.207); the *Angyál*, *Capella* and *Limo* are also good for women.

The most popular **cruising spots** on the Buda side are the Vérmező park by Déli Station (though you should take care, as the park is not particularly safe after dark) and the park at the Buda end of the Margit híd, while in Pest it's the Danube promenade from Erzsébet híd to Vigadó tér. The Népliget behind the Planetarium is another meeting place, though it's notoriously dangerous.

The major event in the gay calendar is **Gay Pride Budapest**, a four-day festival taking place at the end of June. Organized by Hattér, this is fast becoming a well-established event in the capital, incorporating a varied programme of film festivals, public discussion forums and gay parties. The event culminates in the colourful Pride March on the final Saturday, which wends its way from Dózsa György út to the Belgrád rakpart via Andrassy út.

The website Ⓦ www.gayguide.net/Europe/Hungary/Budapest has the latest on gay accommodation, bars, clubs, restaurants, baths and any events that might be happening in the city, and the Hattér helpline (daily 6–11pm; ⓣ 329-3380, Ⓔ hatter@ hatter.hu), run by the largest gay and lesbian organization in the country, is another good source of information.

RESTAURANTS

Club 93

Map 4, E9. V, Vas utca 2 ⓣ 338-1119. Astoria (M2). Daily 11am–midnight. A cheap pizzeria, popular with gays and lesbians. Its gallery and window seating make it a good place to people-watch.

Wurlitzer

Map 4, F7. VII, Wesselényi utca 49 ⓣ 351-0231. Blaha Lujza tér (M2). Mon–Sat noon–midnight. Gay-friendly place recently reopened under new management. Serves Hungarian-style food.

RESTAURANTS

BARS

Most of the places listed below levy an **entry fee** or set a minimum consumption level – being gay in Budapest is an expensive privilege. Some, like the *Capella*, give you a card when you enter, which all your drinks are written down on; you then pay for your drinks and the entry fee as you leave – though be warned that if you lose the card you'll have to pay a lot of money.

Action Bár

Map 6, E8. V, Magyar utca 42 ⓦ www.action.gay.hu. Kálvin tér (M3).

Daily 9pm–4am.

The hardest of the gay bars, full of young men looking for one-night stands. Dark room and video room. Minimum consumption 1000Ft.

Amstel River Café

Map 6, C5. V, Párisi utca 6. Ferenciek tere (M3).

Mon–Fri 9am–11pm.

Not on the river, but between Váci and Petőfi utcas, this Dutch-style pub attracts a large foreign clientele and is welcoming to gays.

Angyál Bár

Map 4, G7. VII, Szövetség utca 33. Tram #4 or #6 from Blaha Lujza tér (M2).

Thurs–Sun 10pm–dawn.

Budapest's premier gay club looks a bit like an airport lounge, but has an interesting crowd. Saturdays are men-only, but Fridays and Sundays are popular with women. Has a dark room. Entry 600–700Ft.

Capella

Map 6, A7. V, Belgrád rakpart 23 ⓦ www.extra.hu/capellacafe. Ferenciek tere (M3).

Mon & Tues 9pm–2am, Wed–Sun 9pm–5am.

Drag queens, jungle music and lots of kitsch. Shows start at 11.30pm and 2am on Friday and Saturday nights, or midnight the rest of the week. A very mixed joint, with men, women and a lot of straights too. Entry 1000Ft.

Chaos

Map 4, E9. V, Dohány utca 38 ⓦ www.chaospub.hu. Astoria (M2).

Daily 9pm–5am.

The most cultured of the gay bars, this is a friendly place to meet. The ground floor is a gallery, but downstairs there's a bar and a small dance floor. Minimum consumption 700Ft (Fri and Sat).

Darling

Map 6, D6. V, Szép utca 1. Astoria (M2).

Daily 7pm–4am.

A small beer-house and video gallery that gets "warmer" after 9pm and stays open till late. Has a dark room. Attracts a lot of Romanian prostitutes.

Eklektika

Map 6, E5. V, Semmelweis utca 21. Astoria (M2).

Mon–Fri noon–midnight, Sat & Sun 5pm–midnight.

Lesbian-friendly bar – a pleasant space with 1960s furniture – that has a women-only evening on the second Saturday of every month. No entry fee, except on women's night (500Ft).

Heaven 51

Map 4, D5. VI, corner of Jókai utca and Ó utca.

Wed–Sun 10pm–4am.

This friendly, two-level cellar bar hosts popular transvestite shows on Friday and Saturday, with an excellent Britney Spears. You'll find both straights and gays here. Entry 600Ft.

Limo Club

Map 6, A8. V, Belgrád rakpart 9.

Daily noon–5am.

New bar near the *Capella*, attracting a gay-straight mix. Lavishly and imaginatively decorated, with a bar on the ground floor and a dance floor down the spiral staircase.

Mystery Bar-klub

Map 4, C6. V, Nagysándor József utca 3. Arany János utca (M3).

Mon–Fri 10pm–4am, Sat & Sun 6pm–4am.

Very small bar for talking rather than dancing – there's no disco. If the door's locked you might have to wait to be let in. Internet access.

GAY BUDAPEST: BARS

Live music

Live music is one of the city's strengths: most evenings you can choose from classical, folk and jazz performances. Now that Budapest is on the world circuit, a large number of foreign performers include it on their tour schedule.

For "what's on" information consult any of the listings magazines on p.9 or visit the Tourinform office (see p.8). See Directory on p.267 for details of ticket agencies.

If you can't get tickets for a performance, it is always worth persevering with the staff at the ticket office or door, as there is often some way in, even if it costs a bit extra – for instance, the Music Academy puts aside tickets each performance for a fire and a police officer, which are often not used, and it also has space on its top balcony.

OPERA, BALLET AND CLASSICAL MUSIC

You can enjoy **opera** in Budapest at a very reasonable price; the surroundings are magnificent, and you can even afford to treat yourself to several glasses of (Hungarian) champagne in the bar during the interval. Of the two venues, the grandest is the State Opera House, a nine-teenth-century pile on Andrássy út, while the Erkel Theatre is much more modern. Most productions are in Hungarian, a custom introduced by Mahler when he was director of the State Opera House. Fans prefer their opera "old style", with lavish sets and costumes, and they interrupt with ovations after bravura passages. Productions are, however, severely handicapped by lack of money – which means rising stars are lured to foreign opera houses – and by the ridiculously big repertoire that the opera houses maintain. Given Hungarians' preference for lavish productions, it's not surprising that **operetta** should be so popular: its combination of music, dancing and general melodrama is something that Hungary excels at.

The city offers a wide variety of **classical music** performances, although the pre-Baroque period is poorly represented. There are several concerts every night of the year, especially during the two main festivals – the Budapest Spring and Autumn festivals (see p.235 and p.238 respectively). Look out for performances by the **Budapest Festival Orchestra**, the city's only privately financed orchestra, conducted by the charismatic Iván Fischer, and the **Radio and Television Symphony Orchestra**, conducted by Tamás Vásáry – though both orchestras are below par when their inspirational directors are not at the helm – as well as two excellent **chamber ensembles**: the Liszt Ferenc Chamber Orchestra and the Weiner Száz Orchestra. Pianists Péter Frankl, Zoltán Kócsis, András Schiff and Desző Ránki, violinist Vilmos Szabadi and cellist Miklós Perényi are other names to look out for.

Places of worship that regularly host concerts include the **Mátyás Church** on Várhegy (see p.23); the **Lutheran Church** on Deák tér (see p.81), including free performances of Bach before Easter – information for these is posted by the church entrance; and the **Dohány utca synagogue** (see p.115).

The opera, theatre and concert halls all close at the end of May for the summer, reopening in mid-September, though there is a summer season of outdoor concerts at the open-air venues in town.

Bartók Memorial House (Bartók Emlékház)

Map 2, C4. II, Csalán utca 29.

Concerts, not just of Bartók's music, are held in the villa where the composer used to live, most Fridays at 11am.

Budapest Convention Centre (Budapest Kongresszusi Központ)

Map 3, B12. XII, Jagelló út 1–3 ☏209-1990.

Modern and uninspiring concert hall behind the *Novotel*, hosting big concerts.

Erkel Theatre

Map 4, H9. VIII, Köztársaság tér 30 ☏333-0540.

A modern venue for operas, ballet and musicals, near Blaha Lujza tér (M2).

Hungarian State Opera (Magyar Állami Operaház)

Map 4, D6. VI, Andrássy út 22 ☏353-0170.

Budapest's grandest venue, with gilded frescoes and three-tonne chandeliers – a place to dress up for.

Music Academy (Zeneakadémia)

Map 4, E6. VI, Liszt Ferenc tér 8 ☏342-0179.

Nightly concerts and recitals in the magnificent gold-covered *Nagyterem* (Great Hall) or the smaller *Kisterem*. The music is excellent and the place has a real buzz.

Old Music Academy (Régi Zeneakadémia)

Map 4, F5. VI, Vörösmarty utca 35.

Concerts every Saturday

morning by young musicians in the concert hall in the Liszt Memorial Museum.

who achieved international fame with their work, as well as more modern musicals.

Operetta Theatre
Map 4, D6. VI, Nagymező utca 17 ⓣ332-0535.
The stunningly refurbished home of operetta. Here you can see works by Lehár, Kálmán and other local stars

Pesti Vigadó
Map 6, B3. V, Vigadó tér 1 ⓣ327-4322.
Another fabulously decorated hall, though the acoustics are inferior. Box office opens at 1pm.

FOLK MUSIC AND TÁNCHÁZ

Hungarian **folk music and dancing** underwent a revival in the 1970s, drawing inspiration from Hungarian communities in Transylvania, regarded as pure wellsprings of Magyar culture. Enthusiasts formed "dance houses" or **táncház** to revive traditional instruments and dances, and get people involved. Visitors are welcome to attend the weekly gatherings (350–800Ft admission) and learn the steps. Groups such as Muzsikás, Téka, Ökrös and Kalamajka play Hungarian folk music, while other groups are inspired by South Slav music from Serbia, Croatia and Bulgaria, or, in the case of Di Naye Kapelye, klezmer music from around the region.

Details of events are available in listings magazines or on the website ⓦ www.tanchaz.hu. Bear in mind that many cultural centres close for the summer, so check before you go.

Almássy téri Szabadidő Központ
Map 4, G7. VII, Almássy tér 6 ⓣ342-0387,

ⓦ www.datanet.hu/~almassy.
Closed July & Aug.
Greek and African dance houses; there are often big

Hungarian or gypsy (Roma) gatherings too.

City Cultural Centre (Belvárosi Művelődési Ház)

Map 4, C11. V, Molnár utca 9 ⑦ 317-5928.
Closed early June–late Sept.
The Kalamajka ensemble plays to a packed dance floor on Saturday nights at this downtown Pest cultural centre. Instruction from 7pm. There is also music in the bar upstairs, and as the evening rolls on a jamming session often gets going.

Fonó Budai Zeneház

Map 2, E7. XI, Sztregova utca 3 ⑦ 206-5300, ⑩ www.fono.hu.
Tram #18 or #47; get off at stop at Fehérvári út 108.
This large, lively concert venue out in Kelenföld is a twenty-minute tram ride from Deák tér, but one of the best folk venues in town, with old groups from different parts of the Carpathian Basin appearing every Wednesday. Concerts start 8pm.

Rézmál

Map 3, B2. II, Marcibányi tér 5/A ⑦ 315-0592, ⑩ www.pipacs.hu/rezmal.
Members of the top folk band Muzsikás often play on Thursday night from 8pm – check in *Pesti Est*. Not a dance house as such – the group just plays and people sit around in a very informal atmosphere.

JAZZ

Don't be fooled by the small number of regular jazz venues in Budapest – the country boasts some brilliant jazz players, some of them well known abroad. Keep an eye out in particular for pianists Béla Szakcsi Lakatos, György Szabados, Karoly Binder, Janos Nagy and György Vukán, double bassist Aladár Pege, guitarist Gabor Juhasz and saxophonists Mihaly Dresch (who can play an ethno variety if in the mood) and Istvan Grencso. Two groups worth catching are

Trio Midnight (Kalman Olah on piano who is brilliant) and the Dél-alföldi Saxophone Ensemble.

Details of performances can be found in *Pesti Est* listings. Apart from the venues listed below, performances take place at local cultural centres (see p.215) and in a number of the places listed on pp.200–203 under "Clubs and discos", such as the *Petőfi Csarnok*.

Benkó Dixieland Klub
Map 4, D12. IX, Török Pál utca 3.
Daily 5–10pm.
The world-famous Benkó Dixieland Band plays here every Wednesday evening when not touring abroad.

Dokk Jazz Bistro
Map 7, I2. III, Hajógyári sziget 122 ☎457-1023.
Mon–Thurs & Sun noon–midnight, Fri & Sat noon–dawn.
Bar/restaurant on an island by Óbuda (easiest access is by taxi). Regular attractions include acid jazz pianist Zsolt Kaltenecker.

Fonó Budai Zeneház
Map 2, E7. XI, Sztregova utca 3 ☎206-5300, ⓦwww.fono.hu. Tram #18 or #47; get off at stop at Fehérvári út 108.

Has the best ethno-jazz and avantgarde in the city.

Hades Jazztaurant
Map 4, F5. VI, Vörösmarty utca 31 ☎352-1503.
Mon–Fri noon–2am, Sat 5pm–2am.
Pleasant bar/restaurant with a jazz trio (Mon & Fri) and piano music (Tues–Thurs). No live music June–August. Open till 2am (midnight on Sun).

Jazz Garden
Map 6, C9. V, Veres Pálné utca 44/A ☎266-7364.
Daily noon–1am.
Jazz bar and restaurant. Guests include Béla Szakcsi Lakatos and Aladár Pege, as well as local resident American blues guitarist Bruce Lewis.

JAZZ

213

**John Bull Pub
"Automobile"**
Map 3, A5. XII. Maros utca 28
⊤ 356 3565.
The interior is mock British pub, but it has high-quality, quiet, cool combo jazz most nights. Five minutes' walk up Csaba utca from Moszkva tér.

New Orleans Jazz Club
Map 4, D5. VI, Lovag utca 5

⊤ 354-1130.
Daily noon–2am.
New, modern bar attracting big international names – but tickets can be astronomical even by Western standards.

Pesti Est Café
Map 4, E6. VI. Liszt Ferenc ter 5.
The club downstairs does not always have jazz but it can get good performers.

POP AND CONTEMPORARY DANCE MUSIC

Budapest attracts every Hungarian band worth its amplifiers and a growing roll-call of international stars, making it the best place for **rock concerts** in Hungary. Major foreign acts appear at the vast Népstadion, the smaller Kisstadion or the SAP arena, all in the same complex (see p.224), and their appearances are well publicized in the media and in posters around town. Don't get too excited by flyposters advertising Michael Jackson or the Cure, however, as these usually refer to light shows or DJs at clubs and discos. Prices range from 1000Ft up to as much as 10,000Ft for international superstars. For an authentically grim Magyar rock-opera, you can't beat *István a király* (Stephen the King) or the *Attila Sword of God*, both of which are about the early heroes of the Hungarian nation.

Many of the clubs and bars on pp.197–203 have live music – see the listings in the free weekly *Pesti Est*. The following major cultural centres are also regular venues.

Almássy téri Szabadidő Központ

Map 4, G7. VII, Almássy tér 6 ⊕342-0387, ⓦwww.datanet.hu/~almassy. Closed July & Aug.
One of the city's main district cultural centres, located in downtown Pest.

Fonó Budai Zeneház

Map 2, E7. XI, Sztregova utca 3 ⊕206-5300, ⓦwww.fono.hu. Tram #18 or #47; get off at stop at Fehérvári út 108.
Lively concert venue out past Móricz Zsigmond körtér.

Petőfi Csarnok

Map 2, F5. XIV, Zichy Mihály út 14 ⊕342-4327.
Huge, purpose-built youth centre near the back of the Városliget, hosting concerts by local and big-name foreign bands and contemporary dance performances.

Trafó

Map 4, G14. IX, Liliom utca 41 ⊕456-2054, ⓦwww.trafo.hu.
Major contemporary arts centre attracting top foreign acts, with an excellent bar downstairs.

POP AND CONTEMPORARY DANCE MUSIC

Theatre and cinema

Budapest has some stunning theatres and cinemas that are worth visiting for their architecture alone. If you are undeterred by the language barrier, an evening at the theatre can be a rewarding experience. Language is less of a problem at cinemas; foreign films are usually screened in their original language.

To find out **what's on**, look out for flyers and check the listings magazines (see p.9). Full cinema listings are given in the Hungarian publications *Pesti Est* (free) and *Pesti Műsor (PM)* under the heading *Budapesti mozik műsora*. The free theatre listings publication, *Súgó*, available from theatre foyers, is published in English in July and August.

See Directory on p.267 for details of ticket agencies.

THEATRE

Hungarians show great taste when it comes to building theatres: take the splendid mass of the Comedy Theatre (*Vígszínház*) up the road from Nyugati Station or the **Új Színház** opposite the Opera House. However, mainstream Hungarian theatre itself is in the doldrums at present, and its melodramatic and unsubtle productions in an incomprehensible language are not the most exciting combination for visitors. Generally, you can expect more dynamic performances from provincial theatre companies, such as the one from the town of **Kaposvár** in Transdanubia, which has attracted some good actors and directors disenchanted with theatre in Budapest. Currently, the best Hungarian mainstream theatre is to be found amongst the Hungarian minorities in neighbouring countries, such as Romania, where the theatre still plays a vital role in communication. This might change, however, with the opening of the **National Theatre**, on the Pest riverside near Petőfi bridge (see box on p.218); the culture ministry is pumping in huge funds to turn it into a showcase for the nation's drama, but cynics just expect more of the same dross.

Alternative theatre is where the quality is to be found. One Hungarian group that has received considerable critical acclaim abroad is the **Mozgó haz** (Moving House) theatre company, whose inventive combination of music and movement under the direction of László Hudi won the top award at the International Theatre Festival in Sarajevo in 1998 and was well received at the London International Festival of Theatre in 2001. Sadly, however, the group is struggling to survive: the cultural ministry determinedly refuses to give it any backing, and this lack of support means that, absurdly, the group rarely performs at home – though look out for them at the Trafó (see p.219), the best venue for alternative dance and theatre. Other names to look out for are the **Krétakör** group, under the young director Árpád Schilling, and performances by **Péter Halász**, an actor-director who spent many years in New York before returning to Hungary.

The puppet theatre is covered
under "Kid's Budapest" on p.245.

THEATRE

THE NATIONAL THEATRE

The sorry saga of Budapest's National Theatre (*Nemzeti Színház*) is a source of much shame and amusement in the city. The theatre used to be housed in a grand building on Blaha Lujza tér until the construction of the metro in the 1960s – which many saw as an evil plot by the Communist regime to undermine the nation's identity. For many years the theatre temporarily occupied a hideous building in the backstreets of Pest, while the debate over a permanent home for the theatre continued. In 1997, the centre-left city authorities finally started the construction of a huge development on Erzsébet tér, which incorporated specially constructed and very costly foundations so that an existing underground car park would not disturb the performances. Hardly had the foundations been laid, however, when the new centre-right national government halted construction in 1998 and started a new debate about where to put the theatre. Finally, it chose a site on the Pest riverbank south of the centre – and the new theatre opened in March 2002. The project has not been without controversy, however, with the government minister in charge giving the job of designing the building to the architect who designed his own house. After much wrangling, the city started developing the old site on Erzsébet tér as a conference centre and car park in 2001, but for three years it was just an embarrassment, an abandoned building site named by local wits as the "National Hole" (*nemzeti lyuk*).

Alternative theatre **venues** include the **MU Színház**, XI, Körössy József utca 17 (☎209-4014); **Szkéné Színház**, XI, Műegyetem rakpart 3 (☎463-3741); **Studio K**, IX, Mátyás utca 9 (☎216-7170); and the **Merlin Theatre** in the centre of town at V, Gerlóczy utca 4 (☎266-4632), which often hosts visiting British companies.

THEATRE

During summer there are easy-to-understand performances at the outdoor theatre on Margit sziget.

Szkéné Színház

Map 2, E6. XI, Műegyetem rakpart 3 ☏463-3741.
A small theatre housed in the main building of the Technical University near the *Gellért Hotel*, this has been an alternative venue for many years, dating back to the bad old days of Communism.

Trafó

Map 4, G14. IX, Liliom utca 41 ☏456-2054.
A new contemporary arts centre in a former transformer station under the dedicated direction of cultural impresario György Szabó. It pulls full houses with Hungarian and foreign theatre and dance performances.

Új Színház (New Theatre)

Map 4, D7. VI, Paulay Ede utca 35 ☏351-1406.
Stunning Art Nouveau building across the road from the Opera House. One of the better mainstream theatres, offering reliably polished performances.

Vígszínház

Map 4, B2. XIII, Szent István krt 14 ☏329-2340.
Great place for people-watching: the locals dress up in their finest in this magnificent theatre. The acting is very much in the mainstsream Hungarian style, but visiting companies also perform here.

FILMS AND CINEMA

Hollywood blockbusters and Euro soft-porn films currently dominate Budapest's mainstream **cinemas**, though the city has a chain of "arts cinemas", which specialize in the latest releases and obscure films from Eastern and Western Europe. Their provenance is indicated thus: *angol* (British), *lengyel* (Polish), *német* (German), *olasz* (Italian), and *orosz* (Russian).

FILMS AND CINEMA

HUNGARIAN FILM

Hungarians have an impressive record in film, and many of the Hollywood greats were Hungarian emigrés – Michael Curtiz, George Cukor, and actors Béla Lugosi, Tony Curtis and Leslie Howard to name but a few. In the Communist years Hungarian films continued to make waves, with Károly Makk, István Szabó, Márta Mészáros and others making films that managed to say much about the oppressive regime in spite of its restrictions. Now the main restriction on film makers is chronic underfunding, but what the Hungarian film industry lacks in money it makes up for in ideas. In recent years a number of good films have been released, which unfortunately probably never make it beyond the art-film festivals in the West. Directors to look out for are Peter Gothár, with his absurd humour and love of the fantastic (*Time Stands Still, Let Me Hang Vaska*), Ildikó Enyedi (*My Twentieth Century* and *Simon the Magician*), Béla Tarr (*Werckmeister Harmonies* and the epic eight-hour *Satan Tango*) and János Szász, whose latest film *The Witman Boys* won the best international film at Cannes. Other rising stars to watch for are Kornél Mundroczó, Szabolcs Hajdú and Ferenc Török, whose recent film *Moszkva tér* – about apolitical youths in 1989 – has won many fans.

Budapest Sun runs listings of all movies playing in English. If you understand Hungarian, the fullest **listings** appear in *Pesti Est* and *Pesti Műsor* (*PM*) under the heading *Budapesti mozik műsora*. Here, the times of shows are cryptically abbreviated to *n8* or *1/4 8* for 7.15pm; *f8* or *1/2 8* for 7.30pm; and *h8* or *3/4 8* for 7.45pm. "*Mb.*" indicates the film is dubbed, and "*fel.*" or "*feliratos*" means that it has Hungarian subtitles.

Cinema-going is cheap, with tickets between 600 and 900Ft, and sometimes films arrive in Budapest before they reach New York. In the summer, there are also outdoor and drive-in cinemas on the edge of town.

The three main **film festivals** during the year are the Hungarian Film Festival (*Magyar Filmszemle*; Ⓦ www.magyar .film.hu), a parade of the year's new films in February, and two alternative festivals of Hungarian and foreign films, the Titanic Film Festival (Ⓦ www.datanet.hu/titanic) in October and the Europa Film Festival in December.

A host of **multiplex** cinemas has now also appeared in the city, such as the Corvin and the Westend Ster Megaplex, at Westend City Centre by Nyugati Station (Ⓣ 238-7222).

**Budapest has some beautiful movie houses –
check out the Moorish interior of the Uránia
and the coffered ceiling of Puskin.**

Cirko-gejzir

Map 4, A3. V, Balassi Bálint utca 15–17.
One of the best alternative cinemas. Chinese tea served before showings. Regular selection of films from around the globe. In any given week they might be showing films by Almodovar, Tarkovsky, Jarmusch, Wenders and Rohmer, and even the latest odd classic.

Corvin Budapest Filmpalota

Map 4, F13. VIII, Corvin köz 1

Ⓣ 459-5050, Ⓦ www.corvin.hu.
The glitzy Film Palace, near the Ferenc körút metro station (M3), is a modern jungle of cinemas, popcorn and drinks. You can catch the latest foreign releases here, and in February it hosts the Hungarian Film Festival. Reduced-price tickets on Wednesdays.

Művész

Map 4, D5. VI, Teréz körút 30 Ⓣ 332-6726.
Alternative cinema near the Oktogon, with one larger

and several smaller rooms named after big film personalities.

Puskin

Map 6, E6. V, Kossuth Lajos 18.
Complex of three cinemas in the centre of town with a large café attached.

Toldi

Map 4, C6. V, Bajcsy-Zsilinszky út 36–38 ☎311-2809. Next door to Arany János utca metro station (M3), the Toldi is one of the more dynamic alternative cinemas in town, with a bar and a bookshop where people congregate. One of the venues for the annual Titanic Film Festival.

Uránia

Map 4, E9. VIII, Rákóczi út 21. Magnificent Moorish decorations. Undergoing transformation in 2002 and will emerge as the National Cinema, a showcase for Hungarian films.

Sports

Hungarians are passionate about sport. **Spectator sports** such as Grand Prix racing, soccer and horse-racing are very popular, though years of underfunding have brought the last two nearly to their knees. Participatory sports have suffered similarly from a lack of funding, but you can find tennis, squash and riding facilities dotted around the capital. One area that has seen big investments is **fitness centres**. Most of the larger hotels have them and they are open to non-residents as well. Hungary's strongest showing on an international level is in kayaking, shooting, water polo and fencing – of rather limited appeal perhaps for most foreign visitors. One activity where you can easily join in is **chess**: Hungary has a long tradition of great chess players and you can see the game being keenly played in many parks. The great Bobby Fischer settled down in Hungary and rumour has it you can see him playing in the Széchenyi Baths, in the City Park.

Information about the city's extensive bath and swimming facilities is given on pp.228–232.

SOCCER

Hungary's great footballing days are long past – the golden team of the 1950s that beat England 6–3 with stars such as Ferenc Puskás and József Bozsik is a world away from today's national team that struggles to qualify for any big tournaments. The club scene is also in deep crisis, with teams floundering in a financial desert amid poor infrastructure and bad management. While **international matches** are held at the Népstadion – generally filling just a third of its 76,000 seats – club football revolves around the turf of three **premier league teams**. Ferencvárosi Torna Club (aka FTC or Fradi) is the biggest club in the country, based at IX, Üllői út 129, near the Népliget metro. Fradi is almost a national institution, and its supporters, dressed in the club's colours of green and white, are the loudest presence at international matches too. The club has long had right-wing ties – this was the fascists' team before the war, and in recent years it has attracted a strong skinhead – and anti-Semitic – element. When a businessman of Jewish origin bought the club in 2001, it resulted in an outpouring of violently anti-Semitic comments from the nationalist right wing. Fradi fans try to pick fights with supporters of Újpesti Torna Egylet, whose ground is at IV, Megyeri út 13 (four stops on bus #30 from Újpest Központ metro station). Their main rivals are MTK, whose club is at VIII, Salgótarján utca 12–14 (tram #37 from Blaha Lujza tér).

See the daily paper *Nemzeti Sport* for details of fixtures. The **season** runs from late July to late November and late February to mid-June. Matches are played on Saturday afternoons. Tickets cost around 1200Ft.

HORSE-RACING

Horse-racing has long been popular in Hungary, but is currently in a state of upheaval. It was introduced from

England by Count Széchenyi in 1827 and flourished until 1949, when flat racing (*galopp*) was banned by the Communists. For many years punters could only enjoy **trotting races** at the Ügetőpálya just beyond Keleti Station, but in the mid-1980s flat racing resumed at Kincsem Park, further east of the centre. The sport since then has been dogged by financial problems and misman-agement, and the announcement in 2000 that the trotting track (the Ügetőpálya) was being sold off for redevelopment caused uproar in racing circles.

Despite the protests, the sale is going ahead and Kincsem Park is being redeveloped to handle both flat racing and trotting. While this is happening, flat racing has temporarily transferred to **Alag**, outside the city on the road to Vác. Trotting races, continue to be held for the time being at the Ügetőpálya, Kerepesi út 11 (bus #95 or trolley bus #80 from either Népstadion or Keleti Station). Races start at 2pm on Saturday and 4pm on Wednesday. The atmosphere at the tracks is informal, but photographing the racegoers is frowned upon, since many attend without the knowledge of their spouses or employers. Races are advertised in *Fortuna* magazine. **Betting** operates on a tote system, where your returns are affected by how the odds stood at the close of betting. The different types of bet you can make are *tét* (placing money on the winner); *hely* (on a horse coming in the first three); and the popular *befutó* (a bet on two horses to come in either first and second or first and third). Winnings are paid out about fifteen minutes after the end of the race.

GRAND PRIX RACING

First held in 1986, the **Hungarian Grand Prix** takes place every summer at the purpose-built Formula One rac-ing track at **Mogyoród**, 20km northeast of Budapest. It is usually scheduled for mid-August, and financial uncertainties surrounding the event spark off rumours every year that this is the last year it will be held. Details are available from Tourinform, any listings magazine or the website Ⓦ www.hungaroring.hu. You can reach the track by special buses from the Árpád Bridge bus station; trains from Keleti Station to Fót, and then a bus from there; or by HÉV train from Örs vezér tere to the Szilasliget stop, which is 1800m northeast of Gate C. **Tickets**, available from Ostermann Forma 1 Kft., Apáczai Csere János utca 11, 3rd floor (Ⓣ 317-2844) or from booths in Ferenciek tér, range from 5200Ft for the first day, to between 27,000Ft and 71,500Ft for the final day, and from 28,000Ft to 95,000Ft for a three-day pass – the price being partly determined by the location, and whether you book in advance or risk disappointment on the day.

PARTICIPATORY SPORTS

TENNIS AND SQUASH

Tennis courts can be booked all year round at the Városmajor Tennis Academy in Városmajor Park near Moszkva tér (Ⓣ 202–5337) and at the *Thermal Hotel Helia* in north Pest, XIII, Kárpát utca 62 (Ⓣ 452-5800) – you can also rent racquets – while **squash** enthusiasts should head for the City Squash Club at II, Marcibányi tér 13 (Ⓣ 325-0082). The *Marriott Hotel* in central Pest also has courts, though these cost a bit more.

SKIING AND ICE-SKATING

If it's a snowy winter, you might consider **skiing** at Normafa in the Buda Hills; equipment can be rented

from Suli Sí in the Komjádi
swimming complex at II,
Árpád Fejedelem utca 8
(☎ 212-2750). You could
also join the locals at the
ice rink by Hősök tere in
the Városliget (City Park)
between November and
March; skates can be rented
out.

HORSE-RIDING

For **horse-riding** head out
to the Great Plain, where
there are many small riding
schools; ask at Tourinform
for further information (see
p.8) or contact Pegazus Tours
at V, Ferenciek tere 5, in the
office facing you as you walk
into the courtyard rather

than the one on the street
front (Mon–Thurs 9am–
4pm, Fri 9am–3pm; ☎ 317-
1552, Ⓦ www.pegazus.hu),
or the Hungarian Equestrian
Tourism Association at
Ráday utca 8 (☎ 456-0444,
Ⓕ 456-0445, Ⓦ www.equi
.hu).

CAVING

Hungary has the right geol-
ogy for **caves**, and both
under Budapest and further
afield you'll find plenty to
explore. Contact the
Hungarian Association of
Speleologists at the
Szemlőhegy Cave in Buda
(p.68) on ☎ 346-0494 or
346-0495.

Baths and pools

Budapest has a long bathing tradition going back to Roman times or even earlier, and a visit to the city's baths should not be missed. There are three different types of bath: *gyógyfürdő*, a thermal bath in its original Turkish form, as at the Rudas and Király, or the magnificent nineteenth-century settings of the Gellért and Széchenyi; *uszoda*, a proper swimming pool like the Sport; and *strand*, a summer pool in a verdant setting, like the Palatinus or Csillaghegy. Most baths are divided into a swimming area and a separate section for thermal baths (*gyógyfürdő* or the *göz*, as they are popularly known).

Csillaghegyi Strand

Map 2, E2. III, Pusztakúti út 3.
May 10–Sept 15 daily
6am–7pm; Sept 16–May 9
Mon–Fri 6am–7pm, Sat
6am–3pm, Sun 6am–noon;
500Ft.
Large outdoor complex spreading up the hillside north of Óbuda. Ten minutes by train from Batthyány tér,

and close to the Csillaghegy HÉV stop, with a large main pool and smaller warmer pools. Nude sunbathing on the upper slopes.

Gellért Gyógyfürdő

Map 4, B14. XI, Kelenhegyi út 4 ☎466-6166.
Mixed pool May–Sept daily 6am–7pm, July & Aug Fri & Sat

BATHING MATTERS

The Budapest bath experience can be daunting, as little is written in English once you are inside and attendants are unlikely to speak much more than Hungarian and a smattering of German. However, the basic system of attendants and cabins is the same in most baths, and once you get the hang of the rituals, it is most rewarding. A standard ticket from the ticket office (*pénztár*) covers two hours in the sauna, steam rooms and pools; supplementary tickets will buy you a massage (*masszázs*), tub (*kádfürdő*) or mud bath (*iszapfürdő*). Inside the changing room (*öltöző*) an attendant will direct you to a cabin, and in single-sex steam baths where swimsuits are still rare, they will give you a *kötény* – a small loincloth for men or an apron for women – which offers a vestige of cover. Once you've changed, find the attendant again, who will lock your door. You will get a key which you should tie to the strings of your *kötény* as you set off – making a note of your cabin number and taking with you any other tickets for massages etc. The best way to enjoy the steam baths is to move from room to room, moving on when the heat gets too much. A popular sequence in the thermal baths is: sauna, warm pool, steam room, cold plunge, hot plunge (the last makes your skin tingle wonderfully), followed by a dip in warm water, and then the whole sequence again. However, it's entirely up to you, and the main thing is not to stay longer in any one section if you feel uncomfortable. As you leave, take a sheet to dry yourself, relax in the rest room if you feel exhausted, and then find the attendant to unlock your cabin. It is usual to tip the attendant a couple of hundred forints. In many pools bathing caps (*uszósapka*) are compulsory; like swimsuits and towels, they can be rented at the *pénztár*.

also 8pm–midnight; Oct–April
Mon–Fri 6am–7pm, Sat & Sun
6am–5pm. Thermal baths –
men and women separate: daily
6am–6pm. 1600Ft for thermal
section only, 1800Ft for access
to all areas.

The most popular of the
city's baths, the Gellért has it
all: a magnificent main pool
for swimming, hot pools for
sitting around in both inside
and outside on the terrace,
fabulous Art Nouveau steam
baths, and a large outdoor
area, including a wave
machine in the main pool
and shaded terraces – and, of
course, a restaurant where
you can get your daily dose
of meat fried in breadcrumbs.
In the main pool, swimming
caps are compulsory; you can
get free blue plastic ones by
the exit from the changing
rooms. The baths attract a lot
of foreigners, and staff usually
speak German or English.

Hajós Alfred Uszoda (aka Sport)
Map 3, G1. Margit sziget.
Daily 6am–6pm; 500Ft.
One of the nicest places for
proper swimming – a

beautiful 1930s lido at the
southern end of the island
that was renovated for the
2001 European water polo
championships. Has a small
sauna, and two large outdoor
pools against a backdrop of
trees; one is normally given
over to water polo. In the
winter you can swim out
along a channel to the larger
of the pools without walking
outside. The buffets on the
terrace and in the entrance
hall serve excellent pastries.

Király Gyógyfürdő
Map 3, E3. II, Fő utca 84.
Men: Mon, Wed & Fri
9am–8pm; women Tues &
Thurs same hours, Sat
6.30am–noon; 600Ft.
Fabulous Turkish baths. Of
the steam baths, this is the
one most popular with the
gay community.

Lukács Fürdő
Map 3, E1. II, Frankl Leó út
25–29.
Outdoor mixed swimming pool
with sauna (Mon–Sat
6am–7pm, Sun 6am–5pm);
thermal baths (men: Tues,
Thurs, Sat & Sun 6.30am–8pm;

BATHS AND POOLS

women: Mon, Wed & Fri same hours); 800Ft entry to both. Two small but delightful pools in the grounds of this bath-cum-hospital complex. Buy your tickets in the folly entrance hall (ask for the *uszoda* if you want the pool) and follow the courtyard round to the left, past the plaques put up by grateful patients. It also has steam and mud baths (*iszapfürdő*), the latter being particularly popular with gays.

Palatinus Strand
Map 7, H7. Margit sziget.
May–mid-Sept daily 8am–7pm; 600Ft.
Halfway up the islands on the west, the Palatinus has a large outdoor set of pools, including a wave pool and children's pools, all set in a big expanse of grass. The sunroof above the changing rooms is a gay centre.

Rác Gyógyfürdő
Map 3, F11. I, Hadnagy utca 8–10.
Men: Tues, Thurs & Sat 6.30am–6pm; women: Mon, Wed & Fri 6.30am–6pm; 600Ft.

Small, modernized Turkish baths on the southern edge of the Tabán, in one of the few remaining buildings of the old Serb quarter. Popular with gays as a meeting place.

Rudas Gyógyfürdő
Map 3, G12. I, Döbrentei tér 9.
Mon–Fri 6am–7pm, Sat & Sun 6am–1pm; 700Ft.
One of the original Turkish baths in the city, at its best when the sun shines through the hole in the dome to light up the beautiful interior. Still operates the apron system, so swimming togs are not needed in the steam section; in the larger pool to the left of the entrance the usual rules apply. The steam baths are for men only – women can only get a look when *Cinetrip* raves are held in the baths (see p.200).

Széchenyi Fürdő
Map 4, I1. XIV, Állatkerti körút 11 (entrance opposite the Circus).
Mid-May–mid-Sept daily 6am–6pm; mid-Sept–mid-May Mon–Fri 6am–6pm, Sat & Sun 6am–4pm; 1200Ft.

Magnificent nineteenth-century complex in the Városliget with sixteen pools in all, including the various medicinal sections. You'll probably use just the three outdoor pools – the hot one with people playing chess that appears in so many photos of the city, a pool for swimming, and the jacuzzi/whirling pool. There is also a mixed sauna with a maze of hot and cold pools across the far side of the hot pool from the changing rooms. Chess sets are not provided – bring your own if you want to play. There are separate steam baths for men on Mondays, Wednesdays and Fridays, and for women on Tuesdays, Thursdays and Saturdays.

Festivals

Whatever time of the year you visit Budapest, there's almost certain to be something happening. Of the events listed in this chapter, the biggest are the Spring Festival in late March/early April, and the Autumn Festival from late September to late October – both of which feature music, ballet and drama, including star acts from abroad. Many theatres, concert halls and dance houses close down during the long, hot months of July and August, though open-air performances are staged in their place. The city's population returns from the countryside for the fireworks on August 20, and life returns to normal as school starts the following week. The new arts season holds fire until the last week of September, when there is a rash of music festivals and political anniversaries. The opening performance at the State Opera House is traditionally *Bánk Bán*, by Ferenc Erkel.

JANUARY

Farsang
January 6 to Ash Wednesday. This is the season of carnivals and balls, and Farsang is the Hungarian way of saying farewell to winter, as well as fattening everyone up before fasting

begins in Lent (carnevale – the farewell to meat). Revellers usually take to the streets in fancy dress during one weekend in January; they process across the Lánchíd and down to Vörösmarty tér, where prizes are given for the best-dressed. Unfortunately the inclement weather at this time of year often dampens the event's spirit.

FEBRUARY

Bears and Spring

February 2. Tradition has it that if the bears in Budapest Zoo come out of their cave on this date and catch sight of their shadows, they will return to their lairs to sleep, and the winter will be a long one. If the sun doesn't shine, it means that spring is just around the corner.

Hungarian Film Festival

Two weeks of the latest films from the Hungarian studios. Tickets can be bought at the central venue, the Corvin Filmpalota on Ferenc körút (see p.221), which usually shows films with English translations.

MARCH–APRIL

Declaration of Independence of 1848

March 15. A public holiday in honour of the 1848 Revolution, which began with Petőfi's declaration of the *National Song* from the steps of the National Museum. Budapest decks itself out with Hungarian tricolours, and there are speeches and gatherings outside the museum and by Petőfi's statue on Marcius 15 tér. The more patriotic citizens wear little cockades in the national colours (red, white and green) pinned to their lapels.

Budapest Spring Festival

Late March/early April. The city's major arts festival: classical music concerts in venues across the city, as well as some jazz and folk; exhibitions, including the World Press Photos show; dance, including the folk dance festival; theatre and cinema, with a series of Hungarian films with English subtitles often showing in one cinema in town.

EASTER

Late March/early April. Easter has strong folk traditions in Hungary. Easter Saturday is marked by processions in churches, while on Easter Monday *locsolkodás* (splashing) takes place, when men and boys visit their female friends to spray them with cologne. Kids get a painted egg or money in return for splashing, while the men receive *pálinka* (schnapps). This is a tamer version of an older village tradition where a bucket of water was used instead of the perfume bottle. Regular events in the weeks preceding Easter are arts and craft fairs in the Museum of Ethnography, with traditional folk skills like egg painting on display; and free performances of the Bach Passions in the big, yellow Lutheran church on Deák tér.

MAY

Labour Day

May 1. Though still a public holiday, citizens are no longer obliged to parade past the Lenin statue near the Városliget. Instead the major trade unions put on a big do in the park, with shows, games, talks, and of course food and drink in large quantities.

FESTIVALS: MAY

235

JUNE

Book Week

Early June. Vörösmarty tér is lined with stalls, as Hungarian writers gather from neighbouring countries and further afield. Authors sign books for the punters – politicians have now joined the book circus, competing to see who can attract the largest number of people wanting their books autographed – and there is singing and dancing on the temporary stages in the two squares.

WOMUFE

Early June. A two- to three-day event at the Budai Parkszínpad in the park by Kosztolányi Dezső tér, hosting a collection of world music stars.

Worldwide Music Day

Nearest weekend to June 21. Musical events around town mark this day, thought up by the French to celebrate music around the world.

Bridge Festival (Hid Fesztval)

End of June. A new event that commemorates the building of the Chain Bridge in the 1840s. The bridge itself is closed to traffic for the festival, and there is a river cavalcade, fireworks and general festivities.

Budapesti Bucsú

Last weekend. "Bucsú" means farewell in Hungarian, and the first Budapesti Bucsú was held in 1991 to celebrate the departure of Soviet troops from the country. Now it's an annual city-wide celebration of music, with events in the Tabán, the park at the Buda side of the Erzsébet híd, and in Hősök tere, where there is a large outdoor classical music performance.

JULY

Bastille Day
July 14. Street ball outside the French Institute near the Lánchíd in Buda, with music, dancing and fireworks.

AUGUST

Hungarian Grand Prix
Usually second weekend. The Hungarian Grand Prix takes place at the Hungaroring circuit at Mogyoród on the northeastern edge of the city.

Budafest
Mid-August. Opera and ballet festival in the State Opera House.

Sziget Festival
Mid-August. One of the biggest rock and pop festivals in Europe takes place on Óbudai-sziget, an island north of the centre. Rock, pop, world music, dance, theatre, films and children's events. Further information on ⓦ www.sziget.hu.

St Stephen's Day
August 20. A public holiday in honour of Hungary's national saint and founder, with day-long rites at his Basilica, a craft fair and folk dancing at different venues in the Várhegy, and a spectacular fireworks display at 9pm. Over a million people line the Danube to watch the fireworks fired off between the Erzsébet and Margit bridges, and the traffic jam that follows is equally mind-blowing. Restaurants are also packed that night, so book well ahead if you want to eat out.

Budapest Parade
August 25. A mini version of London's Notting Hill Carnival, when a procession of floats set up by radio stations and clubs parades through the city, ending up on Dózsa György út by City Park

for a rave into the early hours.
Ⓦ www.budapestparade.hu.

The Jewish Festival
End of August. Attracts an
international range of artists
presenting classical, jazz and
klezmer music and
exhibitions.
Ⓦ www.jewishfestival.com

SEPTEMBER

Budapest Wine Festival
Early September. The
centrepiece of this festival is
on Vörösmarty tér, where
you can walk around the
wine stalls tasting and buying
wines. There may also be
concerts and a procession.

**BNV: Budapest National
Fair**
Early September.
Hungary's largest consumer
trade fair of the year takes
place in the Budapest
International Fair Centre at
X, Albertirsai út 10 (☎263-
6000).

European Heritage Days
Late September. A Council
of Europe initiative which
takes place all over the
Continent, with public
buildings opened up for a
weekend. Tours (in
Hungarian) take you round
the Art Nouveau Geological
Institute on Stefánia út, the
former Post Office Savings
Bank in Hold utca, and the
Interior Ministry on
Roosevelt tér.

Budapest Music Weeks
**Late September to early
November.** City-wide music
events starting around the
anniversary of Bartók's death
on September 25.

**Budapest Autumn
Festival**
**Late September to mid-
October.** This is the lesser of
the two big arts festivals, but
stronger on contemporary
music. There are also
exhibitions, opera and theatre
performances.

OCTOBER

Music of Our Time
Early October. Two weeks of contemporary music played by Hungarian and foreign artists.

Titanic Film Festival
Early October. An annual show of independent films shown over ten days in October, usually at the Toldi Cinema by Arany János utca metro station (M3).

Arad martyrs anniversary
October 6. Commemoration of the shooting of the thirteen Hungarian generals in 1849 in Arad in present-day Romania, when the 1848 revolution was crushed by the Austrians with Russian help. Wreaths are laid at the "Eternal Flame" at the junction of Báthory and Hold utca (Map 4, B5), erected on the spot where Count Lajos Batthyány, the Prime Minister of the short-lived independent government, was shot.

Commemoration of the Uprising
October 23. A national holiday to commemorate the 1956 Uprising and the declaration of the Republic in 1990. Ceremonies take place in Kossuth tér, by the Nagy Imre statue nearby, and at Nagy's grave in the New Cemetery (see p.137).

NOVEMBER

All Souls' Day
November 1. Cemeteries stay open late around this day and candles are lit in memory of departed souls, making for an incredible sight as darkness falls.

DECEMBER

Mikulás

December 5–6. St Nicholas's Day. On December 5, children clean their shoes and put them in the window for "Mikulás", the Santa Claus figure, to fill with sweets. Naughty children are warned that if they behave badly, all they will get is *virgács*, a gold-painted bunch of twigs from Mikulás' little helpers. Nowadays most children get sweets, twigs and presents.

Christmas

December 24–25. The main celebration is on December 24, when the city becomes eerily silent by late afternoon. Children are taken out while their parents decorate the Christmas tree (until then the trees are stored outside, and on housing estates you can often see them dangling from windows). When the children return home, they wait outside until the bell rings, which tells them that "little Jesus" (*Jézuska*) has come. Inside, they sing carols by the tree, open presents, and start the big Christmas meal, which is traditionally spicy fish soup, amongst other things. In the preceding weeks there are Christmas fairs in several locations in town, the best being in the Museum of Ethnography, where traditional crafts are demonstrated.

New Year's Eve

December 31. Revellers gather on the Nagykörút, engaging in trumpet battles at the junction with Rákóczi út. In the Opera House there is an all-night ball; tickets, which are expensive, can be bought from the usual tickets agencies on p.267.

Kids' Budapest

Budapest offers a healthy range of activities for kids from state-of-the-art playgrounds to roller-skating parks, with concessions on most entry tickets for under-14s. Don't expect anything too high-tech, however, as a lack of cash dogs the facilities and some of the city's playgrounds have become pretty run-down. There is no doubting the average Hungarian's love of children, though. They will talk to children on buses and give up their seats for parents carrying small babies; old ladies will loudly berate parents for not dressing their babies adequately (which for Hungarians means not putting a hat on in the mildest of weather); and if you are pushing a baby buggy, help is usually quickly forthcoming when you're trying to negotiate stairs.

Shops selling toys and games are listed
under "Shopping" on p.260.

Since the city is still very much lived in and offices have not yet taken over the centre of town, there are a lot of **playgrounds** in squares and parks, such as in Klauzál tér and the Károlyi kert near Astoria. But the best of the adventure playgrounds are in the **Millenarium Park** (p.57) and in the **Zoo** (p.112). If your children want to jump around and get rid of excess energy there are **trampolines** in big cages at the Buda end of the Margit híd and in the Városliget, south of the Széchenyi baths.

PARKS AND OUTDOOR ACTIVITIES

Caves

There are several **caves** in the Buda Hills that are open to the public, and which are good fun for children as long as they aren't scared of the dark. The **Labyrinth of Buda Castle** under the Várhegy (see p.31) offers some exciting exploration for 6- to 12-year-olds, while the Pálvölgy Stalactite Caves at Szépvölgyi út 162 (*Pálvölgyi cseppkőbarlang*; map 7, A5; hourly tours Tues–Sun 10am–4pm; 40min; 400Ft) and the Szemlő-hegy Caves at Pusztaszeri út 35 (*Szemlőhegyi barlang*; map 7, C7; Mon & Wed–Fri 10am–5pm, Sat & Sun 10am–4pm; 300Ft) display dramatic geological formations.

Görzenál Skatepark

Map 7, H6. III, Árpád fejedelem útja ☏250-4800.

Szentendre HÉV to Timár utca. March–Oct Mon–Fri 9am–7pm, Sat & Sun 9am–9pm; Nov–Feb Sat & Sun 9am–6pm.

Space to rollerblade, skateboard and cycle, with ramps and jumps, all to your heart's content.

Margit sziget

Map 2, E4.

A great open space where you can rent **bikes** and four-person **trikes**, or take a trip round the island on the train on wheels that leaves from the strange sculpture at the southern end of the island.

The **Palatinus open-air baths** (p.231), halfway down on the west of the island, have a wave machine and lots of small pools for kids. The low point of the island is the zoo across on the east – a smelly and sorry-looking place. Otherwise the island's scenery is varied, with a rose garden, ruins, and big open spaces for frisbee and ball games, all creating a very pleasant atmosphere. If you go back once the children are in bed you can hear the nightingales sing.

Városliget
Map 4, I1.

This is where you'll find the largest concentration of activities for children. Besides the park itself you have the **zoo** (*Állatkert*; daily: May–Aug 9am–7pm; April & Sept 9am–6pm; Oct & March 9am–5pm; Nov–Feb 9am–4pm). Recent improvements to the zoo have made it a great place to visit; kids can feed the camels and giraffes, tickle the rhinos, stroke the goats, sheep and farm animals and explore the new Palm House. The adventure playground is excellent too. Next door is the **circus** (mid-April–end Aug: Wed, Fri & Sun 3pm & 7pm, Thurs 3pm, Sat 10am, 3pm & 7pm; ☏ 342-8300 for bookings), and beyond that the **Amusement Park** (*Vidám Park*; May–Sept daily 9am–8pm; Oct–April Mon–Fri 10am–6.45pm, Sat & Sun 10am–7.15pm), which is enjoyable in its shabby way – in summer there is a section for younger kids with suitably tame rides (*Kisvidám Park*). Across the road from the circus is the outdoor **Széchenyi Baths** (p.231). For those who prefer to stay above water level, there's rowing in summer and ice-skating in winter on the lake by Hősök tere (Nov–March Mon–Fri 9am–1pm & 4–8pm, Sat & Sun 10am–2pm & 4–8pm depending on the weather). Out of the park's many museums the best for kids is the **Transport Museum** (*Közlekedési Múzeum*; Tues–Sun 10am–6pm), with vehicles of all kinds and a model train set that runs on the hour every hour until 5pm. Across the way, on the first floor of the Petőfi Csarnok, is its **Aviation and Space** display (*Repüléstörténeti és űrhajózási kiállítás*; April–Nov Tues–Fri 10am–5pm, Sat & Sun 10am–6pm).

MUSEUMS

Underground Railway Museum (Földalattivasút Múzeum)

Map 6, E3. Below ground at Deák tér.

Tues–Sun 10am–6pm. 120Ft or one BKV ticket.

The small *Földalattivasút Múzeum* next to the metro station still preserves some of the original track the trains first ran on, as well as the original wooden carriages, decorated with old advertisements.

Palace of Miracles (Csodák palotája)

Map 4, D1. XIII, Váci út 19. Lehel tér (M3).

Jan–mid-April Tues–Fri 9am–5pm, Sat & Sun 10am–6pm; mid-April–Dec Mon–Fri 10am–5pm, Sat & Sun 10am–6pm; 500Ft.

The brainchild of two Hungarian physicists, this interactive playhouse aims to explain scientific principles to 6- to 12-year-olds, using optical illusions, a bed of nails, a simulated low-gravity "moonwalk" and a "miracle bicycle" on a tightrope – though the scarcity of explanations in English may leave you none the wiser.

Szentendre Village Museum

Map 8, A1.

April–Oct Tues–Sun 9am–5pm; 200Ft.

Children's programmes every weekend, a playground and frequent folk-craft and folk-dancing displays in this museum outside Szentendre, north of the city.

Telephone Museum (Telefónia Múzeum)

Map 5, C2. I, Úri utca 49.

Tues–Sun 10am–6pm.

A hands-on museum, which is a rarity in Budapest. You can send faxes and call one another on vintage phones.

The Rail Heritage Museum described on p.134 is also likely to appeal to children.

THEATRE, DANCE AND OTHER ACTIVITIES

Folk dancing

Kids brave enough to try their steps at Hungarian folk dancing can go to a children's *tánchaz*. The same top musicians who play for the adults play for the children too at the **Kalamajka dance house** event (Sat 5–6pm) at the City Cultural House (Map 6, B7; Belvárosi Művelődési Ház at V, Molnár utca 9).

"Kidstown" (Kölyökvár)

Map 4, G7. VII, Almássy tér Leisure Centre, Almássy tér 6 ☎267-8709.
Mid-Oct–April Sun 10am–1pm.
A play centre offering all sorts of activities from face-painting to model-building – plus films, music and drama.

Puppet theatre (Bábszínház)

Map 4, F5. VI, Andrássy út 69 ☎321-5200.
Budapest has a strong tradition in puppetry, but at present has only one puppet theatre (*bábszínház*), which occasionally puts on English-language performances. Morning and matinee performances are for kids, while the evening's occasional masked grotesqueries or renditions of Bartók's *The Wooden Prince* and *The Miraculous Mandarin* are intended for adults. Tickets are available from the puppet theatre itself or the Central Box Office at Andrássy út 15 (☎267-1267).

PUBLIC TRANSPORT

A cheap and reliable form of amusement are the different forms of **public transport** in the city, and children under six travel free. **Trams** are an endless source of fun, the best ride being along the embankment in tram #2. Across the water, the **Siklò** (see p.53) is a great experience, running up from the Lánchíd to the Royal Palace, with the view of Pest suddenly appearing before your eyes. A popular way to spend an afternoon in the Buda Hills is to go on the "**railway circuit**" – the Cogwheel Railway, the Children's Railway and the chairlift (see p.66). In the summer (April–Oct) there's the added thrill of **boat rides** on the Danube – either short tours of the city up to Margit sziget and back, or further afield to Szentendre and on to Esztergom. The only problem with these is that if your child gets bored, you will be trapped on the boat with no escape. Another summertime source of delight are the **steam trains** that run from Nyugati Station up to Vác.

Shopping

Budapest's shopping scene has been transformed in recent years by the mushrooming of international stores such as Benetton, Marks and Spencer and Mexx and the opening of modern shopping malls across the city. The malls have brought in long opening hours and a bright new style that sets the pace for other shops – not that many locals can afford to shop here – prices are high by Hungarian standards. Holding their own, however, against the international brands, numerous, small backstreet shops continue to preserve local crafts and traditions.

Most shops are **open** Monday to Friday 10am–6pm, and Saturday until 1pm, with foodstores generally operating from 8am to 6pm or 7pm. Recently some shops in the centre of the city have been staying open later on Saturdays. Shopping malls on the edge of the city have longer opening hours: 10am–9pm every day of the week. You can usually find a 24-hour *non-stop* shop serving alcohol, cigarettes and some food in the centre of town.

The main **shopping areas** are located to the south of Vörösmarty tér in central Pest, in particular in and around pedestrianized Váci utca and Petőfi Sándor utca, which have the biggest concentration of glamorous and expensive shops. The main streets radiating out from the centre – Bajcsy-Zsilinszky, Andrássy and Rákóczi út – are other major shopping focuses, as are the two ring boulevards, the Great Boulevard (especially from Margit Bridge to Blaha Lujza tér) and the Kiskörút, while some of the old craftsmen and workshops are still operating in the backstreets inside the Nagykörút. Shops in the Várhegy are almost exclusively given over to providing foreign tourists with folksy souvenirs such as embroidered tablecloths, hussar pots and fancy bottles of Tokaji wine.

Falk Miksa utca, running south off Szent István körút, near the Pest end of the Margit híd (Map 4, A3), is known as Budapest's "Street of Antiques", and is where you'll find the biggest collection of **antique stores** and galleries. Kossuth Lajos utca between Ferenciek tere and the *Astoria Hotel* also has a couple of shops. If it's books and prints you want, head for Múzeum körút, where there are several **secondhand bookshops** (*antikvárium*) clustered opposite the Hungarian National Museum. Most shops should be able to advise on what you can export from the country and how to go about it. Several shops organize **auctions**; the best months for these are April, May, September and December – check the monthly free hotel magazine *Where Budapest* (see p.9) for dates. Another great source of antiques are the flea markets listed on p.254, though you'll need to be wary about parting with large sums of money, as stallholders can charge hugely inflated prices.

Budapest also has a set of distinguished **market halls** (*vásárcsarnok*) dating from the late nineteenth century, some of which still function as general markets, while others have been turned into supermarkets, though you can still admire their structure. There are also some outdoor markets (*piac*), which are a more lively proposition, with old folk coming into town to sell their produce. Most of the markets are busy, crowded places, so you should mind your pockets and bags at all times.

SHOPPING

Unless otherwise stated, opening hours of the shops
listed below are Mon–Fri 10am–6pm, Sat 10am–1pm.
Most shops in Budapest accept credit and charge cards.

ANTIQUES AND SECONDHAND BOOKS

BÁV
Map 6, C3, V, Bécsi utca 1–3
(for paintings); Map 6 C5, VI,
Andrássy út 27 (for *objets
d'art*); Map 4, D7, V, Ferenciek
tere 10 (for carpets).
Mon–Fri 10am–6pm, Sat
9am–1pm.
There are eighteen outlets,
including the three above, in
this large chain of assorted
antique shops, which also
holds regular auctions at
Lonyay utca 30–32.

Forgács
Map 6, D3. Kempinski
Corvinus Hotel, V, Erzsébet tér
7–8 ⊕429-3379.
Mon–Fri 1–8pm, Sat 2–7pm.
A good range of old books,
prints and antiques from a
friendly dealer.

Honterus
Map 6, E8. V, Múzeum körút
35 ⊕317-3270.

Mon–Fri 10am–6pm, Sat
10am–2pm.
Engravings, postcards and
secondhand books, opposite
the National Museum.

Központi Antikvárium (Central Antiquarian Bookshop)
Map 6, E7. V, Múzeum körút
17 ⊕317-3781.
Large secondhand bookshop
opposite the Hungarian
National Museum, with
some antiquarian books and
prints too.

Pless & Fox
Map 4, B3. XIII, Szent István
körút 18 ⊕312-1238.
Old jewellery and rare metals,
just down the road from the
Margit híd.

Sóos
Map 6, D2. V, József Attila
utca 22.

Mon–Fri 9am–5pm, Sat 10am–1pm.
An excellent place to pick up secondhand photographic goods at bargain rates, as well as assorted junk.

ART AND PHOTOGRAPHY GALLERIES

Dovin Galéria
Map 6, B5. V, Galamb utca 6 ⊤318-3673.
Tues–Fri noon–6pm, Sat 11am–2pm.
Elegant gallery in central Pest selling contemporary Hungarian art.

Godot Studio
Map 6, F4. VII, Madach Imre út 8 ⊤322-5272.
Contemporary art gallery.

Mai Manó
Map 4, D6. VI, Nagymező utca 20 ⊤302-4398.
Mon–Fri 2–6pm.
On the first floor of the former Arizona Club, now restored as the Photography Museum and selling contemporary and old Hungarian photographs.

Miró
Map 4, E6. VI, Teréz körút 11–13 ⊤322-4041 ext 38.
Mon–Fri 2–6pm.
Displays of contemporary photography.

Várfok Galéria
Map 3, C5. I, Várfok utca 14 ⊤213-5155.
Tues–Sat 11am–6pm.
One of three small galleries just off Moszkva tér. Displays work by the younger generation of Hungarian artists.

BOOKS AND MAPS

Bestsellers
Map 4, B7. V, Október 6 utca 11 ⊤312-1295, ⓦwww.bestsellers .com (ordering is not possible via the website).
Mon–Fri 9am–6.30pm, Sat 10am–6pm, Sun 10am–4pm.
Excellent range of English books, with English and Hungarian literature, travel,

and reference books, and newspapers too. Friendly staff can order books for you.

Cártográfia

Map 4, C5. VI, Bajcsy-Zsilinszky út 37.
Mon–Wed 9am–5pm, Thurs 9am–6.30pm, Fri 9am–3.30pm.
A map shop with a good range, but it's not self-service – you have to ask for the maps you want from the stern staff, which makes browsing difficult.

CEU Bookshop

Map 4, B7. Central European University, Nádor utca 9
℡ 327-3096.
Mon–Fri 9am–6pm, Sat 10am–5pm.
University bookshop with a good range of English academic, business, international relations and reference titles.

Írók Boltja

Map 4, E6. VI, Andrássy út 45.
Mon–Fri 10am–6pm, Sat 10am–1pm (July & Aug closed Sat).
The "Writers' Bookshop" is on the premises of the prewar *Japán* coffee house. There's a

wide range of English-language books at the back, and a good selection of photography, art and architecture books in the main part of the shop. You can drink coffee and read at the tables in the front of the shop.

Király Books

Map 3, E4. II, Fő utca 79
℡ 214-0972.
Mon–Fri 9am–6pm, Sat 10am–5pm.
Run by the same people as Bestsellers across the river, a very good selection of books – in French as well as English – and newspapers.

Libri

Map 6, C5. V, Váci utca 22 and Rákóczi út 12.
Mon–Fri 10am–6.30pm, Sat & Sun 10am–3pm.
There's a good range of English-language books on Hungary straight ahead as you walk into the shop at Váci utca 22. English-language and travel books are upstairs at Rákóczi út 12, where you'll also find a small internet café.

Litea
Map 5, D3. I, Hess András tér 4 (Fortuna Passage).
Daily 10am–6pm.
This well-lit shop has a good stock of English books on Hungary, some CDs and cassettes, and a coffee bar with tables.

Rhythm 'n' Books
Map 6, D8. V, Szerb utca 21–23.
Mon–Fri noon–7pm.

CLOTHES AND SHOES

Agens Cannabis
Map 3, E4. II, Fő utca 73.
Mon–Fri 1–7pm, Sat 10am–1.30pm.
Jackets and other smart clothes all made out of hemp.

Ciankáli
Map 4, D12. IX, Vámház körút 9.
Stylish secondhand clothes are sold in this basement shop at the back of the courtyard.

Cipőszerviz
Map 4, D5. VI, Jókai utca 10.
Mon–Fri 8.30am–5pm.

At the far end of the courtyard as you enter from the street, offering a good selection of new and secondhand English-language books, as well as some CDs and tapes.

Térképkirály
Map 6, E2. V, Sas utca 1.
Mon–Fri 9am–5.30pm.
Range of maps and guidebooks near Deák tér.

Shoe repairs near the Oktogon.

Csángó
Map 6, C4. V, Szervita tér 4.
Signposted in through a courtyard in central Pest. Bags of all shapes in a shop that has been going for sixty years.

Emilia Anda
Map 6, C4. V, Váci utca 16/b, Fortuna Passage.
☎318-7512 & 337-2354.
Classy, well-designed day and evening wear for women, and jewellery including chunky rings and beautiful pendants.

Fleischer Shirts
Map 4, D6. V, Paulay Ede utca 53.
Old-fashioned shirt-maker selling handmade shirts at good prices. On the corner of Nagymező utca, five minutes' walk from the Opera House.

Kaláka
Map 6, C5. V, Haris köz 2.
Women's clothes, shoes and accessories by Hungarian designers.

Manier
Map 6, B7. V, Váci utca 48 (entrance on Nyári Pál utca).
Zany but appealing clothes from young fashion designer Ágnes Németh.

Marácz Kalapbolt
Map 4, F8. VII, Wesselényi utca 41.
Mon–Fri 11am–6pm.
Old-fashioned hat shop with steamers and other old equipment in the back room. Sells beautiful fedoras in black and grey.

Marks & Spencer
Map 6, C3. VI, West End Centre, Váci út 1–3.
Daily 10am–9pm.
The largest M&S outside London, they claim.

Paroka bolt
Map 6, C3. VII, Kazinczy utca 26.
Wig-makers in the heart of the old Jewish quarter, moving to nearby premises: check the sign on the door. Wigs don't come much cheaper between here and Brooklyn.

Vass
Map 6, C5. V, Haris köz 2
℡318-2375.
A traditional shoemaker, just behind Ferenciek tere, producing handmade shoes to order and ready-to-wear.

Zábrák
Map 6, D3. V, Kempinski Hotel Corvinus, Erzsébet tér 7/8
℡329-7979.
Daily 9am–6pm.
Handmade shoes, ready-to-wear and made-to-order, in a hotel boutique near Deák tér.

SHOPPING: CLOTHES AND SHOES

FLEA MARKETS

Ecseri piac

Map 2, H8. XIX, Nagykörösi út, on the southeast edge of the city. Access by bus #54 (red) from the Határ út metro stop on the blue line, or bus #54 (black) from Boráros tér by Petőfi Bridge. Mon–Fri 8am–4pm, Sat 8am–noon.

This flea market has become a well-known spot for tourists – and for ripping them off. Stalls sell everything from bike parts and jackboots to nineteenth-century peasant clothing and hand-carved pipes, with a few genuine antiques in amongst the tat. You'll need to bargain hard.

Petőfi Csarnok

Map 2, F5. XIV, Zichy Mihály utca 14.

Sun 8am–2pm

Sunday flea market in and around the ugly cultural centre in the Városliget. Smaller than Ecseri, and less established, with stallholders laying out their wares every week. Lots of junk but some good bargains too. Small entry fee.

Nowák piac

Map 2, F5. VII, Dózsa Gy. utca 1–3.

The newest of the flea markets, a short walk from Keleti Station up Verseny utca. Excellent bargains and shady characters, although surprisingly for Budapest it is still weak in the snack department.

FOOD AND WINE

Bio ABC

Map 6, E7. V, Múzeum körút 19.
Mon–Fri 10am–7pm, Sat 10am–2pm.
Natural oils, organic fruits, juices, cheeses and snacks, opposite the Hungarian National Museum.

Budapest Wine Society

Map 3, C5. V, Batthyány utca

59 ⓣ 212-2569.

Mon–Fri 10am–8pm, Sat 10am–6pm.

In a basement just up the street from Moszkva tér, offering some of Hungary's best wines from private producers across the country, good advice in English, and free tastings on Saturday afternoons.

Chez Daniel

Map 4, E4. VI, Sziv utca 32 ⓣ 302-4039.

Daily 11.30am–midnight.

The gourmet food shop attached to this top French restaurant offers Hungarian wines, as well as excellent pâtés and other fine foods.

Demijohn

Map 3, E2. II, Margit körút 23. Mon–Fri 11am–7pm, Sat 10am–4pm.

Excellent wines in this outlet for the Hilltop Neszmely vineyard. Has received good marks from wine buffs abroad.

La Boutique des Vins

Map 6, D1. V, József Attila utca 12 ⓣ 117-5919.

Mon–Fri 10am–6pm, Sat 10am–3pm.

Founded by the former *sommelier* of the *Gundel* restaurant, who now has a vineyard of his own. Strongest in wines from Villány and Tokaj.

Lekvárium

Map 4, E9. VII, Dohány utca 39.

Mon–Fri 10am–6pm.

Hungarians have a strong tradition of pickling and preserving, with most families laying up jars of plum and apricot jam (*lekvár*), pickled cucumbers and peppers for the winter. This shop also sells some more interesting varieties, like quince compote and tobacco flower honey.

Rothschild

Map 6, G4. VII, Dob utca 12. Mon–Thurs 8.30am–6pm, Fri 8.30am–2pm.

On the edge of the Jewish quarter, a couple of minutes' walk from the Dohány utca synagogue, this is one of the few shops in Budapest selling kosher Hungarian and imported wines and foods.

SHOPPING: FOOD AND WINE

GIFTS, CRAFTS AND CHINA

Haas & Czjzek
Map 4, C6. VI, Bajcsy-Zsilinszky út 23 ☎311-4094.
Full selection of Hungarian porcelain, including Hollóháza, Alföld and Zsolnay, and some glassware. The shop dates back to 1792, as the small display at the back of the shop documents.

Hephaistos
Map 6, B8. V, Molnár utca 27.
Mon–Fri 11am–6pm, Sat 10am–2pm.
Sells all kinds of wrought-iron objects from candlesticks to bookshelves. The latter might present transport difficulties, but the smaller items make great gifts. All goods are made in their Szentendre foundry.

Herend
Map 6, D2. V, József nádor tér 11 ☎317-2622.
Very fancy – some would say twee – and expensive porcelain from the Herend factory in western Hungary, collected by the likes of Queen Victoria.

Holló Folk Art Gallery
Map 6, E5. V, Vitkovics Mihály utca 10 ☎317-8103.
This beautiful early nineteenth-century shop near the Astoria is a very pleasant place to browse in, and you can also buy good presents, such as wooden furniture, boxes, eggs and candlesticks all hand-painted with bird, tulip and heart folk motifs, and intricately iced gingerbread figures.

Zsolnay
Map 6, C5. V, Kigyó utca 4 and Ferenciek tere 11.
Mon–Fri 10am–6pm, Sat 10am–1pm.
Art Nouveau-style porcelain that is less kitsch than some other Hungarian porcelains. Made at the factory in Pécs in southern Hungary that made its name designing the tiles on buildings such as the Applied Arts Museum.

HOUSEHOLD GOODS

Brush shop
Map 6, F5. VII, Dob utca 3.
Every kind of brush you can think off in this very traditional artisan's shop.

Kátay
Map 4, D5. VI, Teréz körút 28.
Amidst the fantastic range of plates, bowls, saucepans and electrical goods you can find excellent presents such as a wooden spoon stand and wooden bowls.

MALLS

Mammut and Mammut II
Map 3, C4. II, Széna tér.
Recently doubled in size with the opening of Mammut II. Amidst the plethora of glam boutiques are some useful shops: in the basement of the original Mammut you have a smoothie bar, a seconds shop selling brands such as Mexx and Martinique and a foreign newspaper stall. There is internet access on the first floor at Matávpont, and at the back is an excellent market.

West End City Centre
Map 4, C3. VI, Váci út 1–3, next to Nyugati Station (M3).
Past the grand Niagara Falls, an indoor waterfall cascading down by the southern entrance, you'll find brands such as Mango, Mexx and Springfield, as well as M&S.

Duna Plaza
Map 2, F3. XIII, Váci út 178. Gyöngyös utca (M3).
Large mall further out of the centre with an ice rink and a multi-screen cinema. Local fashion outlets include Kaláka Design Studio and Art'z Modell.

MARKETS AND MARKET HALLS

Fény utca
Map 3, B4. XII, at the back of the Mammut mall, by Moszkva tér.
Mon–Fri 6am–4pm, Sat 6am–1pm.
Popular market that has survived a transfer to a modern setting. Excellent cheese shop on the top floor, where you'll also find what is perhaps the best *lángos* in town – fried dough eaten with garlic, sour cream, cheese or all three together.

Hold utca
Map 4, B5. V, Hold utca 13.
Mon–Fri 6am–5pm, Sat 6am–1pm.
Right behind the American Embassy, this is one of the fine nineteenth-century market halls and still has some smaller stalls.

István tér
Map 2, F3. IV, István tér.
Mon–Fri 7am–5pm, Sat 7am–1pm.
Large market in the square behind the town hall in the northern suburb of Újpest, at the northern end of the blue metro line (M3). It attracts a large number of farmers from the countryside, making it one of the most atmospheric markets in the city.

Klauzál tér
Map 4, E8. VII, Klauzál tér.
Mon–Fri 6am–5pm, Sat 6am–1pm.
In the heart of the old Jewish quarter. A supermarket has squeezed the fruit and veg stands out into the entrance passage.

Lehel tér
Map 4, D1. XIII, Lehel tér (M3).
Mon–Fri 6am–5pm, Sat 6am–1pm, Sun 6am–noon.
Large, popular market temporarily housed in the streets north of the square and set to move into a newly built market hall.

Main Market Hall
Map 6, B9. IX, Vámház körút 2.
Mon 6am–4pm, Tues–Fri

6am–6pm, Sat 6am–2pm.
By the Szabadság híd at the bottom end of Váci utca, the *Nagycsarnok* is the largest and finest market hall of them all, as well as being the most expensive. It also has good stalls upstairs, selling knives and wood craft, amidst the touristy embroideries and tat.

PHOTOGRAPHY

Fotólabor
Map 4, F10. VIII, Gyulai Pál utca 14.
Mon–Fri 8am–6pm.
Top-quality black and white prints done very cheaply, and photos developed and enlarged.

Fotolux
Map 6, E4. VII, Károly körút 21.
Mon–Fri 9am–9pm, Sat 9am–7pm.
Good-quality photographic developing and printing, and professional films.

RECORDS AND CDS

Amadeus
Map 6. B2. V, Szende Pál utca 1.
Daily 9am–9pm.
Good store for classical and jazz music, and also stocks bargain Hungaroton CDs. Entrance from the Danube promenade. No credit cards.

CD Bar
Map 4, F11. VIII, Krúdy Gyula utca 6 ☎338-4281.
Mon–Fri 10am–8pm, Sat 10am–4pm.
Classical and jazz records in this basement shop in an increasingly fashionable backstreet a couple of streets behind the Hungarian National Museum.

Fonó
Map 2, E7. XI, Sztregova utca 3 ☎206-5300.
Sun–Fri 10am–11pm, Sat 6–11pm.
It's a twenty-minute tram

ride from Deák tér on #47 to get to the shop in the bar of this folk club, but it's worth it for the range of jazz, ethno-jazz blues and world music, and, above all, Hungarian folk music CDs. Stays open into the evening during concerts.

Kodály Zoltán Zeneműbolt
Map 6, E7. V, Múzeum körút 17 & 21.
Scores and secondhand records, tapes and CDs, opposite the Hungarian National Museum.

Rózsavölgyi Zeneműbolt
Map 6, C4. V, Szervita tér 5.
Mon–Fri 9.30am–7pm, Wed 10am–7pm, Sat 10am–5pm.
Established record shop with a knowledgeable staff, near Vörösmarty tér. Classical music on the ground floor, rock and folk downstairs. Good for sheet music as well.

TOYS

Fakopáncs
Map 4, F12. VIII, Baross utca 50 and József körút 50 ☎337-0992.
Mon–Fri 9am–7pm, Sat 9am–4pm, Sun 9am–2pm.
A massive array of wooden puzzles and toys is crammed into the two "Woodpecker" shops, both at the junction of Baross utca and the Nagykörút.

Gondolkodó Logikai Játékok
Map 4, D7. VII, Király utca 25.
Mon–Fri 10am–6pm, Sat 10am–1pm.
"Thinking Logical Games" is the wordy name of the shop, so naturally it sells puzzles, Rubik's cubes, chess sets, logic games and other toys to make you think. You can also get the Hungarian version of Monopoly.

Játékszerek anno
Map 4, D4. VI, Teréz körút 54.
Mon–Fri 10am–6pm, Sat 9am–1pm.
Beautifully made

reproductions of toys and games from the turn of the last century, including wooden tops, kaleidoscopes, and a spectacular wind-up duck on a bicycle.

Puppet Store
Map 6, C5. V, Párizsi utca 3.

Mon–Fri 10am–6pm, Sat 10am–1pm.

A handful of dragons and a nestful of birds are just two of the hand puppets available in this outlet hidden away in the courtyard. The shop assistants often go onto the street to demonstrate their "pets".

Directory

Airlines Aeroflot, V, Váci utca 4 ☏318-5955; Air France, V, Kristóf tér 6 ☏318-0411; Alitalia, V, Bajcsy-Zsilinszky út 12 ☏483-2170; British Airways, V, East-West Business Centre, VIII, Rákóczi út 1–3 ☏411-5555; CSA, V, Vörösmarty tér 2 ☏318-3175; KLM, VIII, Rákóczi út 1–3 ☏373-7737; Lufthansa, V, Váci utca 19–21 ☏266-4511; Malév, V, Dorottya utca 2 ☏235-3565; SAS, V, Bajcsy-Zsilinszky út 12 ☏266-2633.

Airport information Terminal 2A: ☏296-7000 for departures, ☏296 8000 for arrivals. Terminal 2B: ☏296-5053 for departures, ☏296-5882 for arrivals.

Banks and exchanges Cash dispensers can be found across the city. The best places for changing money are the larger banks: the Magyar Külkereskedelmí Bank at Türr István utca 9, by the top of Váci utca, or the small Gönc és vidéke Bank at Rákóczi út 5 offer the best rates, while the exchange offices around Vörösmarty tér have the worst ones. There is a 24-hour exchange service at Tribus, Apáczai Csere János utca 1. You can transfer money from abroad through the Magyar Külkereskedelmí Bank, V, Szent István tér 11; through Interchange, the regional agents for Western Union, which have branches at the main stations and in the city centre ☏266-4995; and through the American Express Moneygram service (minimum $100), V, Deák utca 10 ☏235-4330. Money transfers allegedly take only a few minutes. The

Magyar Külkereskedelmi Bank also has safe-deposit boxes for storing valuables.

Bike rentals and repairs Try Charles Rent-a-Bike at *Charles Apartments*, XI, Hegyalja út 23 Ⓣ202-3414; and Nella Bikes off Bajcsy-Zsilinszky út at V, Kálmán Imre utca 23 Ⓣ331-3184. The Bike Store at VI, Nagymezo utca 43 Ⓣ312-5073, and Kerékvár at I, Hunyadi János utca 4, at the Buda end of the Lánchíd Ⓣ214-8814, both sell and repair bikes.

British Council VI, Benczúr utca 26 Ⓣ478-4700, Ⓕ342-5728, Ⓦwww.britishcouncil.hu. Library, newspapers and a noticeboard. Mon–Thurs 11am–6pm, Fri 11am–5pm; closed Aug.

Camping and Caravanning club VIII, Baross utca 21 Ⓣ317-1711 (Mon–Fri 10am–6pm). Can supply canoeing maps of the Danube, advise on equipment and arrange reductions for FICC members.

Car breakdown The Magyar Autóklub runs a 24-hour breakdown assistance Ⓣ188.

Car rental Avis at V, Szervita tér 8 (by the Jet petrol station

under the multistorey car park) Ⓣ381-4685, Ⓕ318-4859, Ⓦwww.avis.hu; Budget at the *Hotel Mercure Buda*, I, Krisztina körút 41–43 Ⓣ & Ⓕ214-0420, Ⓦwww.budget.hu; Europcar at Ülloi út 62 Ⓣ477-1080; Hertz at V, Aranykéz utca 4–8 Ⓣ296-0999, Ⓕ296-0998, Ⓦwww.hertz.hu. All these companies also have offices at the airport.

Couriers International) DHL, VIII, Rákóczi út 1-3 Ⓣ266-2640; Fedex, IX, Nádasdy utca 2–4 Ⓣ216-3606; UPS, X, Kozma utca 4 Ⓣ0640-262-000, Ⓕ432-2210.

Electric power 220 volts. Round two-pin plugs are used. Bring an adaptor.

Embassies Australia, XII, Királyhágó tér 8–9 Ⓣ457-9777; Austria, VI, Benczúr utca 16 Ⓣ351-6700; Bulgaria, VI, Andrássy út 115 Ⓣ322-0824; Canada, XII, Budakeszi út 32 Ⓣ392-3360; Czech Republic, VI, Rózsa utca 6 Ⓣ351-0539; Denmark, XII, Határor út 37 Ⓣ355-7320; Germany, XIV, Stefánia út 101–3 Ⓣ467-3500; Ireland, V, Szabadság tér 7, Bank Center, 7th floor Ⓣ302-

9600; Israel, II, Fullánk utca 8 ⊤200-0781; Netherlands, II Füge utca 5–7 ⊤326-5301; New Zealand, VI, Teréz körút 38, 4th floor ⊤331-4908 (by appointment only); Norway, I, Ostrom utca 13 ⊤212-9400; Romania, XIV, Thököly út 72 ⊤352-0271; Russian Federation, Bajza utca 35 ⊤312-6608; Slovakia, XIV, Stefánia út 22 ⊤460-9010; Slovenia, II Cseppko utca 68 ⊤438-5600; Sweden, XIV, Ajtósi sor 27A ⊤460-6020; UK, V, Harmincad utca 6 ⊤266-2888; USA, V, Szabadság tér 12 ⊤475-4400.

Emergencies Ambulance ⊤104; Police ⊤107; Fire service ⊤105.

Hospitals and dentistry
Embassies can recommend private, foreign-language-speaking doctors and dentists. There are 24-hour casualty departments at V, Hold utca 19, behind the US embassy ⊤311-6816, and at II, Ganz utca 13–15 ⊤202-1370. The Országos Baleseti Intézet VIII, Fiumei út 17 ⊤333-7599, specializes in broken limbs and accidents; Profident, VII, Károly

körut 1, is a round-the-clock dentist where they speak English. A private clinic with English-speaking personnel is the IMS (International Medical Services) at XIII, Váci út 202 ⊤329-8423 (Mon–Fri 7.30am–7pm) and at III, Vihar utca 29 ⊤388-8257 (24-hour).

International buses and trains
International train tickets should be purchased 24–36 hours in advance, at the stations or the MÁV booking office, VI, Andrássy út 35 (Mon–Fri 9am–5pm, until 6pm April–Sept; ⊤461-5500, ⓦwww.mav.hu). Bookings are required on all international train routes. Although some international trains also stop at Kobánya-Kispest and Zugló stations, you cannot buy international tickets at these smaller stations, only at the main termini. The Vienna-bound *Wiener Waltzer* often runs late, so reserve sleepers on from Austria in Budapest. Also bring drinks, as the buffet staff overcharge shamelessly. Tickets for international buses must be purchased at the bus station in hard currency, and should be booked 24 hours in advance.

The majority of international bus services currently depart from the Erzsébet tér bus station (℡485-2100), though this bus station will eventually move elsewhere; see p.6 for more information.

Internet access Internet cafés are not difficult to find. Some have English keyboards – indicated below. (The main difference on Hungarian keyboards is that the y and z are swapped round and you have an assortment of accented vowels at the right-hand end of the keyboard in place of inverted commas and colons.) One of the biggest set-ups is *Ami*, V, Váci utca 40 (daily 9am–2am; 700Ft an hour; some English keyboards), with fifty terminals, plus games available. Other options include *Click*, VI, Jókai tér 3 (24hr; twenty terminals; 700Ft an hour, or 500Ft 2–10am); *Enternet* at V, Deák Ferenc u. 15 on the corner of Vörösmarty tér (daily 10am–9pm; nine stand-up terminals – 15min only which means a fast-moving queue, and it's free, so ideal for just checking emails); *Libri*

Könyvpalota, VII, Rákóczi út 12, upstairs in the bookshop (Mon–Fri 10am–7.30pm, Sat 10am–3pm; ten terminals; 300Ft an hour); and *Vista Visitor Center*, VI, Paulay Ede utca 7 (Mon–Fri 8am–8pm, Sat & Sun 10am–6pm; eight terminals, some English keyboards; 600Ft an hour).

Laundry Házimosoda, V, Galamb utca 9 ℡200-5305 (Mon–Fri 8am–7.30pm, Sat 9am–1pm), offers laundry and dry cleaning; Irisz Szalon, V, Városház utca 3–5 (Mon–Fri 7am–7pm, Sat 7am–1pm), is one of the few self-service launderettes left in the city.

Lost property For items left on public transport go to the office at VII, Akácfa utca 18 ℡267-5299 (Mon, Tues & Thurs 7.30am–3pm, Wed 7.30am–7pm, Fri 7.30am–2pm). Lost or stolen passports should be reported to the police station in the district where they were lost. Any found are handed to the relevant embassy.

Names Surnames precede forenames in Hungary, to the confusion of foreigners. In this book, the names of historical personages are rendered in the Western fashion, for instance, Lajos Kossuth rather than Kossuth Lajos (Hungarian-style), except when referring to the names of buildings, streets, etc.

Newspapers British papers (in their international editions) and the *International Herald Tribune* are on sale in many places in the centre of town, including stalls on Vörösmarty tér and bookshops such as Bestsellers (see p.250).

Pharmacies Details of each district's 24-hour pharmacy are posted in every pharmacy's window. Central 24-hour pharmacies include those at Alkotás utca 2, opposite Déli station, and at Teréz körút 41, near Oktogon. For herbal remedies try Herbária, VIII, Rákóczi út 49, and V, Bajcsy-Zsilinszky út 58.

Photo booths Passport-sized photos are available from automatic booths in Deák tér, Kálvin tér, Nyugati tér and Moszkva tér metro stations (400Ft for four colour photos); Sooter's at V, Deák Ferenc. utca 22 (399Ft for four colour shots);

and the third floor of the Corvin department store on Blaha Lujza tér.

Photocopying Copy General, XI, Karinthy Frigyes utca 4–6 (open 24hr).

Post Main office/poste restante at V, Petofi Sándor utca 13 (Mon–Fri 8am–8pm & Sat 8am–2pm), and a late-night post office by Keleti Station at VII, Baross tér 11/c (daily 7am–9pm).

Religious services in English Anglican: Sun 11am – ring the rectory at ☏0623/452-023 for details of where the service is being held; Baptist: Sun 10.30am, International Baptist Church, II, Törökvész út 48–54 (Móricz Zsigmond Gimnázium) ☏1/319-8525; Roman Catholic: Sat 5pm, Pesti Jézus Szíve Templom, VIII, Mária utca 25 ☏318-3479.

Taxis Citytaxi has an English-speaking service ☏211-1111, but other reliable companies include: Volántaxi ☏466-6666; Fotaxi ☏222-2222; Buda-taxi ☏233-3333; and Tele-5-taxi ☏355-5555.

Telephones International calls can be made from any phone booth on the street or from the Telephone and Telegram Bureau, V, Petofi utca 17–19 (Mon–Fri 8am–8pm, Sat 10am–4pm). The international operator can be reached on ☎199, though it can be a long wait to get the number you want.

Ticket offices (*jegyiroda*) Central Box Office at VI, Andrássy út 15 (*Központi Jegyiroda*; Mon–Fri 9am–6pm; ☎267-9737); TicketExpress, VI, Andrássy út 18 (Mon–Fri 9.30am–6.30pm, Sat 9am–1pm; ☎312-0000, ⓦwww.ticketexpress.hu); Filharmónia at V, Mérleg utca 10 (Mon–Fri 10am–6pm; ☎318-0281); Music Mix at V, Váci utca 33 and in the Mammut Shopping Centre (☎266-7070,

ⓦwww.musicmix.hu; Publika at VII, Károly körút 9 ☎322-2010; and the Vigadó Jegyiroda at V, Vörösmarty tér 1 (Mon–Fri 9am–7pm, Sat & Sun 10am–3pm; ☎327-4322). The Opera House has its own box office (Mon–Sat 11am–5pm, Sun 4–7pm) for events there and in the Erkel Theatre.

Time Hungary is one hour ahead of GMT, six hours ahead of Eastern Standard Time and nine ahead of Pacific Standard Time in North America. A word of caution: Hungarians express time in a way that might confuse the anglophone traveller. For example, 10.30am is expressed as "half eleven" (written 1/2 11 or f11), 10.45am is "three-quarter eleven" (3/4 11 or h11), and 10.15am is "a quarter of eleven" (1/4 11 or n11)

CONTEXTS

History

A lthough Budapest has only formally existed since 1873, when the twin cities of Buda and Pest were united in a single municipality together with the smaller Óbuda, the locality has been settled since **prehistory**. *Homo sapiens* appeared here around 8000 BC, and a succession of peoples overran the region during the first Age of Migrations, the most important of whom were the Celtic Eravisci who settled on Gellért-hegy in about 400 BC.

In 35 BC the Danube Basin was conquered by the **Romans** and subsequently incorporated within their empire as the province of Pannonia, whose northern half was governed from the town of **Aquincum** on the west bank of the Danube. Ruins of a camp, villas, baths and an amphitheatre can still be seen today in Óbuda and Római-Fürdő. Roman rule lasted until 430 AD, when Pannonia was ceded to **Attila the Hun**. Attila's planned assault on Rome was averted by his death on his wedding night, and thereafter Pannonia was carved up by Germanic tribes until they were ousted by the Turkic-speaking Avars, who were in turn assailed by the Bulgars, another warlike race from the Eurasian steppes.

The coming of the Magyars

The most significant of the invaders from the east were the **Magyars**, who stamped their language and identity on Hungary. Their original homeland was between the Volga and the Urals, where today two Siberian peoples still speak languages that are the closest linguistic relatives to Hungarian; along with Finnish, Turkish and Mongolian, these languages make up the Altaic family. Many of these Magyars migrated south, where they eventually became vassals of the Khazar empire and mingled with the Bulgars as both peoples moved westwards to escape the marauding Petchenegs.

In 895 or 896 AD, seven Magyar tribes led by Árpád entered the Carpathian Basin and spread out across the plain, in what Hungarians call the "**landtaking**" (*hon-foglalàs*). They settled here, though they remained raiders for the next seventy years, striking terror as far afield as France (where people thought them to be Huns), until a series of defeats persuaded them to settle for assimilating their gains. According to the medieval chronicler, known as Anonymous, the clan of Árpád settled on Csepel sziget, and it was Árpád's brother, Buda, who purportedly gave his name to the west bank of the new settlement.

The Árpád dynasty

Civilization developed gradually after Árpád's great-grandson **Prince Géza** established links with Bavaria and invited Catholic missionaries to Hungary. His son **Stephen** took the decisive step of applying to Pope Sylvester for recognition, and on Christmas Day in the year 1000 AD was crowned as a Christian king. With the help of Bishop Gellért, he then set about converting his pagan subjects. Stephen was subsequently credited with the **foundation of**

Hungary and canonized after his death in 1038. His mummified hand and the crown of St Stephen have since been revered as both holy and national relics.

Despite succession struggles after Stephen's death, the absence of external threats during the eleventh and twelfth centuries enabled the **development of Buda and Pest** to begin in earnest, largely thanks to French, Walloon and German settlers who worked and traded here under royal protection. However, the growth in royal power caused tribal leaders to rebel in 1222 AD, and Andrew II was forced to recognize the noble status and rights of the **natio** – landed freemen exempt from taxation – in the Golden Bull, a kind of Hungarian Magna Carta.

Andrew's son **Béla IV** tried to restore royal authority, but the **Mongol invasion** of 1241 devastated the country and left even the royal palace of Esztergom in ruins. Only the timely death of Genghis Khan spared Hungary from further ravages. Mindful of a return visit, Béla selected **Várhegy** as a more defensible seat and encouraged foreign artisans to rebuild Buda, which German colonists called *Ofen* after its numerous limekilns (the name Pest, which is of Slav origin, also means "oven").

Renaissance and decline

After the Árpád dynasty expired in 1301, foreign powers advanced their own claims to the throne and for a while there were three competing kings, all duly crowned. Eventually **Charles Robert** of the French Angevin (or Anjou) dynasty triumphed. Peacetime gave him the opportunity to develop the gold mines of Transylvania and northern Hungary – the richest in Europe – and Charles bequeathed a robust exchequer to his son **Louis the Great**, whose reign saw the population of Hungary rise to three million, and the crown territories expanded to include much of what are now Croatia and Poland. The oldest extant strata of the Buda Palace on Várhegy date from this time.

After Louis's demise, the throne was claimed by **Sigismund of Luxembourg**, Prince of Bohemia, whom the nobility despised as the "Czech swine". His failure to check the advance of the Turks through the Balkans was only redeemed by the Transylvanian warlord **János Hunyadi**, whose lifting of the siege of Belgrade caused rejoicing throughout Christendom. Vajdahunyad Castle in the Városliget is a romantic nineteenth-century replica of Hunyadi's ancestral seat in Transylvania.

Hunyadi's nephew, **Mátyás Corvinus**, is remembered as the **Renaissance king**, who, together with his second wife Beatrice of Naples, enticed humanists and artists from Italy to their court. Mátyás was an enlightened despot, renowned for his fairness, but when he died in 1490 leaving no legitimate heir the nobles took control, choosing a pliable successor and exploiting the peasantry. However, in 1514 the peasants, led by **György Dósza**, rebelled against the oppression. The savage repression of this **revolt** (over 70,000 peasants were killed and Dózsa was roasted alive) and subsequent laws imposing "perpetual serfdom" alienated the mass of the population – a situation hardly improved by the coronation of the 9-year-old **Louis II**, who was barely 16 when he had to face the full might of the Turks under Sultan Süleyman "the Magnificent".

The Turkish conquest: Hungary divided

The battle of **Mohács** in 1526 was a shattering defeat for the Hungarians. After sacking Buda, the Turks withdrew to muster forces for their real objective, Vienna. To forestall this, Ferdinand of Habsburg proclaimed himself king of

Hungary and occupied western Hungary, while in Buda the nobles put János Zápolyai on the throne. Following Zápolyai's death in 1541, Ferdinand claimed full sovereignty, but the Sultan occupied Buda and central Hungary and made Zápolyai's son ruler of Transylvania, which henceforth became a semi-autonomous principality – a **tripartite division** formally recognized in 1568. Despite various truces, warfare became a fact of life for the next 150 years, and national independence was not to be recovered for centuries afterwards.

Turkish-occupied Hungary was ruled by a Pasha in Buda, with much of the land either deeded to the Sultan's soldiers and officials, or run directly as a state fief. The towns, however, enjoyed some rights and were encouraged to trade, and the Turks were largely indifferent to the sectarian bigotry practised in Habsburg-ruled Hungary. The Habsburg **liberation of Buda** in 1686 was actually a disaster for its inhabitants, as the victors massacred Jews, pillaged at will and reduced Buda and Pest to rubble. The city's Turkish baths and the tomb of Gül Baba were almost the only surviving buildings.

Habsburg rule

Habsburg rule was a bitter pill, which the Hungarians attempted to reject in the **War of Independence** of 1703–11, led by **Ferenc Rákóczi II**. Though it was unsuccessful, the Habsburgs began to soften their autocracy with paternalism as a result. The revival of towns and villages during this time owed much to settlers from all over the empire, hence the Serb and Greek churches that remain in Pest and Szentendre. Yet while the aristocracy commissioned over two hundred palaces, and Baroque town centres and orchestras flourished, the masses remained all but serfs, mired in isolated villages.

Such contradictions impelled the **Reform movement** led by Count **István Széchenyi**. His vision of progress was embodied in the construction of the **Lánchíd** (Chain Bridge) between Buda and Pest, which proved an enormous spur to the development of the two districts. The National Museum, the Academy of Sciences and many other institutions were founded at this time, while the coffee houses of Pest became a hotbed of radical politics.

When the empire was shaken by revolutions which broke out across Europe in **March 1848**, local radicals seized the moment. **Lajos Kossuth** dominated parliament, while **Sándor Petőfi** mobilized crowds on the streets of Pest. A second war of independence followed, which again ended in defeat and Habsburg repression, epitomized by the execution of Prime Minister Batthyàny in 1849, and the Citadella atop Gellért-hegy, built to intimidate citizens with its guns.

Budapest's Belle Époque

Following the historic Compromise of 1867, which established the **Dual Monarchy** of Austria-Hungary, Buda and Pest underwent rapid **expansion** and formally merged. Pest was extensively remodelled, acquiring the Nagykörút (Great Boulevard) and Andrássy út, a grand approach to the Városliget, where Hungary's **millennial anniversary celebrations** were staged in 1896. New suburbs were created to house the burgeoning population, which was by now predominantly Magyar, though there were still large German and Jewish communities. Both elegance and squalor abounded, café society reached its apogee, and Budapest experienced a **cultural efflorescence** in the early years of the twentieth century to rival that of Vienna. Today, the most tangible reminders are the remarkable buildings by Ödön Lechner, Béla Lajtha and other masters of Art Nouveau and National Romanticism – the styles that characterized the era.

The Horthy years

World War I spelt disaster for Hungary; of the 3.8 million men mobilized, 661,000 were killed, 743,000 injured, and 734,000 taken as POWs. With the collapse of the Dual Monarchy, the liberal Count Károlyi was rapidly superseded by a revolutionary **Republic of Councils** that terrified the landowning classes. The Republic collapsed in 1919 after the Romanian army routed it on the battlefield and occupied Budapest, whereupon the status quo ante was restored by **Admiral Horthy**, self-appointed regent for Karl IV, who had been exiled by the Western allies ("the Admiral without a fleet, for the king without a kingdom"). His regency was characterized by gala balls and hunger marches, revanchism and anti-Semitism. Yet Horthy was a moderate compared to the **Arrow Cross** Fascists waiting in the wings, whose power grew as **World War II** raged.

Anticipating Horthy's defection from the Axis in October 1944, Nazi Germany staged a coup, installing an Arrow Cross government, which enabled them to begin the massacre of the **Jews** of Budapest. It was only thanks to the valiant efforts of foreign diplomats like Wallenberg and Lutz that half of them survived, when ninety percent of Hungary's provincial Jews perished. In the same year, the five-month-long **siege of Budapest** was a time of terrible hardships for the city's inhabitants, during which the Danube bridges were blown up and Várhegy reduced to rubble, as the Red Army battered the *Wehrmacht* into submission.

The Communist takeover and the 1956 Uprising

As Budapesters struggled to rebuild their lives after the war, the Soviet-backed **Communists** took control by "salami tactics" – stealthily reducing the power of other forces in society, and using the threat of the Red Army and the ÁVO secret police, who took over the former Arrow Cross torture chambers on Andrássy út. By 1948, their hold on Hungary was total, symbolized by the red stars that replaced the crown of St Stephen everywhere, and a huge statue of Stalin beside the Városliget, where citizens were obliged to parade before Hungary's "Little Stalin", **Mátyás Rákosi**.

As elsewhere in Eastern Europe, the Communist Party was racked by power struggles, and after the death of Stalin in 1953 Rákosi was replaced by **Imre Nagy**. Nagy's "New Course" allowed Hungarians an easier life before Rákosi struck back by expelling him from the Party for "deviationism". However, the nation had taken heart from the respite and intellectuals held increasingly outspoken public debates during the summer of 1956. The mood came to a head in October, when 200,000 people attended the funeral of László Rajk, a victim of the show trials in 1949, in Kerepesi Cemetery, and Budapest's students decided to march to the General Bem statue near the Margit híd.

On October 23, demonstrators chanting anti-Rákosi slogans crossed the Danube to mass outside Parliament. As dusk fell, students demanding access to the Radio Building were fired upon by the ÁVO, and a spontaneous **Uprising** began that rapidly took hold throughout Budapest and spread across Hungary. The newly restored Nagy found himself in a maelstrom, as popular demands were irreconcilable with realpolitik. It was Hungary's misfortune that the UN was preoccupied with the Suez Crisis when the

Soviets reinvaded and crushed the Uprising, causing 200,000 Hungarians to flee abroad. Of those who didn't, 400 were sentenced to death and 30,000 imprisoned or deported.

"Goulash socialism" and the end of Communism

After Soviet power had been bloodily restored, **János Kádár** gradually normalized conditions, embarking on cautious reforms, nicknamed "**goulash socialism**", that made Hungary the envy of its Warsaw Pact neighbours and the West's favourite Communist state in the late 1970s. Though everyone knew the limits of the "Hungarian condition", there was enough freedom and consumer goods to keep the majority content. During the 1980s, however, it became apparent that the attempt to reconcile a command economy and one-party rule with market forces was unsustainable. Dissidents tested the limits of criticism, and even within the Party there were those who realized that changes were needed. Happily, this coincided with the advent of Gorbachev, which made it much easier for the reform Communists to shunt Kádár aside in 1988.

The **end of Communism** was heralded by two events the following summer: the ceremonial reburial of Nagy, and the dismantling of the barbed wire along the border with Austria, which enabled thousands of East Germans to escape while "on holiday". In October 1989, the government announced the legalization of other parties as a prelude to free elections, and the People's Republic was renamed the Republic of Hungary in a ceremony broadcast live on national television. Two weeks later this watershed was eclipsed by the fall of the Berlin Wall, closely followed by the Velvet Revolution in Czechoslovakia and the overthrow of Ceauşescu in Romania.

Budapest today: the post-Communist era

After such events, Hungary's first **free elections** in the spring of 1990 seemed an anticlimax, despite resulting in a rejection of the Socialists (reform Communists), and a centre-right coalition dominated by the **Hungarian Democratic Forum (MDF)** under Premier **József Antall**. The MDF aimed to restore the traditions and hierarchies of prewar Hungary. However, not everyone wanted the Catholic Church to regain its former power, and the MDF's desire to restore the Hungarian nation to its former position sounded to Hungary's neighbours like a revanchist claim on the lost lands of Trianon.

After Antall's death in 1993, his successor was unable to turn the economy around, and the 1994 elections saw the **Socialists return to power**, assisted by sympathetic media. To guard against accusations of abusing power like their predecessors, they included the **Free Democrats (SzDSz)** in government and reassured Hungary's creditors with austerity measures that disillusioned voters who had hoped that the Socialists would reverse the growing inequalities in society. The emergence of a brash new entrepreneurial class and consumer culture, rising crime, unemployment and homelessness were deeply unsettling to many, especially the older generation – yet there seemed no alternative to the onward march of capitalism.

Widespread corruption among the Socialists led to their defeat in the **1998 election**, which was narrowly won by the **Fidesz-Hungarian Civic Party** of **Viktor Orbán**. Like Britain's Tony Blair, whose style of leadership he emulates, Orbán managed to reposition his party to the right by talking about the need to revive national culture and using the buzzword *polgári* (meaning "civic", but redolent of bourgeois middle-class values) to appeal to a broad constituency.

More than a decade after the historic "change of systems" (*rendszervàltas*), Hungary settled down as a capitalist democracy, ready to **join the EU** in 2002 – a move that most Hungarians support, believing that they will benefit from being under Europe's protective mantle. However, many are uneasy about the erosion of their national identity by global capitalism and multiculturalism, and outraged by the EU's refusal to subsidize agriculture in the new member states, or to allow free movement of labour for another seven years. And some regretted their earlier enthusiasm for joining **NATO** after US forces based in Hungary bombed Serbia during the Kosovo conflict.

There is also tension between Orbán's government and the Mayor of Budapest, **Gábor Demszky**, who escaped the fate of his party SzDSz by being re-elected for a third term in 1998. In an effort to undermine Demszky's position, Orbán halted the building of the National Theatre, whose foundations had already been laid at vast expense, and cancelled the city's planned fourth metro line. Besides personal animosity (allegedly dating back to their student days at ELTE), the feud reflects an older conflict between Budapest and the provinces, where the capital has long been viewed as too alien to true Hungarian values – a constituency that Orbán has blatantly tried to monopolise. In spring 2002, Orbán paid for his arrogant style when he was pushed out of office in the general election. Fidesz's high-profile, nationalistic campaign won votes from the right, but perhaps it was too successful: the collapse of the other right-wing parties left Fidesz without a potential coalition partner. This allowed the Socialists, who won a couple of seats less, to form a coalition again with the Free Democrats. The Socialist leader, the moderate Péter Medgyessy, may take a more soothing line to heal the very deep divisions that were left by a bitter election campaign. Meanwhile the quiet but competent Demszky has a very good chance of re-election in autumn 2002 after the left's strong showing in the capital.

Books

There is quite a range of books on Budapest available in the city, particularly books on architecture and translations of Hungarian literature. The Hungarian publisher Corvina publishes a number of books covering Hungary's folk traditions and artistic treasures, mostly translated into English or German, which can be bought fairly cheaply in Budapest.

Publishers are detailed below in the form of British publisher/American publisher, where both exist. Where books are published in one country only, UK or US follows the publisher's name. Out-of-print books are designated o/p.

See p.250 for details of bookshops in Budapest.

Art and architecture

Our Budapest (Budapest City Hall). A very informative series of pocket-size books available from the English-language bookshops listed on pp.250-252. Written in Hungarian, English and other languages by experts in their fields, they cover the city's architecture, baths and parks and cost a mere 300Ft or so each, though unfortunately the standard of English varies.

Györgyi Éri et al, *A Golden Age: Art and Society in Hungary 1896–1914* (Corvina). Hungary's Art Nouveau age captured in a beautifully illustrated coffee-table volume.

János Gerle et al, *Budapest: An Architectural Guide* (6 BT, Budapest). The best of the small new guides to the city's twentieth-century architecture, covering almost three hundred buildings, with brief descriptions in Hungarian and English.

Ruth Gruber, *Jewish Heritage Travel: A Guide to Central and Eastern Europe* (John Wiley o/p). A comprehensive guide to Jewish sights in Budapest and elsewhere.

Edwin Heathcote, *Budapest: A Guide to Twentieth-Century Architecture* (Ellipsis, UK). A useful and informative pocket guide to the city, though with some curious omissions.

Tamás Hofer et al, *Hungarian Peasant Art* (Constable/ International Publications Service o/p). An excellently produced examination of Hungarian folk art, with lots of good photos.

László Lugosi Lugo, *1900 Budapest 2000*, (Vincze, Budapest). A fascinating look at how the city has changed over a hundred years. Photographs of the city taken by a leading photographer of the day, Klösz György, are placed next to pictures taken with the same equipment today.

Imre Móra, *Budapest Then and Now* (New World Publishing, Budapest). A personal and very informative set of accounts of life in the capital, past and present.

Tamás Révész, *Budapest: A City before the Millennium* (Herald, Budapest). Excellent collection of black and white photographs of the city, though the text can be irritating.

Dora Wieberson et al, *The Architecture of Historic Hungary* (MIT Press, US). Comprehensive, illustrated survey of Hungarian architecture through the ages.

History, politics and society

Robert Bideleux, Ian Jeffries, *A History of Eastern Europe: Crisis and Change* (Routledge, UK). An excellent and wide-ranging history of the region.

Judit Frigyesi, *Béla Bartók and Turn-of-the-century Budapest* (University of California Press). Placing Bartók in his cultural milieu, this is an excellent account of the Hungarian intellectual world at the beginning of the last century.

Jörg K Hoensch, *A History of Modern Hungary 1867–1994* (Longman/Addison-Wesley). An authoritative history of the country.

László Kontler, *Millennium in Central Europe: A History of Hungary* (Atlantisz). A very thorough and reliable history, but it's let down by its slightly archaic style.

Bill Lomax, *Hungary 1956* (Allison & Busby/St Martin's Press o/p). Still probably the best – and shortest – book on the Uprising, by an acknowledged expert on modern Hungary. Lomax also edited *Eyewitness in Hungary* (Spokesman, UK), an anthology of accounts by foreign Communists (most of whom were sympathetic to the Uprising) that vividly depicts the elation, confusion and tragedy of the events of October 1956.

John Lukács, *Budapest 1900* (Weidenfeld/Grove Press). A very readable account of the politics and society of Budapest at the turn of the last century, during a golden age that was shortly to come to an end.

George Schöpflin, *Politics in Eastern Europe 1945–92* (Blackwell). An excellent overview of the region in the latter part of the twentieth century by one of the acknowledged experts.

Michael Stewart, *The Time of the Gypsies* (Westview Press). This superb book on gypsy culture is based on anthropological research in a gypsy community in Hungary.

Peter Sugar, (ed), *A History of Hungary* (I B Tauris). A useful, not too academic, survey of Hungarian history from pre-Conquest times to the close of the Kádár era, with a brief epilogue on the transition to democracy.

Biography and travel writing

Magda Dénes, *Castles Burning: A Child's Life in War* (Anchor/Touchstone Books). A moving biographical account of the Budapest ghetto and post-war escape to France, Cuba, and the United States, seen through the eyes of a Jewish girl. The author died in December 1966, shortly before the book she always wanted to write was published.

Brian Hall, *Stealing from a Deep Place* (Heinemann). In 1982, Hall cycled through Hungary, Romania and Bulgaria and came up with this engaging portrait of the region. The account of his time in Budapest is particularly enchanting.

George Lang, *The Truffles I Have Seen* (Penguin/Random House). An autobiography of the Hungarian-born restaurateur, with an absorbing account of Budapest before and during World War II.

Patrick Leigh Fermor, *A Time of Gifts* (Penguin); *Between the Woods and the Water* (Penguin). In 1934, the young Leigh Fermor started walking from Holland to Turkey, reaching Hungary in the closing chapter of *A Time of Gifts*. In *Between the Woods and the Water* the inhabitants of the Great Plain and Transylvania – both gypsies and aristocrats – are superbly evoked. Lyrical and erudite.

George Mikes, *Any Souvenirs?* (Penguin/Harvard Common Press o/p). Born in Siklós in southern Hungary, Mikes fled the country in 1956 and made a new life in Britain as a humorist. This wry account relates his first visit home in fifteen years.

John Paget, *Hungary and Transylvania* (Ayer, US; op). Paget's massive book attempted to explain nineteenth-century Hungary to the English middle class, and, within its aristocratic limitations, succeeded. Occasionally found in second-hand bookshops.

Walter Starkie, *Raggle-Taggle* (John Murray o/p/Transatlantic Arts o/p). The wanderings of a Dublin professor with a fiddle, who bummed around Budapest and the Plain in search of gypsy music in the 1920s. First published in 1933 and last issued in 1964; a secondhand bookshop perennial.

Ernő Szép, *The Smell of Humans* (Central European University Press, Budapest/Arrow, UK). A superb and harrowing memoir of the Holocaust in Hungary.

Literature

Access to **Hungarian literature** has greatly improved in recent years – and the standard of translations is much higher, too. Works by great twentieth-century writers, such as Antal Szerb and Sándor Márai, have appeared in translation recently, as well as contemporary authors like Péter Nádas and Péter Esterházy, whose dense, very Hungarian style presents a formidable challenge to the translator. Numerous collections of short stories are published by Corvina in Budapest, though the quality of translations varies from the sublime to the ridiculous. Works by nineteenth-century authors such as Mór Jókai are most likely found in secondhand bookshops (see p.249).

ANTHOLOGIES

Loránt Czigány (ed), *The Oxford History of Hungarian Literature from the Earliest Times to the Present* (Oxford University Press). Probably the most comprehensive collection in print to date. In chronological order, with good coverage of the political and social background.

György Gömöri (ed), *Colonnade of Teeth* (Bloodaxe/Dufour). In spite of its strange title, this is a good introduction to the work of young Hungarian poets.

Michael March (ed), *Description of a Struggle* (Picador/Vintage). A collection of contemporary Eastern European prose, featuring four pieces by Hungarian writers including Nádas and Esterházy.

POETRY

Endre Ady, *Poems of Endre Ady* (University Press of America). Regarded by many as the finest Hungarian poet of the twentieth century, Ady's allusive verses are notoriously difficult to translate.

George Faludy, *Selected Poems 1933–80* (McClelland & Stewart/University of Georgia Press o/p). Fiery, lyrical poetry by a victim of both Nazi and Soviet repression. Themes of political defiance, the nobility of the human spirit, and the struggle to preserve human values in the face of oppression predominate.

Miklós Radnóti, *Under Gemini: the Selected Poems of Miklós Radnóti, with a Prose Memoir* (Ohio University Press, US); *Foamy Sky: the Major Poems* (Princeton University Press, US). The two best collections of Radnóti's sparse, anguished poetry. His final poems, found in his coat pocket after he had been shot on a forced march to a labour camp, are especially moving.

Zsuzsa Rákovsky, *New Life* (OUP). Well-received volume translated by the Hungarian-born poet George Szirtes.

FICTION

Géza Csáth, *The Magician's Garden and Other Stories* (Penguin/Columbia University Press o/p); *Opium and Other Stories* (Penguin o/p). Disturbing short stories written in the magic realist genre. The author was tormented by insanity and opium addiction, killing his wife and then himself in 1918.

Peter Esterházy, *The Glance of Countess Hahn-Hahn, Down the Danube* (Quartet/Grove). Surreal story by a playful word-smith. *Helping Verbs of the Heart*, *A Little Hungarian Pornography* and *She Loves Me* are three more works by this descendant of the famous aristocratic family.

Tibor Fischer, *Under the Frog* (Penguin/New Press). Hilarious story of Stalinist times and the 1956 Uprising, by the son of two Hungarian escapees. Its title comes from the Magyar expression "Under a frog, down

POETRY • FICTION

287

a coalmine" – meaning that life couldn't get any worse.

Dezső Kosztolányi, *Skylark* (Central European University Press, Budapest). A short and tragic story of an old couple and their beloved child by one of Hungary's top writers of the twentieth century, in a masterly translation by Richard Aczél.

Gyula Krúdy, *Adventures of Sinbad* (Central European University Press, Budapest/Random House). Stories about a gourmand and womanizer by a popular Hungarian author with similar interests to his hero.

Sándor Márai, *Embers* (Viking). An elegiac meditation on friendship, published in Hungary in 1942 and banned after the war. Since Márai's suicide in 1989, his work has enjoyed a revival in Hungary, and more recently in the English-speaking world, thanks to this splendid translation by Carol Brown-Janeway.

Zsigmond Móricz, *Be Faithful Unto Death* (Penguin). This novel by a major late nineteenth-century Hungarian author sheds light on how Hungarians see themselves – both then and now.

Péter Nádas, *A Book of Memories* (Vintage/Overlook Press). This translation of a novel about a novelist writing about a novel caused a sensation when it appeared in 1998. A Proustian account of bisexual relationships, Stalinist repression, and modern-day Hungary in a brilliant translation by Iván Sanders.

Giorgio and Nicola Pressburger, *Homage to the Eighth District* (Readers International). Evocative short stories about Jewish life in Budapest, before, during and after World War II, by twin brothers who fled Hungary in 1956.

Antal Szerb, *Journey by Moonlight* (Pushkin Press, UK). A Hungarian classic, dating from 1937. Four years later, Szerb, a Jew, died in a concentration camp. This superb translation by Len Rix retains all the atmosphere of the original: a Hungarian on his honeymoon in Italy embarking on a mystical journey of self-discovery.

FICTION

Food, wine and miscellaneous

Lesley Chamberlain, *The Food and Cooking of Eastern Europe* (Penguin o/p). A great compendium of recipes, nostrums and gastronomical history, guaranteed to have you experimenting in the kitchen.

Susan Derecskey, *The Hungarian Cookbook* (HarperCollins, US). A good, easy-to-follow selection of traditional and modern recipes.

Gerard Gorman, *The Birds of Hungary* (Christopher Helm). The best book on the rich birdlife of the country and the best places for bird spotting, by a resident expert.

Stephen Kirkland, *The Wine and Vines of Hungary* (New World Publishing, Budapest). Authoritative and accessible guide with tips on what to order. Covers the different wines of the country's regions, and their winemakers too.

George Lang, *The Cuisine of Hungary* (Penguin/Random House). A well-written and beautifully illustrated work, telling you everything you need to know about Hungarian cooking, its history and how to do it yourself.

Glossary of Hungarian terms

ÁFA Goods tax, equivalent to VAT.

Állatkert Zoo.

Áruház Department store.

ÁVO The dreaded secret police of the Rákosi era, renamed the *ÁVH* in 1949.

Barlang Cave.

Borkostoló Wine tasting.

Borozó Wine bar.

Botanikuskert Botanical garden.

Büfé Snack bar.

Cigány Gypsy (can be abusive).

Cigánytelep Gypsy settlement.

Cigányzene Gypsy music.

Csárda Inn; nowadays, a restaurant with rustic decor.

Csárdás Traditional wild dance to violin music.

Cukrászda Cake shop.

Diszterem Ceremonial hall.

Domb Hill.

Duna River Danube.

Egyetem University.

Erdő Forest, wood.

Étterem Restaurant.

Fogadó Inn.

Folyó River.

Forrás Natural spring.

Fürdő Public baths.

Gyógyfürdő Mineral baths fed by thermal springs with therapeutic properties.

Hajó Boat.

Hajóállomás Boat landing stage.

Halászcsárda/halászkert Fish restaurant.

Ház House.

Hegy Hill or low mountain.

HÉV Commuter train running between Budapest and Szentendre.

Híd Bridge.

Honvéd Hungarian army.

Ifjúsági szálló Youth hostel.

Iskola School.

Kápolna Chapel.

Kapu Gate.

Kert Garden, park.

Kerület (ker.) District.

Kiállítás Exhibition.

Kincstár Treasury.

Kollégium Student hostel.

Komp Ferry.

Körút *(krt.)* Literally, ring road, but in Budapest refers to the main boulevards surrounding the Belváros.

Köz Alley, lane; also used to define narrow geographical regions.

Kulcs Key.

Kút Well or fountain.

Lakótelep High-rise housing estate.

Lépcső Flight of steps.

Liget Park, grove or wood.

Lovarda Riding school.

Magyar Hungarian (pronounced "*mod*-yor").

Magyarország Hungary.

Malév Hungarian national airline.

MÁV Hungarian national railways.

Megálló Railway station or bus stop.

Megye County; the county system was originally established by King Stephen to extend his authority over the Magyar tribes.

Mozi Cinema.

Műemlék Historic monument, protected building.

Művelődési ház/központ Arts centre.

Nyilas "Arrow Cross"; Hungarian Fascist movement.

Palota Palace; *püspök-palota*, a bishop's residence.

Pályaudvar *(pu.)* Rail terminus.

Panzió Pension.

Patak Stream.

Pénz Money.

Piac Outdoor market.

Pince Cellar.

Rakpart Embankment or quay.

Református The reformed church, which in Hungary means the Calvinist faith.

Rendőrség Police.

Repülőtér Airport.

Rév Ferry.

Rom Ruined building; sometimes set in a *romkert*, a garden with stonework finds.

Roma The Romany word for gypsy, preferred by many Roma in Hungary.

Sétány "Walk" or promenade.

Söröző Beer hall.

Strand Beach, or any area for sunbathing or swimming.

Szabadtér Open-air.

Szálló or **szálloda** Hotel.

Szent Saint.

Sziget Island.

Szoba kiadó Room to let.

Tájház Old peasant house turned into a museum, often illustrating the folk traditions of a region or ethnic group.

Táncház Venue for Hungarian folk music and dance.

Temető Cemetery.

Templom Church.

Tér Square; *tere* in the possessive case.

Terem Hall.

Tilos Forbidden; *tilos a dohányzás* means "smoking is forbidden".

Tó Lake.

Torony Tower.

Türbe Tomb or mausoleum of a Muslim dignitary.

Turista térkép Hiking map.

Udvar Courtyard.

Út Road; in the possessive case, *útja*.

Utca (*u.*) Street.

Vár Castle.

Város Town.

Városháza Town hall.

Vásár Market.

Vásárcsarnok Market hall.

Vasútállomás Train station.

Vendéglő Restaurant.

Völgy Valley.

Zsidó Jew or Jewish.

Zsinagóga Synagogue.

GLOSSARY OF HUNGARIAN TERMS

INDEX

around the world

Alaska ★ Algarve ★ Amsterdam ★ Andalucía ★ Antigua & Barbuda ★
Argentina ★ Auckland Restaurants ★ Australia ★ Austria ★ Bahamas ★
Bali & Lombok ★ Bangkok ★ Barbados ★ Barcelona ★ Beijing ★ Belgium &
Luxembourg ★ Belize ★ Berlin ★ Big Island of Hawaii ★ Bolivia ★ Boston
★ Brazil ★ Britain ★ Brittany & Normandy ★ Bruges & Ghent ★ Brussels ★
Budapest ★ Bulgaria ★ California ★ Cambodia ★ Canada ★ Cape Town ★
The Caribbean ★ Central America ★ Chile ★ China ★ Copenhagen ★
Corsica ★ Costa Brava ★ Costa Rica ★ Crete ★ Croatia ★ Cuba ★ Cyprus ★
Czech & Slovak Republics ★ Devon & Cornwall ★ Dodecanese & East
Aegean ★ Dominican Republic ★ The Dordogne & the Lot ★ Dublin ★
Ecuador ★ Edinburgh ★ Egypt ★ England ★ Europe ★ First-time Asia ★
First-time Europe ★ Florence ★ Florida ★ France ★ French Hotels &
Restaurants ★ Gay & Lesbian Australia ★ Germany ★ Goa ★ Greece ★
Greek Islands ★ Guatemala ★ Hawaii ★ Holland ★ Hong Kong & Macau ★
Honolulu ★ Hungary ★ Ibiza & Formentera ★ Iceland ★ India ★ Indonesia
★ Ionian Islands ★ Ireland ★ Israel & the Palestinian Territories ★ Italy ★
Jamaica ★ Japan ★ Jerusalem ★ Jordan ★ Kenya ★ The Lake District ★
Languedoc & Roussillon ★ Laos ★ Las Vegas ★ Lisbon ★ London ★

in twenty years

London Mini Guide ★ London Restaurants ★ Los Angeles ★ Madeira ★ Madrid ★ Malaysia, Singapore & Brunei ★ Mallorca ★ Malta & Gozo ★ Maui ★ Maya World ★ Melbourne ★ Menorca ★ Mexico ★ Miami & the Florida Keys ★ Montréal ★ Morocco ★ Moscow ★ Nepal ★ New England ★ New Orleans ★ New York City ★ New York Mini Guide ★ New York Restaurants ★ New Zealand ★ Norway ★ Pacific Northwest ★ Paris ★ Paris Mini Guide ★ Peru ★ Poland ★ Portugal ★ Prague ★ Provence & the Côte d'Azur ★ Pyrenees ★ The Rocky Mountains ★ Romania ★ Rome ★ San Francisco ★ San Francisco Restaurants ★ Sardinia ★ Scandinavia ★ Scotland ★ Scottish Highlands & Islands ★ Seattle ★ Sicily ★ Singapore ★ South Africa, Lesotho & Swaziland ★ South India ★ Southeast Asia ★ Southwest USA ★ Spain ★ St Lucia ★ St Petersburg ★ Sweden ★ Switzerland ★ Sydney ★ Syria ★ Tanzania ★ Tenerife and La Gomera ★ Thailand ★ Thailand's Beaches & Islands ★ Tokyo ★ Toronto ★ Travel Health ★ Trinidad & Tobago ★ Tunisia ★ Turkey ★ Tuscany & Umbria ★ USA ★ Vancouver ★ Venice & the Veneto ★ Vienna ★ Vietnam ★ Wales ★ Washington DC ★ West Africa ★ Women Travel ★ Yosemite ★ Zanzibar ★ Zimbabwe

also look out for our maps, phrasebooks, music guides and reference books

ROUGH GUIDES TWENTY YEARS

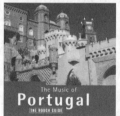 

Don't bury your head in the sand!

Take cover!

with Rough Guide Travel Insurance

Worldwide cover, for Rough Guide readers worldwide

UK Freefone **0800 015 09 06**
US Freefone **1 866 220 5588**
Worldwide **(+44) 1243 621 046**
Check the web at
www.roughguides.com/insurance

ROUGH GUIDES

Insurance organized by Torribles Insurance Brokers Ltd, 21 Prince Street, Bristol, BS1 4PH, England

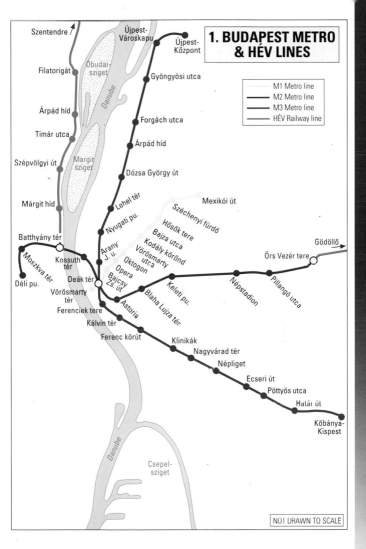

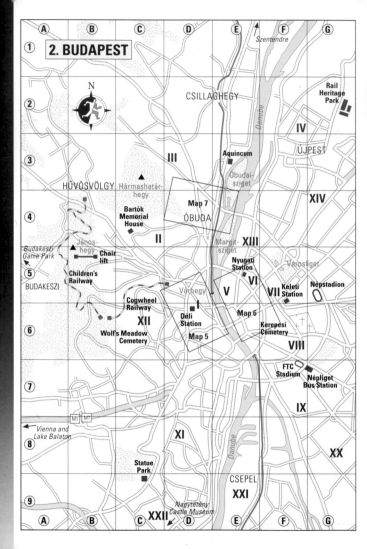

2. BUDAPEST

N

Szentendre

CSILLAGHEGY

Danube

Rail Heritage Park

IV

ÚJPEST

Aquincum

III

Óbudai-sziget

HŰVÖSVÖLGY

Hármashatár-hegy

Bartók Memorial House

Map 7

ÓBUDA

XIV

II

Budakeszi Game Park

Jánoshegy

Chair lift

Children's Railway

Margit-sziget

XIII

Nyugati Station

Városliget

BUDAKESZI

Cogwheel Railway

Várhegy

VI

Keleti Station

VII

Népstadion

XII

I

Déli Station

V

Map 6

Wolf's Meadow Cemetery

Map 5

Kerepesi Cemetery

VIII

FTC Stadium

Népliget Bus Station

Vienna and Lake Balaton

M1 M7

IX

XI

Danube

XX

Statue Park

CSEPEL

XXI

Nagytétény Castle Museum

XXII

A B C D E F G

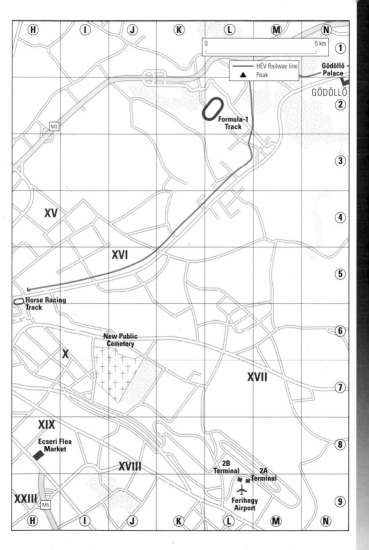

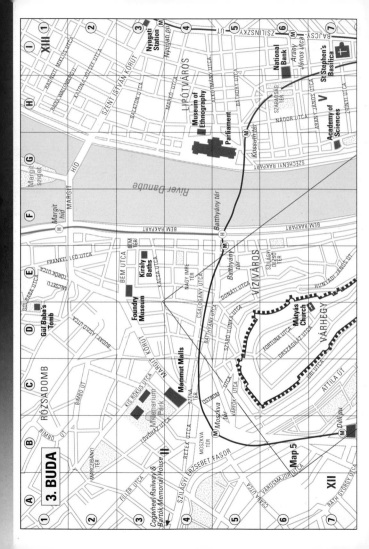

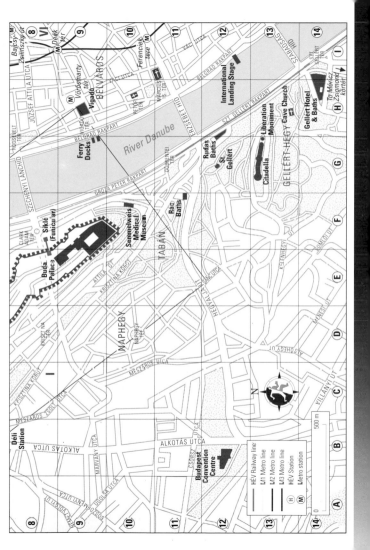

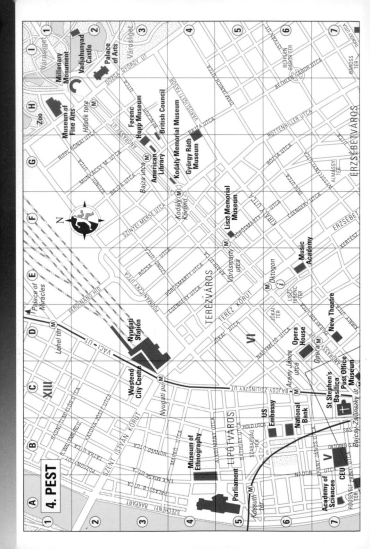

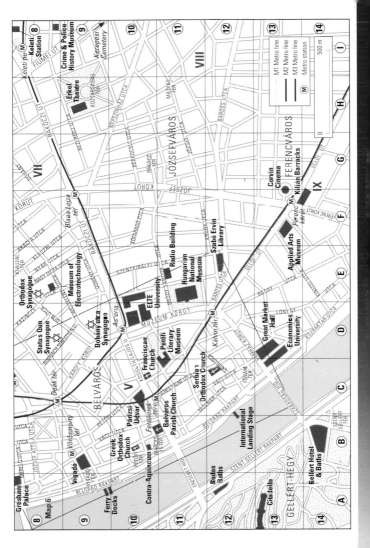

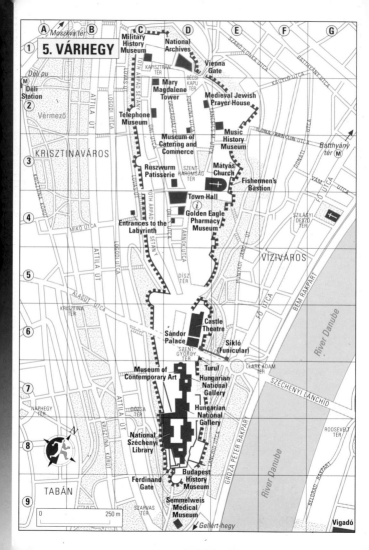

5. VÁRHEGY

Moszkva tér

Déli pu

Déli Station

Vérmező

KRISZTINAVÁROS

Military History Museum

National Archives

Vienna Gate

Mary Magdalene Tower

Telephone Museum

Medieval Jewish Prayer House

Music History Museum

Museum of Catering and Commerce

Ruszwurm Patisserie

Mátyás Church

Fishermen's Bastion

Town Hall

Golden Eagle Pharmacy Museum

Entrances to the Labyrinth

VÍZIVÁROS

Battyány tér

Castle Theatre

Sándor Palace

Sikló (Funicular)

Museum of Contemporary Art

Turul

Hungarian National Gallery

Hungarian National Gallery

National Széchényi Library

Budapest History Museum

Ferdinand Gate

TABÁN

Semmelweis Medical Museum

River Danube

Széchenyi Lánchíd

Roosevelt tér

Gellért-hegy

Vigadó

0 _____ 250 m

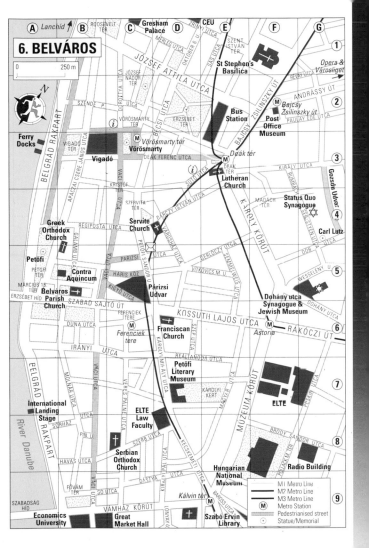

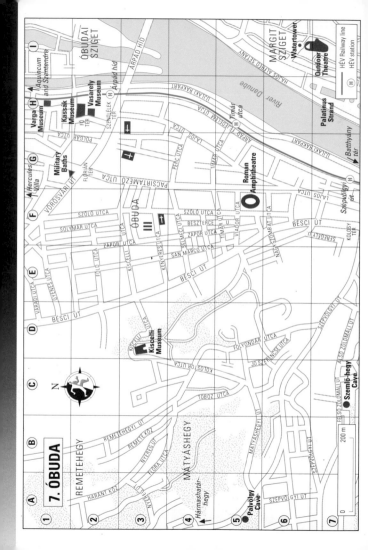

7. ÓBUDA

ÓBUDAI SZIGET

MARGIT SZIGET

Watertower

Outdoor Theatre

(H) HÉV Railway line
HÉV station

ÁRPÁD HÍD

Aquincum and Szentendre

Varga Museum (H)

Kassák Museum

Vasarely Museum

Hercules Villa (G)

Military Baths

FLÓRIÁN TÉR

SZENTLÉLEK TÉR

FŐ TÉR

Árpád híd

POLGÁR UTCA

PACSIRTAMEZŐ UTCA

PERC UTCA

LAJOS UTCA

ÁRPÁD FEJEDELEM ÚTJA

ÚJLAKI RAKPART

River Danube

Palatinus Strand

ÚJLAKI RAKPART

Batthyány tér

Tímár utca

VÖRÖSVÁRI ÚT

FLÓRIÁN UTCA

SZŐLŐ UTCA

SOLYMÁR UTCA

ÓBUDA

ZÁPOR UTCA

KISCELLI UTCA

KÉNYES UTCA

SAN MARCO UTCA

SZŐLŐ UTCA

BESZTERCE UTCA

ZÁPOR UTCA

SELMECI UTCA

TÍMÁR U.

VIADOR UTCA

Roman Amphitheatre

BÉCSI ÚT

SZOMBAT UTCA

BÉCSI ÚT

LAJOS UTCA

SZÉPVÖLGYI út

SZERÉNYI UTCA

KOLOSY TÉR

(H)

Szépvölgyi út

VÁRHEGY UTCA

GYENES UTCA

KISCELLI UTCA

BÉCSI ÚT

Kiscelli Museum

FOLYONDÁR UTCA

JÓ SZERENCSE UTCA

SZÉPVÖLGYI ÚT

KOLOSTOR UTCA

TÖRÖK UTCA

N

REMETEHEGY

REMETEHEGYI ÚT

REMETE KÖZ

NYÉREGY UTCA

FLÓRA UTCA

NYÉREG UTCA

MÁTYÁSHEGY

Harmashatár-hegy

MÁTYÁSHEGYI ÚT

Pálvölgy Cave

SZÉPVÖLGYI ÚT

LEBÓ ZÖLDMÁLI ÚT

FELSŐ ZÖLDMÁLI ÚT

JÓ SZERENCSE UTCA

ALSÓ ZÖLDMÁLI ÚT

Szemlő-hegy Cave

200 m

| A | B | C | D | E | F | G | H | I |

1 2 3 4 5 6 7

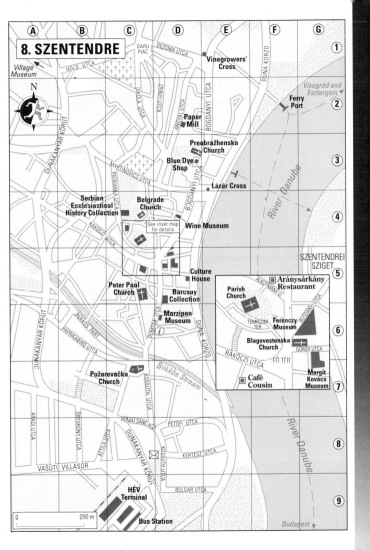

8. SZENTENDRE

A · **B** · **C** · **D** · **E** · **F** · **G**

Village Museum

N

DARU PIAC
DEZSMA UTCA
HOLD UTCA
ISKOLA UTCA
ZENITH UTCA
DUNAKANYAR KÖRÚT
ANGYAL UTCA
BOGDÁNYI UTCA
Vinegrowers' Cross
DUNA KORZÓ

Visegrád and Esztergom

Paper Mill

Ferry Port

Preobrazhenska Church

MARTINOVICS UTCA
PÁTRIARKA UTCA

Blue Dye Shop

Lázár Cross

River Danube

Serbian Ecclesiastical History Collection

Belgrade Church

See inset map for details

Wine Museum

RÁKÓCZI UTCA

SZENTENDREI SZIGET

Culture House

Peter Paul Church

Barcsay Collection

DUNA UTCA

Marzipan Museum

DUNA KORZÓ

DUNAKANYAR KÖRÚT
PAPRIKABÍRÓ UTCA
BÜKKÖS PART

Bükkös Stream

KOSSUTH UTCA

Požarevačka Church

ÁRADI UTCA
ORTOÁNY UTCA
ATTILA UTCA

RÓMAI SÁNC KÖZ
PETÖFI UTCA
KERTÉSZ UTCA

River Danube

VASÚTI VILLASOR

BOLGÁR UTCA

DUNAKANYAR KÖRÚT
KOSSUTH UTCA

HÉV Terminal

Bus Station

Budapest

0 — 200 m

Inset map

Parish Church
Aranysárkány Restaurant
ALKOTMÁNY U.
TEMPLOM TÉR
Ferenczy Museum
BOGDÁNYI UTCA
Blagovestenska Church
GÖRÖG UTCA
RÁKÓCZI UTCA
FÓ TÉR
Café Cousin
Margit Kovács Museum

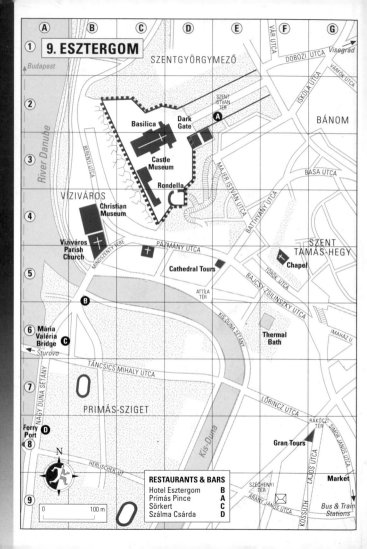

9. ESZTERGOM

Budapest

River Danube

SZENTGYÖRGYMEZŐ

VÁR UTCA
DOBOZI UTCA
Visegrád
ISKOLA UTCA
VÁRFOK UTCA

SZENT ISTVÁN TÉR

Basilica

Dark Gate

BÁNOM

Castle Museum

Rondella

BERÉNYI UTCA

MAJER ISTVÁN UTCA

BASA UTCA

VÍZIVÁROS

Christian Museum

BATTHYÁNY UTCA

SZENT TAMÁS-HEGY

Víziváros Parish Church

MINDSZENTY TÉRE

PÁZMÁNY UTCA

Cathedral Tours

TÖRÖK UTCA

Chapel

ATTILA TÉR

BAJCSY-ZSILINSZKY UTCA

Máría Valéria Bridge

Sturovo

KIS-DUNA SÉTÁNY

IMAHÁZ U.

Thermal Bath

NAGY DUNA SÉTÁNY

TÁNCSICS MIHÁLY UTCA

PRÍMÁS-SZIGET

LŐRINCZ UTCA

Kis-Duna

Ferry Port

RÁKÓCZI TÉR

SIMOR JÁNOS UTCA

Gran Tours

HERLISCHER ÚT

N

SZÉCHENYI TÉR

Market

LAJOS UTCA

KOSSUTH

ARANY JÁNOS UTCA

Bus & Train Stations

0   100 m

RESTAURANTS & BARS

Hotel Esztergom	B
Prímás Pince	A
Sörkert	C
Szálma Csárda	D